Right-Wing Military Government

Twayne's Themes in Right-Wing Politics and Ideology Series
Roger Eatwell, General Editor

Titles in the Series

The Nature of the Right: European and American Politics and Political Thought since 1789, eds. Roger Eatwell and Noël O'Sullivan

Islamic Fundamentalism, Youssef M. Choueiri

The Political Economy of the New Right, Grahame Thompson

Right-Wing Military Government

by
Robert Pinkney

Twayne Publishers · Boston
A Division of G.K. Hall & Co.

© Robert Pinkney, 1990

Published in the United States of America by Twayne Publishers
A Division of G.K. Hall & Co.
70 Lincoln Street
Boston, Massachusetts   02111

Published simultaneously in Great Britain by
Pinter Publishers Limited
25 Floral Street, London WC2E 9DS

Twayne's Themes in Right-Wing Politics and Ideology, no. 3

ISBN 0–8057–9554–5   10 9 8 7 6 5 4 3 2 1
      0–8057–9555–3 (pbk.)   10 9 8 7 6 5 4 3 2 1

Typeset by The Castlefield Press Limited, Wellingborough, Northants
Printed and bound in Great Britain by Biddles Ltd.

Contents

Tables

Acknowledgements

Many people have helped to make the completion of this study possible. Newcastle upon Tyne Polytechnic gave me leave to carry out much of the research, and the Faculty Librarian, Austin McCarthy, made an extensive literature search. Dr Roger Eatwell of the University of Bath originally suggested the subject, helped me to clarify my ideas in the early stages, and offered many constructive criticisms of the first draft. My wife Mary, my daughter Katharine and my father-in-law Oliver Ford helped to spot many of the typing errors in the original draft. I am grateful to everyone who has helped, but take personal responsibility for the opinions expressed and for any errors that remain.

Acknowledgments

Introduction

Right-wing military government is both a familiar and a neglected topic in academic literature. Much of the general literature on the military in politics extends to right-wing regimes, and there are studies of most of the individual countries which have experienced such government, but little attempt has been made to examine the range of right-wing military governments as a distinctive group, as one might examine liberal democracies or communist states. But are they a distinctive type, or are they merely a residual category which cannot be fitted in with the liberal democracies, communist states, populist revolutionary regimes or Third World systems where any sort of political authority is difficult to establish? I argue that they are, even though they appear at first sight to be a more heterogeneous group than the countries in the other categories.

A major justification for the study of military intervention in general is that it highlights the inability of civilian political structures to wield authority or resolve conflicts adequately — 'when no other card is turned up, clubs are trumps'. Such an inability is frequently related to the immaturity of the political structures ('Britain has had a parliament and political parties for much longer than Togo') and the low level of social and economic development ('Most Togolese are poor, illiterate rural dwellers whose political horizons are limited, and who are indifferent as to whether governments are chosen, or political decisions taken, by fair means or foul'), together with a limited sense of nationhood ('The Togolese thinks in terms of the interests of his own family and tribe and has little sense of belonging to a country called 'Togo'). Soldiers may thus overthrow governments in Togo if they feel that governments are not achieving the desired results, or simply because a military takeover would enhance the wealth and prestige of soldiers and their families. The bulk of the population would remain indifferent as to the morality of such a takeover, and its effect on the political process might be negligible outside the ranks of the newly installed soldiers and their immediate contacts, and the deposed politicians and theirs.

But *right-wing* military intervention reveals more than the weaknesses of political structures and the states of society associated with this. The very existence of a 'left–right' polarisation implies a degree of economic development in which workers and peasants with some sense of common identity challenge the power and wealth of landlords and capitalists. If we regard a right-wing government as one which places the emphasis on blocking the demands of the working class and other groups demanding greater political participation and economic equality, and giving prominence to a profit-oriented private sector rather than a welfare-oriented public sector, then most military governments meeting such a definition are found in the relatively developed Third World countries in which there are likely to be political structures which have previously sustained some form of pluralist democracy, and clearer notions of what sort of political behaviour is or is not legitimate, even if not all citizens share the same notions. Right-wing military intervention is therefore not merely a matter of soldiers displacing civilian rulers who themselves had doubtful democratic credentials, and then following broadly similar policies, but of soldiers displacing democratically elected governments and either attempting to reverse previous left-wing policies or ensuring that previously threatened left-wing policies do not materialise. But why does this happen, and why mainly within a cluster of countries outside both the more economically developed liberal democracies and the poorest countries of the world, and what light does it throw on the problems of countries attempting to grapple with the early stages of industrialisation?

Many of the countries of Western Europe and North America began the process of industrialisation at a time when the authority of well-established elites was not seriously challenged, opportunities for mass political participation were limited and there were no other countries permitting such participation which the underprivileged might cite as a model in the pursuit of their own demands. These conditions are much less true of much of modern Latin America and Asia. Many of these countries have, or have had, universal suffrage, competitive elections and political parties and pressure groups to articulate public demands, but the structures have rested on uneasy foundations, either because no indigenous elite was able to win the voluntary allegiance of the masses after independence (much of Latin America, Indonesia, Pakistan and South Korea) or because social changes undermined the authority of earlier elites (Thailand and Turkey). Violence in the pursuit of political demands or in the overthrow of governments is not new to most of these countries, and military intervention was common in many, in the sense of an organised group of soldiers plotting the downfall of the government and then installing one of their members in power. But 'military government', in the sense of the army providing the rulers' main power base, just as we speak of 'party government' or 'aristocratic government', is a much newer phenomenon, reflecting the greater cohesion and resources of twentieth-century armies and the strength of civil resistance which could no longer be overcome by a Bonaparte-type figure alone. Once such a military government is in power, it raises new questions about the basis of authority, the relationship between rulers and both the military constituency, which has the power to remove them in the way that their predecessors were removed, and the civil society which may be reluctant to accept their rule. In the longer term soldiers will find it difficult to rule by force alone, and will be faced with the delicate choice of either 'civilianising' themselves by seeking public support through an election, or finding acceptable civilians to whom to transfer power without their policies, their wealth, their liberty or their lives being jeopardised. Alternatively, power may be snatched from them before they are able to make such a choice, and new political forces will be unleashed. While these dramas are being acted out by soldiers and politicians, what of the significance of right-wing military government for society as a whole? If it is a distinctive way of checking the challenge of the underprivileged in particular types of society, how far does it succeed, both in the short term and the long term, and to what extent does it leave a distinctive impression on the political and social structures which succeed it?

In this study we begin by attempting to clarify the concepts of 'right-wing' and 'military government', and look at empirical evidence of the types of country in which right-wing military government is most commonly found. We then examine the various explanations of military intervention and go on to look at the various processes by which soldiers attempt to establish effective authority, which leads to a fourfold typology of military governments. Any such jump from empirical examination to abstract classification is bound to be difficult, and to involve elements of oversimplification, yet it is necessary if we are to make any sense of the diversity of right-wing military governments. They vary in their degrees of repression, their relationship with their military constituents and with civilian elites and masses, the extent to which they embrace the ideology of the 'new right', and in their perceptions of the sort of society they ultimately want to establish and of the role of the military within it. Our fourfold classification focuses on the power structure established by the military, because this is important in both revealing the strengths and weaknesses of the military in relation to society, and in highlighting the problems they are likely to encounter in maintaining authority and pursuing their desired objectives.

Our four categories are personal rule, military authoritarianism, civil–military authoritarianism and limited democracy. The first of these is relatively rare, and requires not only a skilled individual leader but a disciplined army to follow him which has avoided the factionalism that interpenetration of civil and military institutions often creates. Such a regime gives the leader ample room for manoeuvre in day-to-day government, but places heavy reliance on coercion in the absence of institutionalised contacts with civilians. Military authoritarian regimes have similar strengths and weaknesses, but with the advantage that they are less dependent on the mortality of one individual. Their emergence may be facilitated by the previous remoteness of civil and military elites from one another, or a mutual antipathy between them, or by the weakness of civilian elites and political structures which makes them expendable. As with personal rule, the short-term advantage of being able to rule with a minimum of concessions to civilians may be offset by the absence of institutionalised civilian co-operation. A government heavily dependent on coercion is difficult to sustain over a long period, and the regime may thus attempt to transform itself into one approximating to our third or fourth categories, assuming that it is not driven out of office by popular pressure.

Civil–military authoritarianism implies a greater interdependence of civil and military elites, either because divisions within an army with a relatively low level of professionalism are exploited by civilians, or because well-established civilian groups with strong power bases cannot easily be dislodged. Civil–military interdependence may contribute to the greater longevity of the regime, but not necessarily to its effectiveness. There may be incoherence, discontinuity and instability as power passes between shifting coalitions. Limited democracy implies not merely nominal elections but genuine competition for places in a relatively effective legislature, though not generally for the executive. It may emerge because the country has already had substantial experience of pluralist politics and will not take kindly to authoritarianism, because socioeconomic changes since military intervention have produced new pressures for democracy, or because the military are searching for a broader, more secure base. It would be tempting to think of these regimes as a final phase before the restoration of civilian rule, especially if democratisation gathers a momentum which the military cannot control, as in Brazil, but it is also possible that the military will treat such democracy as exists as a safety valve for public discontent rather than a pathway to civilian liberal democracy, and that, as in Indonesia, they will not allow their own legitimacy to be called into question.

In Part II we explore the politics of some of the countries approximating to each of these categories and test some of the hypotheses we have developed. My concern is not so much to quantify the achievements of military governments, which is a hazardous business in view of both the paucity of data which would enable one to compare key variables at the beginning and end of different periods of civil and military government, and the problem of establishing exactly when such governments begin or end. (For an attempt to compare the performances of civilian and military regimes see McKinlay and Cohan, 1975, pp. 1–30.) Instead I concentrate more on the circumstances in which the various military governments came to power, the ideologies and interests they reflected, their strengths and weaknesses in relation to civil society, and the circumstances making for their withdrawal or (less frequently) their prepetuation in power. The impatient reader may still demand an answer to the question 'What did the military in Chile (or Turkey or El Salvador) actually achieve?' If the question cannot be answered accurately in terms of changes in per capita income, literacy or expenditure on social welfare, and still less in terms of the number of tortures, arbitrary arrests or attacks on striking workers, we can still offer an impressionistic account of such developments as the extent of restoration of order, the strengthening of elites or weakening of mass movements, the strengthening of the private sector at the expense of the public, and of relations with the West in preference to non-alignment or ties with the Eastern Bloc, all of which may have a significance which transcends the duration of military government.

In Part III I attempt to put the episodes of right-wing military government into perspective by looking at the ability or otherwise of soldiers to perpetuate what they have established. If the limitations of rule by force, and the limited capacity of soldiers to resolve political problems, leads to an attempt to transfer power to acceptable civilians, or less frequently to military leaders civilianising themselves, the processes by which this can be done are extremely varied. At one extreme civilian pressure, sometimes aided by rebels from within the armed forces, may dictate a transfer of power which leaves soldiers with little more than their pensions or a single airline ticket to a place of exile. At the other, the military 'withdrawal' may be little more than a strategic move to allow civilians to take responsibility for unpopular policies, while soldiers retain the power to veto any decisions or to re-intervene when it suits their convenience. In between these extremes the transfer of power may produce civilian governments which vary in their strength, stability and autonomy from the army, and vary in their ability to calculate the sort of behaviour which will be necessary to prevent further military intervention. We examine both the variables which are likely to stimulate military attempts to return to barracks, and which will determine the relationship between the successor government and the military. These variables can be looked at from a static point of view (what is the degree of military strength and professionalism, and how strong are civilian political structures, at a particular point in time?), or from a dynamic perspective (what circumstances brought the military to power initially, and how did civil–military relations evolve in consequence?). The first approach enables us to sketch out the extent to which different types of successor regimes will be dependent on the military. The second enables us to focus on the broader question of the nature of post-military political systems.

Right-wing military rulers, for all their diversity, have two sets of beliefs in common. In the short term they claim the need for authoritarian rule because attempts at democracy are deemed to have failed. Yet in the long run (and unlike many left-wing rulers) they proclaim a belief, almost without exception, in the desirability of pluralist democracy, even if this is sometimes qualified by excluding some 'undesirables' from the political process. But does a spell of authoritarianism pave the way for more firmly rooted democracy, as soldiers would like to believe, by eliminating political extremists and the causes of political and economic instability? Or does it make any nominally democratic successor regime inherently unstable because military intervention has set a precedent for political actors to rely on violence if they cannot get their own way by constitutional means? Is military government irrelevant to subsequent political development, either because it is merely a symptom of underlying violence, in a divided society, which will continue whether soldiers are in power or not, or because military intervention represented one brief adventure in an otherwise democratic polity? Or does right-wing military government have a positive impact in a way that soldiers had not envisaged, because people's sufferings are such during the period of repression that they are more determined to preserve democracy, for all its limitations and the personal defeats and compromises it sometimes implies, rather than giving the generals any pretext for returning?

We look at the circumstances which might be conducive to each of these outcomes. The evidence suggests that most right-wing military governments have done little to transform social or economic structures in the way that left-wing rulers have done in Egypt or Libya, so that any notion of soldiers laying the foundations for stable political competition is extremely dubious. In societies where the majority of the population remain poor, rural and illiterate, there is little reason to believe that either military or civilian government will do much to enhance the immediate prospects for pluralist democracy. But it is in the countries where the levels of social and economic development are relatively high, and where there has been some previous experience of pluralist politics, that the most interesting questions arise. These countries have a capacity for producing some of the harshest forms of authoritarianism, because of the strength of the armies and the strength of the opposition they need to crush to establish their authority, but they also have a core of articulate citizens who may be determined that pluralist democracy shall succeed, if only because of the extreme unattractiveness of the obvious alternative. It would be foolhardy to predict the outcome, but it is interesting that most academic explanations of the establishment of democracy at earlier times place the emphasis on the requisite social and economic conditions, many of which still appear to be lacking in the countries we examine, or on the willingness of previously antagonistic groups to recognise that compromise is in their mutual interest, rather than emphasising a positive desire for democracy itself (which was in many cases an unknown quantity anyway until it actually emerged). If some of the countries emerging from right-wing military government do succeed in developing durable political systems based on peaceful competition for power and influence, despite their economic handicaps and their unhappy experiences of pluralist politics in the past, then right-wing military government will have had an impact which few generals and few political observers would have foreseen. As for the soldiers themselves, remarkably few have been punished by their civilian successors for their behaviour when in office, and the promise or expectation of an amnesty often hastens the process of military disengagement. A generous budgetary provision may then persuade them to remain in barracks, but there remains a delicate balance in many countries between the civilian will to prevent further military intervention and the socioeconomic conditions which continue to make civil democracy unstable.

PART I
The Emergence of Right-Wing Military Government

The involvement of soldiers in politics is not new, and can be traced back at least as far as Roman times. The phenomenon of military government, in the sense of a government drawn mainly from the army and using the army as its main power base, is much newer and belongs essentially to the past fifty years. Our task in the first part of the book is to clarify what we understand by the terms 'military government' and 'right-wing', and then map out the parts of the world in which right-wing military governments are most commonly found. The evidence suggests these are most frequently countries which are more socially and economically developed than most of the Third World, but less developed than the First and Second World countries of Europe, North America and Australasia. I try to explain why this should be so, and look at the political, social and military factors which are conducive to the capture of power by right-wing soldiers.

Once soldiers have taken power, there is a variety of ways in which they can attempt to make their authority effective, but I suggest a broad fourfold classification to illustrate the possible relationships between military rulers, the army as a whole and the wider society. Soldiers comprise a small minority of the population, and the soldiers who have taken power a still smaller minority. Unlike many elected civilian governments, they cannot expect to rely on the willing co-operation of the population. They therefore need to retain (or establish) the co-operation of the army as a whole in order to use force effectively when willing co-operation is lacking, but they may also find that circumstances require them to work in co-operation with various civilian groups if the latter can provide additional sources of expertise or reduce the need for dependence on force. Right-wing ideology generally rules out any attempt to build a power base around a specially created mass party (though Generals Franco and Peron attempted something of this sort in earlier times), but if personal rule or military authoritarianism with a minimal civilian involvement are not considered feasible or desirable, there is the alternative of working in tandem with civilian elites in a civil–military authoritarian regime, or of permitting a limited form of democracy in which voters can choose a legislature, subject to the disqualification of unacceptable individuals and parties, while the executive remains in the hands of the military. We shall look at the nature of each of these categories of political system, and the possible reasons for their emergence, before going on to look at actual examples in detail in Part II.

1 Right-Wing Military Government: the Setting, the Antecedents and the Implications

What Is Military Government?

At first glance the phenomenon of right-wing military government seems easy to recognise. For most of us it would conjure up a picture of generals in dark glasses presiding over repressive governments which use the might of the army to advance the privileges of the few at the expense of the welfare of the many. The government of Chile under Pinochet is clearly both military and right-wing; the government of Sweden under Palme was neither. But a closer focus may blur the images. What distinguishes military regimes from those in which the army is merely one influential actor or a power behind the throne, and is there a clear 'left–right' continuum which enables us to classify all governments beyond a certain point as 'right-wing'? Sivard casts the net exceptionally widely in her search for 'countries under military control'. She uses the criteria of:

> Key political leadership by military officers; existence of a state of martial law; extra-judicial authority exercised by security forces; lack of central political control over large sections of the country where official and unofficial security forces rule; control by foreign military forces. (Sivard 1983, p.11)

This classification brings in such countries as Iran, Jordan, Afghanistan, North Korea and Taiwan which are clearly ruled by civilians, even though internal or external threats may give the army a significant role. Such a broad definition seems to rob the concept of much of its value, and leaves us with unanswered questions about the extent to which it is soldiers or civilians who wield effective authority. Military influence behind the scenes, and the exercise of power by soldiers in spheres which in other countries might be controlled by civilians, are interesting phenomena, but they are not the same as military government. It may be argued that the concept of 'military government' is itself as unhelpful as that of 'countries under military control'. O'Kane suggests that we should focus more on governments relying on force rather than power, and that the distinction between 'civil' and 'military' governments is clouded by the fact that the military may wield much power outside political office, even under a government not installed by a coup, whereas a 'military' government installed by a coup will not necessarily guarantee central military control (O'Kane, 1989, pp. 334–5). This may well be true, just as terms such as 'liberal democracy' or 'communism' may cover a variety of political systems, but each can still provide a useful focus of interest since each tells us something about the main basis on which power rests. In the case of 'military government', the focus is on governments which use the army, rather than a mass electorate or a single party, as their main power base. We therefore begin by taking the simple view that military government normally implies the wielding of formal executive authority by soldiers, and then consider what qualifications need to be made to this proposition.

Finer suggests a useful 'family tree' of military regimes, starting with the question 'Is the head of state an ex-coup leader?' and then branching downwards to consider such variables as the presence or absence of a military cabinet, a legislature, political parties and civilians sharing executive authority. (Finer in Kolkowicz and Korbonski, 1982, pp. 298–309). This provides a range of possibilities from 'pure military government' in which a military junta rules unencumbered by civilian ministers, a legislature or political parties, through 'personalist' systems in which the army merely supports a Bonapartist leader without sharing in power, to more 'civilianised' systems in which legislatures, parties and civilian ministers act as constraints. The latter type of arrangement becomes more likely the longer a military government is in power, for reasons which will emerge presently, and raises questions as to when the government ceases to be military. Did General Franco or Colonel Sadat, for example, end their lives as military rulers or as retired officers heading civilian governments? These 'transvestite' regimes are best regarded as 'military' until such time as their power base is civilianised by freely contested elections, though the latter term may itself sometimes give rise to dispute. Whether to include 'personalist' systems is also debatable. Many military regimes tend towards personal dictatorship, but the real test is whether the dictator is at the head of a military junta or merely a lone soldier ruling through civilian institutions. Napoleon was not regarded as the head of a military government, and by the same token we would exclude General Mobutu of Zaire.

If we think of military government as a form of government in which executive power rests with a military junta using the army as its main power base, but sometimes sharing power with or constrained by civilians, we arrive at the list of countries in Table 1.1 which have experienced military government since 1960. There is no ideal starting date for such a study, but an earlier decade would take us closer to the shadows of the Second World War and colonialism, when the military were more preoccupied with other matters, and public opinion in independent nations would probably have been more hostile to the blatant imposition of authoritarian rule. By the 1960s most armies were free of colonial tutelage and elite opinion was less likely to regard the 'freedom' fought for in 1939 as sacrosanct if it failed to deliver public order or material benefits. (There is also the practical point that academic literature on the military only began to burgeon in the 1960s, as political scientists moved beyond an interest in the formal political process.)

Table 1.1 Average rankings of economic and social standing of countries with military governments since 1960.

Country	Position on Sivard's ranking	Political orientations of governments		
		Left	Centre/Indeterminate	Right
Spain	28			+
Greece	32			+
Argentina	37			+
Portugal	39	+		
Libya	40	+		
Uruguay	41			+
Panama	48	+	+	+
Chile	49			+
Fiji	53			+
Iraq	58	+		
Brazil	62			+
Ecuador	63		+	
S. Korea	65			+
Paraguay	66			+
Peru	73	+		
Syria	75	+		
Algeria	77	+		
Turkey	80			+
Nicaragua	81			+
Bolivia	84	+	+	+
Thailand	85			+
Guatemala	86			+
El Salvador	88		+	+
Congo	89	+		
Egypt	93	+		
Honduras	94		+	
Nigeria	94		+	
Lesotho	96		+	
N. Yemen	100		+	
S. Vietnam	103			+
Indonesia	105			+
Madagascar	106	+		
Togo	107		+	
Liberia	108		+	
Uganda	109		+	
S. Yemen	111		+	
Ghana	112	+	+	
Burma	113	+		
Eq. Guinea	114		+	
Sudan	116	+	+	
Haiti	119			+

Contd . . .

Table 1.1 Continued. . . .

Country	Position on Sivard's ranking	Political orientations of governments		
		Left	Centre/Indeterminate	Right
Laos	122			+
Pakistan	123			+
Benin	125	+		
Central Af. Repub.	126		+	
Mauritania	128		+	
Rwanda	128	+		
Sierra Leone	130		+	
Niger	131		+	
Guinea	132		+	
Somalia	133	+		
Burundi	135	+		
Bangladesh	136			+
Burkina Faso	139	+	+	
Mali	139		+	
Ethiopia	141	+		

What Is Right-Wing?

The nature of right-wing ideology is discussed more fully in other volumes in this series. Eatwell suggests a checklist of possible distinguishing features of right-wing ideology, which he then demolishes wholly or partially (Eatwell in Eatwell and O'Sullivan, 1990, pp. 47–60). Some can be demolished relatively easily. Resistance to change, authoritarianism and nationalism are clearly not the sole property of the right. Right-wing governments may make sweeping changes to 'roll back socialism', just as social democracies may undergo periods of quiet consolidation; Stalin was more authoritarian than Churchill, and left-wing Middle Eastern politicians are no less nationalistic than their right-wing counterparts in Latin America. The extent to which those on the right take a more pessimistic view of human nature is interesting, but difficult to relate to the actual behaviour of governments. This leaves distinctions between left and right based on attitudes to capitalism/private property, equality and traditional institutions. Respect, and a belief in a significant role for institutions such as monarchy, aristocracy, church and inherited wealth are ubdoubtedly important elements in conservative thinking in many Western countries, but these institutions, with the possible exception of the church, are weaker and less numerous in the countries prone to military government, where colonialism or European immigration have frequently broken the power of traditional institutions without being able to establish legitimate forms of authority in their place. This has not prevented some Latin American rulers from trying to legitimise themselves by creating myths about a fatherland based on Christian virtues which the left is attempting to undermine, but the shallowness of these 'traditions' is reflected in the short political lives of the rulers who seek to invoke them, and in their heavy reliance on coercion in the absence of deference.

A belief in the virtues of capitalism and private property, and indifference or hostility to social equality (especially where it inhibits freedom to pursue material individual interest), do seem to be more important distinguishing features of right-wing ideology. This is especially true in societies where the conservative who puts the preservation of order and hierarchy, or even a sense of duty to the lower orders, before the accumulation of wealth, is less prominent. This does not mean that we can make a crude distinction between politicians favouring uncontrolled capitalism and those who always give priority to equality, social welfare and production for the 'common good' through state ownership or control, but it seems reasonable to characterise politicians tending towards the former approach as right-wing, and towards the latter as left-wing. While it may be true that elites exist in capitalist and socialist economies alike, those in a capitalist economy owe their positions to the opportunities which it has given them to pursue private profit and enjoy inherited wealth, so that any examination of right-wing politics must also look at the process of restricting or containing popular participation in politics in order to minimise challenges to elite privileges. It might be argued that left-wing rulers also do this, only in more subtle ways within the structure of a one-party state, but right-wing rulers have to do it within the context of a system which at least pretends to believe in legitimacy based on political competition, and in which there is therefore the risk of competition allowing their adversaries to win. Even if ballots are not rigged blatantly, attempts will normally be made to limit the effective political participation of groups articulating the interests of poorer sections of the community.

Support for capitalism, private property and inherited wealth, and for elites enjoying the fruits of these, does not necessarily imply a belief in uncontrolled market forces. Right-wing governments have frequently pursued their objectives through subsidies to private enterprise, the regulation of markets and protectionism, but growing international interdependence over the past two decades has made the maintenance of 'capitalism in one country' more difficult. Even before the death of General Franco, Spain was beginning to open its economy to international capitalism in an attempt to stimulate economic growth, and more recently Chile, and to a lesser extent Argentina and Brazil, have followed similar paths. Free market economics may not be a right-wing end in itself, but it is seen by many right-wing governments as a means to the end of maintaining capitalist elites (though there will be some losers as well as winners within these heterogeneous groups). All this is in contrast to the elements of fascism in the earlier right-wing military governments of Franco and Peron, which involved much more economic nationalism, state economic intervention and popular political mobilisation. One can argue about the extent to which fascism is a right-wing ideology, but in functional terms there are parallels between the fascist interventions in the 1930s and 1940s, to remove or forestall left-wing governments in political systems which had not yet evolved means of peaceful political competition, and the more recent right-wing military interventions in Latin America, Pakistan and South Korea. The ends were similar but the means varied according to economic circumstances.

One further problem in attempting to recognise right-wing politics in countries prone to military government is the dearth of indigenous philosophers, or even political pamphleteers. It is difficult to discover a Guatamalan John Locke, a Bangladeshi Edmund Burke or a Chilean Milton Friedman. While right-wing rulers in general tend to see themselves as pragmatists who do not attempt to justify their behaviour with reference to their spiritual ancestors in the way that their left-wing counterparts invoke Marx, Lenin or Mao, this is especially true in Third World countries where the struggle for political survival takes precedence over philosophical debates on matters such as the moral virtues of private health care or the sale of council houses. The absence of a clearly articulated indigenous ideology, and of an unwillingness to give much prominence to imported right-wing ideologies, together with only a limited presence of the 'traditional' brand of conservatism which venerates old-established institutions, gives the 'right' a certain nakedness in many countries. The pursuit of the interests of elites (and their allies) deriving wealth from private capital, frequency reinforced by violence against their opponents, is not always clothed with ideological justifications in a way comparable with much of Western Europe and North America. We must, however, guard against over-generalisation. Traditional conservative values have survived in Turkey and Thailand, the mixed economy was left largely intact by the military in Indonesia and Uruguay, and military governments in Argentina and Chile have attempted to construct moral justifications for their existence in the face of left-wing threats to order. It therefore seems sensible to use the term 'right-wing' in this book in a broad sense, while noting that some of the features of right-wing politics play a less significant role than in the West. I suggest that the most obvious features of a right-wing regime are:

(a) the exclusion from power, or repression, of working-class groups or groups favouring greater equality;
(b) preference for the private sector;
(c) a willingness to pursue policies which lead to greater social inequality;
(d) discouragement of popular participation in politics (though a few right-wing governments favour the controlled 'mobilisation' which is also found on the authoritarian left);
(e) pro-Western foreign policies;
(f) Anti-socialist and anti-communist rhetoric to legitimise authority.

There are also 'optional extras' which are not common to all right-wing governments but which would clearly mark governments out as right-wing, including:

(g) appeals to 'traditional' values extolling such institutions as the family, the church or past national glory;
(h) claims to legitimacy based on the need for 'order' without any reference to the social causes of disorder;
(i) close links with civilian landed and capitalist elites;
(j) the involvement of soldiers in business activity;
(k) a free market economic policy, in the internal economy and/or in relation to foreign capital.

We are still left with questions on the measuring rod to be used in assessing what is right-wing, and of whether we should judge policies by their intention or their effect. If a government is deemed to be 'right-wing', is it judged by some absolute standard (the proportion of the economy in private hands, the extensiveness of restrictions on trade unions), or in relative terms (the extent of trade union restrictions in Argentina in comparison with Chile) or in dynamic terms (the extent to which a current government has privatised the economy, or curbed unions since it came to power?) The first and second approaches raise problems of comparing like with like. Brazilian rulers may make more generous provision for social welfare than those in Ethiopia, but this might be because of Brazil's better endowment with natural resources and despite the more left-wing commitment of the Ethiopians; Argentinian rulers might share similar right-wing convictions to Chileans, but political constraints or economic circumstances might make the Argentinians apply their policies more moderately.

The dynamic approach seems to be the most useful. We are interested in governments which 'move to the right', or attempt to do so, relative to what has gone before. In some cases the intention is clear from the statements of the rulers; in others right-wing outcomes may be unintended or may come about because governments feel that there is no alternative, despite a preference for equality, social welfare and economic planning. Thus privatisation might come about on account of the absence of competent managers, or greater dependence on world capitalism may be the result of a search for a stimulus to the economy. In so far as a line can be drawn it seems useful to restrict the term 'right-wing' to those regimes which show a clear preference for the policies we have described, rather than those which adopt some of them piecemeal when choices are severely restricted.

And What Is Not Right-Wing?

Governments which resort fitfully to privatisation, free market economics and the repression of the poor, but which still attempt to expand social welfare and economic planning when circumstances permit, are better classified as 'centrist'. Others we can describe as 'indeterminate' because their motivations have little to do with class or ideological conflict and more to do with rewarding friends, relatives, or ethnic or religious groups, as in the case of much of tropical Africa. Beyond these types are military governments which not only have no objection to socialist policies but enthusiastically espouse them. Their ideologies and stated policies are the mirror image of those of the right-wing regimes; social mobilisation, equality, social welfare, state economic intervention, the downgrading of traditional institutions and a non-aligned or pro-Eastern foreign policy. How far such beliefs are, or can be, put into practice is a question outside the scope of this study, but successful mobilisation and planning seem to be the exception. Yet the fact that these regimes choose to clothe themselves, however naively or hypocritically, in left-wing ideology suggests a striking contrast to our right-wing regimes. If they express their distaste for the private sector, traditional elites and major capitalist powers, they are clearly foreclosing some policy options, even if the alternatives they seek are not always clear.

The Conditions for Right-Wing Military Intervention

Our rough definitions of left, right and centre/indeterminate enable us to classify countries experiencing military government over the past thirty years in the way shown in Table 1.1. Much of this is inevitably impressionistic in view of the uneven quality and quantity of the literature. The main sources used for individual countries are shown in the bibliography, and these have been supplemented by general works such as those of Delury and Keegan. Table 1.1 lists the countries in order of Sivard's average rankings of social and economic standing (Sivard, 1983, pp. 36–41) which are based on such variables as per capita income, life expectancy, infant mortality, calorie intake, literacy, and the availability of doctors, teachers, schools and hospitals in proportion to the population. Two obvious facts emerge from the table. Firstly, the 27 most 'developed' countries have remained immune to military government altogether. Only two of the top 36 experienced it and of these, Spain was largely civilianised by the 1970s and Greece's brief excursion into military rule looks like aberration in what has otherwise been a pluralist democracy. Secondly, the main concentration of right-wing military governments is in the countries just beyond the fringe of the 'developed' world but more economically advanced than most of the Third World. Of the 13 most developed countries experiencing military government since 1960, 10 had right-wing governments, as did 16 of the top 22. At the least developed end of the scale, only one of the bottom 14 and 4 of the bottom 26 military governments could be regarded as right-wing. This would seem to support Huntington's much quoted and much disputed assertion that: 'In a world of oligarchy, the soldier is a radical. In a middle class world, he is a participant and arbiter; as mass society looms on the horizon, he becomes a conservative guardian of the existing order' (Huntington, 1968, p. 221).

But again it is easy to jump to conclusions after only a brief glimpse at the scene. Some critics would object to a crude 'ranking' of countries on the grounds that the data is often unreliable and that development is anyway not a one-dimensional process. It is useful to put Libya one place above Uruguay when Uruguay has a long history of pluralist politics while Libya, for all its recently acquired wealth, has only recently emerged from the culture of a semi-feudal kingdom? In terms of economic development the two may be comparable, but can economic development be translated into political development, or is the unique history and culture of each country such that no common measure can be found for such development? 'Development' itself may imply value judgements — the notion of moving towards a desired end such as liberal democracy or stability — when what we should be looking for is the way in which countries adapt to a variety of changes in a variety of circumstances, some of which produce right-wing military governments, which in turn may divert political systems in variety of directions.

If we cannot plot political development along a unilinear scale, we can suggest the sort of conditions which are most conducive to right-wing military intervention and then consider which patterns of political evolution are most likely to give rise to these conditions. The more obvious requirements for such intervention include:

(1) the existence of, or perceived threat of the emergence of, a left-wing government;
(2) a belief that civilians alone will not be able to remove or prevent such a government;
(3) a belief within a substantial section of the army that such a government is a serious threat to its interests or beliefs;
(4) the willingness and ability of military leaders to take control of the relevant structures for formulating and executing policy;
(5) the willingness and ability of key sections of civilian society to co-operate in, or at least not undermine, the establishment and maintenance of the military regime;
(6) an acceptance of the legitimacy of changing governments by unconstitutional means.

These requirements give clues as to the nature of societies in which right-wing military intervention may be found. Such societies can be conceptualised through analyses that emphasise variables in socioeconomic development, political behaviour and civil–military relations. We shall pursue these analyses further in subsequent chapters but here we merely note, without attempting to explain, some of the forces at work, as set out in Table 1.2. We have seen that right-wing military governments are most commonly found in the most economically developed countries of the Third World. Development has been accompanied by the growth of employment in the secondary and tertiary sectors, urbanisation and literacy, and hency by growing demands from mass movements for a greater share of material wealth and political participation. We shall look briefly at the way in which such problems have been tacked in other circumstances before returning to the right-wing military.

The problems were largely resolved in the wealthier countries of Western Europe and North America, economically through a sufficient trickle-down of wealth, and politically through timely concessions to facilitate mass involvement in electoral, party and pressure group activity. Where the masses still remained dissatisfied a police force and, in the last resort, an army dominated by the ruling elite could enforce order. Where elites were less able or willing to make concessions there was the alternative of a communist revolution, followed by a regime which claimed legitimacy on the strength of its position as the instigator of the revolution and the source of ideological wisdom. Mass political activity was contained within the process of party mobilisation, and challenges to authority beaten off by an army and police force penetrated by the party. At the opposite developmental pole we have noted that right-wing military government is exceptional in the poorest countries of the world. One pattern of development is for the army as a 'modern' institution in a semi-feudal kingdom such as Egypt or Libya to revolt against the elite in pursuit of demands for economic development and

Table 1.2 Patterns of political evolution

	Twentieth-century semi-feudal society	Nineteenth-century oligarchy		Nineteenth- or twentieth-century oligarchy or autocracy, often inheriting power from a colonial authority	
	Pressures from modern sectors for economic development and egalitarian distribution.	Few concessions to demands from lower social groups for economic or political participation.	Gradual socio-economic change enabling elites to co-opt and socialise additional social groups.	Intra-elite revolt at time of low socioeconomic development.	Rise of mass movements at time of higher socioeconomic development. Absence of concessions to these movements.
	Left-wing military government.	Communist revolution.	Liberal democracy.	Centrist or indeterminate military government.	Right-wing military government.
Consequences of economic changes. Development largely controlled by the state, which can control distribution of rewards.		Development controlled by party-state structure.	Sufficient trickle-down of wealth to retain mass loyalty to existing, political structure.	Change limited by international dependence and weakness of indigenous structures.	Economic policies are aimed at protecting elites and containing non-elite demands at a time when capital accumulation is crucial.
Sources of legitimacy. Government as revolutionary, nationalist liberator.		Party as instigator of revolution and source of ideological wisdom.	Universal suffrage; competitive elections.	Disputed within the elite.	Dispute between elite and masses.
Responses to mass demands for participation and material benefits. Initial culture restricts demands. Single parties are often facades, with power resting with military and bureaucratic elites.		Mobilisation within party structure.	Timely concessions to permit electoral and pressure group activity	Demands are poorly articulated outside the elite.	Demobilisation; suppression of working-class and radical movements.

an egalitarian distribution of the fruits of such development. Left-wing military governments thus emerge, claiming legitimacy as nationalist liberators and often forestalling potential mass demands by producing economic benefits which, at least initially, exceed popular expectations. This minimises the problems of maintaining order, unless the challenges come from religious or ethnic, rather than class bases, as in Ethiopia. The existence of a warrior tradition, or the importance of the country's strategic position in international politics, frequently ensures that there is a large army to maintain order. Other countries may be equally poor but lacking in a traditional ruling elite capable of wielding authority after the departure of the colonial power. In these, notably in tropical Africa, armies are part of the state bureaucracy inherited at independence, and generally lack a long history or distinctive culture. Any dissatisfaction with governments is likely to come not from the masses, who are mainly illiterate rural dwellers, or from soldiers claiming to represent their aspirations, but from groups within the elite who are dissatisfied with their share of the spoils but do not seek radical changes of policy. If soldiers precipitate a change of government, the new regime is likely to be centrist or indeterminate, although it is becoming more fashionable for such regimes to indulge in left-wing rhetoric. (This model is not, of course, intended to be comprehensive. I have ignored the emergence of civilian fascist regimes which, like their communist counterparts, attempt to tackle problems of legitimacy, participation and enforcement through a party/state structure, but without directly controlling the economy. I have also neglected the case of countires which appear to be ripe for military intervention but which manage to retain civilian government, and have not fitted in the countries of southern Europe which succumbed to right-wing military government in the twentieth century despite a long history of independent nationhood.)

The antecedents of right-wing military governments are different from the other types we have described. In contrast to the incipient liberal democracies, the hold of ruling elites was more tenuous. New elites frequently took over from departing colonialists, whether Iberians or powerful Latin American neighbours in the nineteenth century, or northern Europeans and Japanese in the twentieth, but neither successful liberation nor receipt of a constitution from the departing power conferred long-term legitimacy. Changes of government by unconstitutional means became commonplace in Latin America, often involving military coups and the installation of a soldier as head of state (the 'Caudillo'), although military government in the sense in which we have defined the term did not occur until well into the twentieth century. Whether the nation state had a long history, as in much of Latin America, or a brief one as in South Korea, it was faced with a similar problem as economic development passed well beyond the stages found in the countries with left-wing and centrist military governments. Emerging social groups were demanding economic benefits and political rights within an economic system in which concessions to mass demands might undermine the capital accumulation on which the ruling elite depended ('How could indigenous businesses gain a foothold if workers were given higher wages?') and a political system in which there was little consensus on the regulation of political conflict, let alone the incorporation of new groups into the political process ('Why should governments let oppositions win elections if this threatened their wealth, and possibly their life and liberty?') Hence the list of features conducive to right-wing military intervention suggested earlier in this Chapter. The potential damage that a left-wing government could do to elites in an economy which could not easily afford increased social welfare and equality without damaging economic expansion is clear, as is the frequent inability of civilian elites to prevent such an occurrence if they lack a clear legitimate base, but why should the army come to their rescue? This is another question to which we shall return in more detail, but there are a few obvious possibilities. In terms of pay, status and social contacts, army officers are likely to have more in common with civilian elites than workers and peasants. Their professional commitment to the maintenance of order may make them intolerant of militant left-wing opposition and impatient with left-wing governments if their efforts at mass mobilisations are seen to disturb the status quo. The complex hardware required by a relatively developed army may be dependent on the economic development that civilian elites are trying to foster. But we must beware of assuming that a right-wing orientation is inevitable. What we do need to emphasise is that once a military leadership has taken power and adopted a largely right-wing position, the consequences both for the immediate government of the country and for its long-term political evolution may make its history very different from that of countries under civilian governments and under left-wing or centrist military rule. If civilian elites, unlike those in liberal democracies, have failed to socialise or co-opt the masses or satisfy their material demands, then extensive repression is likely to be necessary — much more so than by military governments presiding over countries where popular demands have not reached such a high level. Yet we are faced with the paradox that the countries suffering extensive repression are often those in which the pressure for the emergence (or re-emergence) of pluralist politics is likely to be greatest. Argentina, Brazil, Turkey and Spain had all known pre-coup political competition in a way that Libya and Togo had not. Other countries such as South Korea appeared to be ripe for such competition by virtue of their social and economic structure, even if their previous experience had been limited.

The study of right-wing military government is therefore interesting not merely as a self-contained episode between coup and election, but as a study of ways in which crises precipitated by particular types of economic development, conflicts over legitimacy and participation, and attempts by soldiers to resolve political conflicts without losing their effectiveness as part of a disciplined professional force, can or cannot be resolved. The outcomes will determine whether much of Latin America, Asia and even southern Europe will be subject to further alternations between authoritarianism and disorder, or whether some other form of polity can emerge. In what circumstances will right-wing military intervention leave a long-term shadow over the political system by ensuring that any restoration of civilian rule is on terms acceptable to the military leadership and civilian elites, with many left-wing politicians and parties disqualified from competing for office and with a continued threat of military re-intervention if the civilian regime deviates too far from the path chosen for it? Alternatively, will the failure of the military to make concessions to mass demands lead to a popular revolt and the installation of a left-wing government which is equally authoritarian, if only on account of the need to meet threats of counter-revolution and external subversion? Or will experience of the widespread repression I have mentioned enhance the prospects for pluralist democracy because pressure from many sections of society forces the military to withdraw, and political actors then become determined to resolve conflicts within a democratic framework, rather than resorting to the traditional practice of enlisting the support of the army to defeat their opponents and thus risking the return of a regime that would repress friend and foe alike? And if such pluralist democracy does emerge, will it still have to pay due regard to the demands of soldiers in order to discourage them from intervening again, and will right-wing groupings and elites nurtured by the military enjoy a head start which they can exploit under the new order? An expectation of such an outcome might even be important in facilitating voluntary military disengagement. Alternatively, will a reaction against the military regime lead to an eclipse of right-wing groupings once they have to compete for votes instead of enjoying special protection? With the departure of right-wing military governments from Spain, Greece and much of Latin America, these questions are increasingly important if we ask not just Huntingdon's broad question 'Will More Countries Become More Democratic?' (1984, pp. 193–218) but questions as to the nature of pluralist politics in countries where the system has evolved via the military route, in comparison with those countries where there has been either revolution, or evolution via a civilian elite broadening its base.

2 Soldiers as Political Animals: Their Entry into Politics

Introduction

To speak of the 'entry' of soldiers into politics is to risk provoking the observation that they have always been there, even if they have not always been visible. It would certainly be difficult to write a political history of Turkey or Brazil or Bangladesh without giving prominence to the army. Armies clearly have a role both as part of the formal state bureaucracy which contributes to decision-making and as pressure groups able to threaten sanctions in pursuit of their demands but, as we saw in the previous chapter, the phenomenon of armies actually taking over government belongs mainly to the second half of the twentieth century.

Of the pioneers in the literature on military government, Huntington was in a minority in arguing that: 'The most important causes of military intervention in politics are not military but political and reflect not the social and organisational characteristics of the military establishment, but the political and institutional structure of society' (Huntington. 1968, p.194).

Most other authors accepted the need to look at explanations in both society and the army. Finer looked at such military motivations for intervention as the pursuit of sectional interests and a sense of national mission, against a civilian background which took into account both the prevailing political culture and immediate political crises (Finer, 1962, Chs 4–9). Like many pioneers, he encountered criticism for the crudeness of his prototype. If a high level of political culture reduced the likelihood of military intervention, how could one subsequently explain coups in Greece ('the cradle of democracy'), Uruguay ('the Switzerland of Latin America') or Chile, with its equally long tradition of pluralism and military aloofness from politics? If political crises precipitated coups, were these caused by economic crises, or by the inability of political or social systems to resolve conflicts? And if the role of the military fluctuated between self-appointed guardianship of the national interest and naked self-interest, how did one explain the attitudes and behaviour of soldiers and their interaction with civil society? Subsequent scholars moved on from Finer's bold outlines to plot in more detail the varied circumstances associated with military intervention, and the sort of military governments to which they gave rise, though it is still doubtful whether we are much nearer to a general theoretical explanation of right-wing military intervention, let alone military intervention in general. At least four overlapping areas of explanation have been pursued: economic, political, social and military.

Economic Explanations

Functionalists and Marxists are agreed that the transition from a predominantly rural, primary producing economy to the beginnings of an industrial economy imposes social and political strains. Huntington and Nelson draw attention to the conflict between the goals of economic growth and participation in the 'later stages of modernisation' (Huntington and Nelson, 1976, p. 168). In nineteenth-century Europe participation was contained because the expectations of the masses were lower in the absence of more developed economies to emulate, and in the absence of structures such as mass parties, popular pressure groups and welfare-minded bureaucracies which might be expected to deliver material benefits. In contrast Weiner points out the way in which elites in 'late developing countries' have created such an institutional framework in imitation of the existing developed countries, only to find that such institutions become strained as economic change produces a growing articulate working class. Because the institutions were created as imitations rather than in response to indigenous demands, they lack durability and are liable to be removed by military coups (Weiner in Binder *et al.*, 1971, p. 176). From a different ideological standpoint, radical Latin American scholars have developed the 'bureaucratic authoritarian model' to explain both military intervention and what follows it. The political system is seen to pass from a populist phase in which a multi-class coalition of urban and industrial interests, including the working class, use the state to promote industrialisation around consumer goods, to a bureaucratic authoritarian phase in which the coalition consists of high-level military and civilian technocrats working with foreign capital. Electoral competition and popular participation are now suppressed, and public policy is concerned with promoting advanced industrialisation. Such a process is said to come about because the market for simple manufactured goods has been satisfied and the market dictates a 'deepening' of industrialisation through the domestic manufacture of intermediate and capital goods through highly capitalised enterprises, often affiliated to multinational corporations. Brazil after 1964, Argentina after 1976, Chile after 1973 and Uruguay after 1975 are presented as examples (see especially Collier, 1979, pp. 19–32; O'Donnell in ibid., pp. 285–318; Cammack in O'Brien and Cammack, 1985, pp. 1–36; Im, 1987, pp. 2, 39–41). The political implication of such a process is that since a mass electorate is unlikely to vote for a package of policies which will reduce living standards in the immediate future, only an authoritarian government will be able to impose it and, in the absence of traditional elites enjoying any legitimacy or coercive power, only a military takeover can ensure that capitalist development takes precedence over popular demands.

The bureaucratic authoritarian model has been criticised on the grounds that it is difficult to fit the facts of individual countries to the processes described, and that anyway the policies of the governments concerned have varied from the extremes of free market economics and political suppression in Chile to the more interventionist and pluralist policies in Brazil. In yet other cases, such as Colombia and Venezuela, democratic regimes have achieved economic restructuring without bureaucratic authoritarianism, presumably because elites were able to obtain popular consent (see O'Donnell in O'Donnell *et al.*, 1986, Part II, p. 9). The 'bureaucratic' element in the concept is itself unclear, since it is not self-evident that bureaucrats will prefer capitalist economic development to social welfare and the processes of political bargaining. More serious from our point of view is the question of how the army fits in, given the dependence of the whole venture on military coercion. It may be true, as acknowledged in the previous chapter, that soldiers are apprehensive about the rise of populist politics and the instability associated with it, and may therefore want to terminate the populist phase which is said to precede bureaucratic authoritarianism, but this does not necessarily imply that they intervene to promote a particular type of capitalist development. It may be argued that a complex army needs the benefits of modern technology (guns rather than butter) just as much as capitalist investors, but it is not certain that this outcome is positively sought.

Yet both the functionalists and the buraucratic authoritarian school clearly have a point. The growth of an entrepreneurial class and an urban labour force wrought by economic development is likely to make for new political pressures with which the formal political structure may find it difficult to cope. Cammack offers a more modest perspective in referring to 'the political economy of delayed and dependent capitalist development' in South America in which military governments in Argentina, Chile and Uruguay have (or had) a common desire for the transformation of 'the dynamic of the state apparatuses of class relations' (Cammack in O'Brien and Cammack, 1985, p. 28). If the rise of populist, participatory politics was not to the army's liking, it needed to seek alternative arrangements and civilian allies to help it pursue new directions, but the doubt raised by reading much of the literature is whether soldiers saw a clear path awaiting them once they had taken power or whether military intervention was more a response to immediate threats to their interests and values, with little thought given to future alliances or policies. If the restoration of 'order' is a major reason for military intervention, the question arises as to whether the disorder which precedes intervention is the inevitable product of economic strains or something dependent on the failure of politicians and elites to handle conflicts with sufficient skill, or the inadequacy of the political structure for facilitating crisis resolution.

A more modest economic explanation of military intervention would be one of economic failure by a civilian government rather than radical economic transformation. McDonald explains intervention in Uruguay partly in terms of the desire to 'revive the stagnant economy' (1985, p. 58) and Mitchell (1981, p. 75) explains the 1964 coup in Bolivia partly in terms of the civilian government's inability to deliver the promised prosperity, but such explanations do not have the same prominence in the literature on right-wing coups as they do in connection with the less developed countries where soldiers are less explicitly right-wing. In tropical Africa a devaluation or an austerity budget are often enough to bring troops out into the streets. The difference would seem to lie in the different functions of coups in different types of country. In the less developed countries coups are designed to do little more than replace a limited number of personnel and their dependants, and to reverse the policies which have caused the immediate grievances, such as a budget which has reduced officers' allowances. In the more developed countries where right-wing coups predominate, a more complex socio-economic structure has given rise to greater political polarisation, and coups are likely to reflect attempts at more radical changes. Intervention to redress lesser grievances would involve too heavy a sledgehammer to crack a nut. While a few hundred soldiers can remove governments in Ghana and Togo on the flimsiest of pretexts with little civilian resistance, such an operation in South America or southern Europe would be more complex. Civilians and large sections of the army would be much more likely to resist, or at least withhold support, unless the coup could be justified on the grounds that it was aimed at resolving a major crisis in society.

Political Explanations

Political explanations have to do with both the inadequacy of political structures and the behaviour of political actors. There are few comprehensive models here comparable with bureaucratic authoritarianism, but analyses of individual countries suggest ideas which might have a wider application. There is also the 'crises and sequences in development' approach put forward by Binder *et al.* which, although not concerned primarily with military intervention, suggests that particular combinations of institutional arrangements at particular stages of socioeconomic development may precipitate crises in which violent unconstitutional change is likely. In simple terms the thesis is that non-Western countries adopted structures such as elections by universal suffrage, mass parties, pressure groups and the development of welfare-oriented bureaucracies at a relatively early stage in economic development, and in an environment in which (in contrast to the early years of industrialisation in the West) internal and international communications facilitated a rapid transmission of information and demands. The information made for an awareness of living standards and political rights in more developed countries and thus fed into growing public demands on authority. The structures came into being for a variety of reasons. They were badges of nationhood and symbols of legitimacy in largely new nations which could not resort to traditional aristocratic bases of legitimacy, yet they reflected neither the reality of elite power nor the achievements of the masses in extracting democratic concessions — a baby, as it were, for whom no one acknowledged parentage and which might grow into a wayward adolescent in the absence of parental affection. Economic development would by itself precipitate a political crisis, it is argued, but if this development is accompanied by the opportunity for pressure via the ballot box, mass movements or the bureaucracy for a redistribution of resources which is not to the liking of the ruling elite or the army, then the subsequent crisis can be explained both by the fact that the existence of the political structures has facilitated such pressures and the fact that the base of the structures is too insecure for them to resist counter-attack from elites wanting to protect their interests. Thus in South Korea in 1972: 'The popular sector was politically excluded; competitive elections were abolished; strikes were prohibited; the organisation of labour unions was severely restricted; and basic human rights were violated arbitrarily' (Im, 1987, p. 239).

The need for such repression can be gauged from the threat which a pluralist political structure had posed in the previous year:

> The opposition party candidate, Dae Jung Kim, included popular democratic demands in the New Democratic Party's platform. His campaign theme was the realisation of the pupulist era based on a populist economy. According to Kim, popular democracy would be in opposition to the developmental dictatorship of the Park regime, and a populist economy would be based on popular welfare, fair distribution of the fruits of economic growth, an employee share-owing system, agrarian revolution and new taxes on the rich. (Im, 1987, p. 254)

Similarly in Argentina and, more especially Chile, political structures which had facilitated popular participation in a way that would not have been possible during the early stages of industrialisation in Europe, proved too much of a threat to elites, and seemed too brittle to facilitate any compromise between the elites and populist demands.

If there is a general argument that the importation of Western political structures can precipitate conditions conducive to military intervention, there is also a particular argument that the similarity of the imported product to the Western equivalent is only superficial. In Brazil Cohen argued that military autocracy was not due mainly to economic forces but to a democracy 'imposed from above' which discouraged stable political competition. This was apparently the result of a more positive state role in economic development than was common in the earlier industrialising countries, which could afford a more *laissez-faire* approach. Parties and pressure groups developed from the top down in response to state activities rather than from the bottom up in response to popular demands, and this left the opposition weak, and discouraged stable political competition (Cohen, 1987, pp. 30–54).

> Caught between the extremes, the growing lower classes were drawn into a struggle that was not really theirs. Having no political organisations of their own, they had to express and defend their interests either through the left, which was benefitting from the polarisation it was creating in conjunction with the extreme right. When autonomous working class organisations were formed, they were formed under the auspices of the left. And the left used them in the battle of extremes that ultimately destroyed in one stroke and for a long time to come, both democracy and the prospects for an autonomous labour movement. (ibid., p. 54)

In functionalist language the problem was one of a weak 'political sub-system' — the area of voluntary praticipatory bodies such as mass parties and pressure groups which normally reinforce a democratic system. Without it, a largely passive population is left at the mercy of elite manipulation. The basic features of such a model could be applied to many of our countries prone to right-wing military intervention. Virtually all of them had democratic written constitutions before the military intervened, and the outward appearance of political sub-systems, but parties, pressure groups and electoral processes did not attract the necessary sense of commitment to enable them to resist authoritarian forces. At first sight this might seem to conflict with the earlier 'structural' view that it is an overabundance of participatory structures that makes for instability, but it may be that the participation is not sufficiently institutionalised in a way that makes for predictability of behaviour and consensus. Thus trade unionism may be only a fitful activity, with few regular meetings or subscription payments or negotiations with governments, but unions may provide a channel through which violence against persons and property can erupt.

Our final political explanation is to do with political behaviour. Perhaps the political structures, however imperfect, provide a means by which military intervention could be averted if only the actors achieve the right sort of consensus. Chalmers argues boldly that the imposition of military-dominated regimes in Latin America has been the product not of the general characteristics of the state, society or culture, but of particular historical crises and the choices men made during those crises (Chalmers in Malloy, 1977, p. 38). Valenzuela argues that in Chile a political crisis preceded (and presumably contributed to) the socioeconomic crisis, with naive 'democrats' preferring to allow the military to destabilise the system rather than working for compromise within traditional mediating institutions (Valenzuela in Linz and Stepan, 1978, pp. 81–110). Without being so explicit, other literature also stresses the failure of political actors to reach consensus rather than the adequacy or otherwise of the structures for doing so. Loveman emphasises the variety of groups in Chile which were willing to destroy the whole political structure if that was the price to be paid for destroying the Allende regime (Loveman, 1988, pp. 261–2); Sunar and Sayari note the incompatible courses pursued by the main parties in Turkey, with the ruling Democratic Party determined to exploit the authoritarian structures it had inherited, and the opposition Republican People's Party determined to politicise the army as a means of challenging authority (Sunar and Sayari in O'Donnell *et al.*, 1986, pp. 165–86). As we move to the more immediate causes of intervention, the behavioural element will obviously become more prominent. A coup was sparked off in Thailand by the return from exile of a controversial ex-prime minister (Marks, 1980, p. 620), and General Noriega's coup in Panama in 1988 is explicable largely in terms of the personal whims of the general, but such events are possible only if the underlying conditions for military intervention are present.

Social Explanations

The social structure will frequently be transformed by economic changes and will set limits to the working of political structures and the behaviour of political actors, so we shall deal with it only briefly to avoid repetition. But there are cases where the social structure may take on a life of its own. We noted Finer's early attempts to relate the likelihood and nature of military intervention to levels of political culture and, even though we can point to exceptions to his rules, it does seem plausible to argue that a largely poor, illiterate population is less likely to want to resist military intervention than one which has evolved complex means of dealing with political conflict, based on a belief in democratic consent. A society does not necessarily move in a predictable way from one set of social institutions and values to another simply as a result of economic development, as witness the survival of fierce ethnic, religious or linguistic conflicts even in economically advanced countries. In some cases political structures will fail to adapt to social changes, while in others the social structure inhibits political change. As an example of the first case, Morris notes the way in which the traditional elites around the two main parties in Honduras were losing their viability by the 1950s as the rising urban middle class, organised labour, rural peasants and varied private enterprise organisations made new demands for participation. The armed forces began to fill the vacuum created, originally as arbiter and later through direct military government (Morris, 1984, pp. 121–6). As an example of the second, Malloy describes the clientelistic system in Bolivia, in which material benefits depended on the favours of influential patrons, as inhibiting the growth of horizontal organisations such as trade unions (1977, pp. 462–72). This takes us back to the problem of a weak political sub-system, which in this case left the country vulnerable to military intervention. The 'crises and sequences in development' school might explain this incongruence between political and social institutions in terms of either the arrival of parties and universal suffrage before industrialisation, or the intransigence of old elites in the face of mass movements, as a 'crises of participation', but a blunter explanation might look to external influences. American fears of popular revolution have helped to preserve often anachronistic elites which might have been toppled if internal forces had been allowed free play. Popular revolution has been averted, except in Cuba and Nicaragua, but largely through externally backed armed force.

Military Influence and Civil–Military Relations

Military explanations of military intervention are in many ways the most complicated. While we can speculate on which broad social, economic or political trends are most or least conducive to intervention, when we focus on soldiers we are looking at individuals who may play an infinite variety of roles. The soldier is an individual with thoughts of his own career prospects and life expectancy, a member of a formal institution, the army, which will vary in its sense of professional and corporate interest between different times and places, and a member of primary institutions such as family, church and ethnic group whose claims will sometimes reinforce and sometimes conflict with his loyalty to the army. At an institutional level, the army will interact with a variety of groups such as politicians, bureaucrats, businesses, and even foreign governments and their armies, and within this pattern will be individual soldiers or groups of soldiers acting with varying degrees of autonomy from the army as a whole. To try to explain military intervention within these varied contexts, we can do no more than look at a few possible relationships.

'Military intervention' assumes at least a minimal separation of soldiers from civilians. Where every man is his own soldier, as in the Wild West before the arrival of the sheriff or in a revolutionary movement, no such separation is possible, and it is difficult to make even in a major modern war with universal conscription. As separation becomes clearer, it becomes easier to think of an army with beliefs and interests of its own. The interests include maximising the acquisition of resources, including pay and conditions of service, but beyond that the army's perception of what is in its interests becomes more subjective. We have, then a twofold problem: to explain the degree of differentiation of the military from civil society, and to explain how the interaction between the military and civilians, at both individual and institutional levels, may encourage right-wing military intervention.

Luckham was one of the first scholars to attempt a comprehensive typology of civil–military relations, using the variables of the extent of civil and military power and the nature of 'boundaries' between the army and society (1971, pp. 8–34). In his analysis, military government is precluded in countries where civil power is 'high' because of either the legitimacy and effectiveness enjoyed by distinctive civil institutions (the Western liberal democratic model) or the way in which military and civil institutions cannot be disentangled from one another (the communist and revolutionary models). Where civil power is 'not high', military government becomes a possibility but its form will be influenced by the extent of military power, and on whether civil–military boundaries are 'integral' or 'fragmented'. Extensive military power, in terms of coercive organisational and political resources, can give rise to a 'garrison state' in which the armed forces can demand as large a share of decision-making as they require — Greece under the colonels was cited as an example. Where military power is only medium but boundaries are still integral, a 'guardian state' may emerge. The army still has some self-steering capacity, in the absence of strong civil institutions, and an ability to advance its own clearly perceived interests. Examples included South Korea, Pakistan in 1958 and Turkey in 1960. Where civil–military boundaries are fragmented, in the sense that civil and military institutions do not always have clearly defined roles, a 'praetorian state' may emerge in which military organisations lose their unity and purpose as particular military factions pursue power and influence in coalition with particular civilian factions. Much of Central America would fit this model.

Luckham's main purpose was to map out the varied forms of civil–military relations rather than to explain military intervention, but in looking at variables in civil and military strengths and at civil–military boundaries, there are questions we can ask in relation to right-wing military intervention. If the army has achieved a degree of differentiation from civil society (integral boundaries) we can begin to ask about how far its perceived corporate interests might lead it to a right-wing position. If military power is 'high', in terms of access to complex resources and the existence of a disciplined force to make these effective, in what circumstances is this the cause, or even the effect, of a right-wing ideological position? If civil–military boundaries are more fragmented, what sort of conditions give the upper hand to right-wing civil–military alliances?

We have noted that a military government is more likely to be right-wing if it is situated in a relatively developed country. Such countries are more likely to have integral civil–military boundaries because greater structural differentiation generally goes with development. This impression is reinforced empirically when we look at the long historical evolution of armies in these countries, most of which have enjoyed over a century of independence — Spain, Greece and much of South America. Here, though not necessarily in countries with newer armies, we might concur with Finer that

> The army differs in function from the society that surrounds it and its function requires that it be separated and segregated. It requires a common uniform and this immediately distinguishes it from the civilian masses. It requires separate housing, in purely military quarters, the barracks. It demands a systematised nomadism, moving from one garrison to another. *It demands a separate code of morals and manners from that of the civilian population* . . . all this tends to enhance military solidarity by making the military life self-centred . It is easy, even, to inspire contempt for one's own nationals — the civvies. (Finer, 1962, p. 9; emphasis added)

This notion of 'separateness' has helped the development of the concept of 'professionalism' — the notion that soldiers, like doctors or lawyers, see themselves as belonging to a distinctive hierarchy which has distinctive relations with its clients. The difficulty is that whereas the doctor's or lawyer's clients are easily identifiable, the army's client is the state on whose behalf it fights, and defining what is in the client's interests is a matter of political judgement. Early literature suggested that greater professionalism would lead to greater abstinence from political intervention, since such activity would be outside the army's self-defined role, but actual experience suggests otherwise. Intervention by highly professional armies has been explained in terms of the failure of the client to discharge his functions adequately, especially the failure, or likely future failure, to maintain order and suppress subversion (See especially Makin, 1984, p. 230; Philip, 1984, p. 8). While disorder and subversion are not new, the professional ethos since the Second World War has led to their presentation in a new light. Officer training under United States auspices led to the implanting of Cold War rhetoric about communist threats, which loomed larger with the Cuban Revolution and the rise of guerrilla movements in Latin America. In the cases of Greece and Korea and, a generation earlier Spain, civil wars fought against communists offered an even more visible reason for using the communist threat as a justification for intervention. The professional soldier did not wait for civilians to call on his professional expertise: he used his professional judgement to decide when the time was ripe.

Intervention in response to a left-wing threat is not in itself evidence of professionalism, but there is much evidence that coups in these countries, especially South America, are the work of armies acting as coherent groups rather than groups of malcontents. One rough indicator of professionalism would be the extent to which coups were led by officers from the top of the military hierarchy rather than more junior officers or NCOs bypassing their superiors. Data taken mainly from Keegan's *World Armies* suggests that 76 per cent of the coups ushering in military governments which we have described as 'right-wing' were led by generals, as against only 27 per cent of the coups leading to non-right military governments (Keegan, 1983). Philip shows how professionalism in South America can be traced back to the nineteenth century when rulers tried to achieve stability by converting personally controlled bands of armed men into standing armies. After 1945 these already professional armies were further moulded through the use of military academies to preach the gospel of national security against the communist threat (Philip in Clapham and Philip, 1985, pp. 129–33). The army's *raison d'être* shifted from external defence to internal security. The former might imply a professionalism which left civilians to take the key decisions, since armies do not normally take decisions on when or whether to go to war, whereas the latter gave soldiers more scope in judging when threats to security warranted their intervention in politics.

> 'Old professionalism' (classical professionalism of the Huntingtonian vintage) responds to threats to external security and is highly specialised, its scope of action is restricted, socialisation is neutral, and its general attitude is apolitical. The new professionalism responds primarily to problems of internal security; its military skills are police-like and managerial, and there are no restrictions on the scope of its action. (Stepan, 1978, p. 130)

This is not to suggest the existence of a golden age when 'classical' military professionals abstained from politics. The argument is more that soldiers used to intervene in politics in spite of their professionalism; now they intervene because of it.

If relative development, military professionalism and right-wing military governments generally go together in South America (despite the deviant case of Peru in 1968), the picture is more complicated in other regions of right-wing military government. Pakistan is perhaps closest to the South American model, with the army retaining the professionalism inherited from the British Raj, but most of the literature on Central America suggests something closer to Luckham's fragmented civil–military boundaries. At the risk of oversimplifying, the picture is one of armies emerging as part of the repressive apparatus of landed elites in plantation economies and then moving into government to fill a political vacuum when no other institutions existed to check the rise of mass movements and terrorism (See especially Dunkerley in Clapham and Philip, 1985, pp. 171–200; Rosenberg in Malloy and Seligson, 1987, pp. 193–215). In Greece military intervention reflected the grievances of a close-knit faction within the officer corps and not just the professional perceptions of the army as a whole (Veremis in Featherstone and Katsoudas, 1987, pp. 214–29; Veremis in Clapham and Philip, 1985, pp. 27–45), and in

Asia outside Pakistan professionalism is even more difficult to identify as a source of military intervention.

If the concept of professionalism has limitations in explaining the motives for right-wing coups, we need to look at the roles which an officer may occupy other than membership of a profession. At least three arguments are discernible:

1. That soldiers have distinctive interests which they wish to defend or advance. (This is not the same as asserting the existence of 'professionalism', since the interests may be concerned with the material wealth of individual soldiers rather than a corporate ethos.)
2. That in relatively developed countries, soldiers are part of a larger elite whose interests are threatened by the rise of mass society.
3. That foreign aid, training or collaboration imparts 'imported' values which give soldiers new perceptions on the inadequacy of civilian governments.

On the first argument Calvert sees Latin American officers as members of a military elite, not subordinate to the civilian elite. They are members of a military class in a distinctive relationship to the productive process, able to command it without forming part of it. Welded together by personal links of military discipline, peer group loyalties, intermarriage and awareness of their special privileges, they behave as military men first, rather than bearers of a political ideology (Calvert, 1985, p. 32). In less professionalised armies, the special privileges often show through more clearly than the disciplined loyalty. In Bangladesh the attempt by a populist government to pare down an over-large army, find an economically more productive role for it, and place it under the control of provincial governors in a decentralised structure, led to a coup in 1975 (Rizvi in Clapham and Philip, 1985, pp. 224). In much of Central America, and even Argentina, extensive control of businesses by armies as a whole and by individual officers, gives soldiers immediate reasons for intervention if their interests are threatened. Collective military survival and individual greed may both be factors in military intervention, but so too may a broader notion that a threat of national disintegration exists which endangers the survival of the army. Civil political factions may be unable or unwilling to contain conflict for reasons described earlier in this chapter. The army, whether highly professionalised, as in Turkey, or held together very loosely, as in Indonesia, may have enough collective sense of self-interest to impose its own solution.

A difficulty with any analysis which emphasises the distinctive interests of the military is it begs questions of how the army came to enjoy such autonomy which, in turn, raises questions about the nature of civil–military relations. Did soldiers acquire their relative autonomy because civilians were too weak to resist them, or was it part of a 'trade-off' which excluded them from other areas of activity? In Indonesia the former seems to fit, and this takes us back to a search for explanations of the failure of the political process to institutionalise conflict resolution. In South America we are driven back to the establishment of standing armies, in preference to personally led armed gangs, in the (largely unfulfilled) hope of depriving contenders for political power of military force. In Central America, landed elites were content to let the army take care of violent challenges to their privileges while they enjoyed the fruits of their investment. Even where Luckham's 'integral' civil–military boundaries prevail it does not necessarily mean that the military keep out of politics, only that the boundaries are 'stabilised'. This allows for a variety of relationships which, even if they cannot be dignified with the adjective 'legitimate', may exist as a regular part of the political process. These are manifested by civil factions pressing soldiers to overthrow unwanted governments or soldiers intervening if their self-defined interests have not been adequately looked after by civilian governments. Such manifestations may lead to the argument that soldiers are part of a larger elite.

> There is [in Latin America] . . . a coalition of interests between . . . economic and political elites and the military when both feel their interests threatened on whatever grounds — ideological, economic security or social change — under civilian governments. Military intervention, in its very different forms in the separate states, occurs against a common background. (Blakemore, 1986, p. 1078)

Perhaps this is labouring to demonstrate the obvious. Just as one might expect landowners, accountants, stockbrokers and industrialists in any relatively developed country to close ranks in the event of any populist or egalitarian threat to their interests, it is hardly remarkable that professional men in khaki with comparable salaries and social backgrounds should be part of such a coalition, even if their own interests are not completely congruent with those of the other groups. This is especially the case in South America where, as Philip points out, social stratification is based on class rather than ethnicity or religion, so that class factors unite the officer corps, just as ethnic and religious factors divide them elsewhere (Philip, 1985, p. 357). A minority of officers may be left-wing, just as a minority of stockbrokers may vote for left-wing parties, but the most common effect of military intervention is to install right-wing governments. Within the long-term right-wing trend there will be periods when the military break ranks. Stepan suggests that despite the middle-class background of the Brazilian officer corps, officers see themselves as classless, with a 'mission of promoting the national good' (1971, p. 270). This self-image, he argues, means that the Latin American military will not automatically take up a class position on a particular issue when their own interests are at stake, hence the Peruvian military's stand on land reform: 'The same military institution can shift from far left to far right, and back again, in regard to economic policy' (ibid., p. 270).

Pakistan again appears to share common ground with Latin America, but otherwise civil–military relations in other regions may be more complex. Officers have allied themselves with left-wing or moderate civilians at various times in all the Central American states which have experienced military government, and in Bolivia, Ecuador and Peru, which occupy lower positions in terms of indicators of development than Brazil and the Southern Cone. This may indicate both a greater promiscuity on the part of officers seeking productive liaisons in less clearly stratified societies, with their choice influenced by considerations of short-term gain in coalition bargaining, and a greater ideological heterogeneity within the officer corps, with some members preferring state-sponsored development, greater equality and expanded political participation as means of securing their position against external economic competition and internal terrorism.

In southern Europe and Asia outside Pakistan, the 'army as part of the elite' model is also difficult to sustain. In Greece it was more the colonels' sense of inferiority that precipitated their coup, and Tachau has shown how most Turkish officers come from non-elite families outside the main urban centres (1984, p.83). In so far as they had a class affiliation, it was to the more 'traditional' elite which had been eclipsed as a result of economic development and the defeat of Ataturk's Republican People's Party. In South Korea, officers may have become an elite group after taking power but their initial intervention was concerned more with removing governments which were seen as partial in their handling of the economy and incompetent in their running of the country (Kim, 1971, pp. 93–4). In Indonesia, Crouch describes the army as 'part of the political elite' when it took power (1978, p. 23) but the emphasis should perhaps be on the word 'political'. The problems of a strife-torn country recovering from both Japanese and Dutch occupation elevated the army to a prominent role alongside other state institutions, but its relationship with civilian elites appears to have been as much competitive as complementary.

Foreign influence, our third influence on military behaviour, is often an attractive explanation of military intervention. It may work through attempts to destabilise civil institutions by such means as reducing economic aid or investment, but short of actually organising an invasion from abroad, as in Guatemala in 1954, success still depends on the willingness of the indigenous army to attack the presidential palace. Foriegn influence on such a decision depends on both short-term pressures, including offers of generous support if the coup succeeds, and long-term influences in the form of socialisation through training, shared combat experience and regular contacts. Latin American armies provide obvious examples of this, and Veremis suggests that Greek soldiers' contempt for civilian politicians was encouraged by their American allies during the civil war (Veremis in Featherstone and Katsoudas, 1987, pp. 214–29). No one would deny that such influences may reinforce pressures for military intervention, but those educated at the same school do not always come away learning the same lessons. Stepan contrasts the influence of the military training of Brazilian officers in the United States in reinforcing many right-wing views, with a similar training or Peruvian officers who staged a left-wing coup. 'Total career experiences and national situations', he argues, predominate over attitudes derived exclusively from training (Stepan, 1971, pp. 247–8). Even when officers do behave in ways approved of by their foreign contacts, it is difficult to disentangle the influence of military contacts from the more extensive pattern of foreign relations, including trade, aid and civilian political links, or from the factors which bring the military into conflict with existing civilian governments.

Conclusion

If we want to explain the broad conditions conducive to right-wing military intervention, as opposed to immediate causes, all four influences clearly play a part, but to varying degrees in different regions of the world. The economic changes implicit in early industrialisation in the more developed South American countries, especially Argentina, Brazil and Chile, have clearly produced strains in society with which it would be difficult for any political system to cope. When elites in the system enjoy only a tenuous legitimacy and mass movements threaten established order without generally having the strength to take power themselves, right-wing officers may be tempted to take power on the pretext of restoring order, and in the interests of maintaining elite privileges. The long-standing fragility of the political systems may be a necessary condition for intervention, but the fact that such intervention produces long-term right-wing military governments rather than 'Bonapartist' leaders or Caudillos, has much to do with the dilemmas of distribution that go with industrialisation. Political factors have exerted a more independent influence in southern Europe and parts of Asia. There were no obvious qualitative economic changes in Greece and Turkey comparable with South America, but the inability of politicians to resolve basic constitutional crises which affected the army and its allies brought the military into government. As we move to the countries which were least developed at the time of intervention, such as Pakistan, Bangladesh, Indonesia and South Korea, political factors loom still larger (although South Korean military governments began to resemble their South American counterparts as economic development gathered momentum). When political ineptitude in trying to resolve conflicts in heterogeneous, newly independent countries was combined with upsetting military interests or values, civilian government came to an end. The right-wing credentials of the coup makers were less obvious than in South America, but socialisation under the British Raj and a record of combat against communists who were seen as a threat to the integrity of the nation, made right-wing governments a likely outcome.

Social factors are especially evident in Central America and less developed South American countries such as Bolivia and Ecuador. Although relatively little literature pursues the subject directly, the problem appears to be one of incongruence between social and political structures. If political parties fail to reflect or accommodate new social forces, or if old-fashioned political clientelism inhibits the growth of such forces, political conflict will flow along irregular and unpredictable channels. Equilibrium, if such a concept can be used in politics, might have been restored through a popular revolution against a vulnerable elite, or even by a reforming government chosen in a free election, but United States support for the elite, and for soldiers sustaining it, has generally ruled out such possibilities.

The aspirations of the military themselves have had a bearing on most right-wing military interventions, but in vastly different ways in different parts of the world. It is generally agreed that 'professionalism' has developed furthest in South America and Pakistan, and that this has stimulated intervention when soldiers have perceived a threat to order or internal security. Opinion is divided on how far military interests form part of a larger elite interest, but threats of terrorism and populist politics are likely to give military and civil elites a large area of common ground. In contrast, the military in southern

Europe are more like one of yesterday's elites, upset not by Huntington's 'mass society' looming on the horizon but by the actual excesses produced by well-established liberal democracy. In Central America the current interests of individual officers and military factions are often a better explanation of intervention than a sense of professional integrity, while in Asia outside Pakistan military explanations of intervention are dwarfed by the threats of national disintegration which have created a power vacuum.

Even without covering the whole universe of military governments it is difficult to generalise from such a diversity of cases, but in Table 2.1 a preliminary attempt is made to set out the problems perceived by incoming military rulers, the tasks they set themselves, and the forms of government they establish. (The last of these will be pursued in detail in the next chapter.) Some of the explanations of intervention may give us clues as to what the subsequent military governments were attempting to do. Greece, as the most economically advanced country to experience a successful coup since the war, stands out as an exceptional case, not conforming to any wider pattern. Leaving it aside, the most developed countries to experience military intervention were in South America where the failure of the political system to cope with economic changes left military governments with the long-terms task of social demobilisation in alliance with civilian elites and foreign capital. At the other developmental extreme, the actual or threatened national disintegration of Bangladesh, Indonesia and Pakistan left military governments with the more basic task of holding the nation together, if only to ensure the army's survival. In between were the cases of South Korea, Turkey and Central America. In the first two, the army intervened initially because it saw the behaviour of civilian governments as both a cause of disorder and a threat to military autonomy. But thereafter South Korea and Turkey diverged, with the South Korean army imposing its own political solution through authoritarian development and the Turkish army, loyal to the Atatürk tradition of separating military and political roles, seeking a largely authoritarian civilian political consensus within boundaries defined by the military. The Central American cases have been closer to 'business as usual'. As in the South, Caudillo rule has given way to governments ruling through the army, but the distinction between civil and military governments is much less clear than in other regions. Military presidents often try to legitimise their authority by allowing competitive, though rigged, elections and limited party competition, while nominally civilian governments are restricted by the veto powers of the military, and often include military men in key posts. In these countries we need to look at military governments less as governments which have taken power to steer the country in a new direction than as elements in a shifting coalition. Here, more than in most of the world, the behaviour of military governments depends on the pursuit of the individual and collective interests of soldiers rather than on clarity of ideology or political consistency.

The final column of Table 2.1 leaves us with four broad types of right-wing military government, but the reasons why diverse countries with diverse histories approximate to any of these types has still to be explored. It is to this task that we turn in the next chapter.

Table 2.1 The perceived problems and tasks of right-wing military governments

Country/region	Problems perceived by the military	Tasks of military governments	Types of military government
Greece	Political crisis. Decadence caused by liberal democracy. Insecurity of right-wing officers.	Authoritarian government to restore traditional values.	Military authoritarian.
South America	Terrorism, disorder. Threat of mass demands.	Social demobilisation in co-operation with civil elites and foreign capital.	Personal rule; military authoritarian.
South Korea	Disorder, political interference with the military.	Authoritarian government to harness developmental potential.	Civil–military authoritarian; limited democracy.
Turkey	Disorder. Threat to autonomy of the military and their civilian allies.	Early handover to relatively authoritarian civil government within pluralist system.	Limited democracy.
Thailand	Civilian incompetence. Maldistribution of resources.	Preservation of civil and military elite interests.	Limited democracy.
Central America	Terrorism, communism. Threats to survival of officers by popular movements.	Containing mass movements	Civil–military authoritarian.
Indonesia Pakistan Bangladesh	Civil threats to military privileges. National disintegration.	Immediate task of national survival, which frequently involves suppressing radical groups.	Limited democracy (Indonesia), military authoritarian.

3 How Can Soldiers Govern? The Dynamics of Right-Wing Military Government

Introduction

Any military government taking power is faced with immediate problems of survival and long-term problems of either 'civilianising' itself or handing over power to acceptable civilians. 'Pure' military government, unencumbered by civilian partners or co-optees, is not feasible except for short periods. Clapham and Philip suggest that the weakness is one of political management rather than lack of legitimacy (1985, p. 3), but the acquisition of a legitimate base will obviously improve the regime's prospects of survival and effectiveness. Certain basic requirements of a government which has taken power by force, in a country with at least some previous experience of pluralist politics, can be enumerated. Apart from legitimacy, it needs access to expertise, the means of implementing decisions, means of communicating with the population and means of coercion. If it is led by military men it also needs to retain or restore the hierarchy within its military constituency. If it is right-wing it will want to close down or severely restrict any potential structures which promote autonomous popular participation or a more egalitarian distribution of resources. In this chapter we shall explore the possible styles of government which are open to right-wing soldiers; the reasons why particular styles are chosen; the possible roles for the army and civilians; the relations with civil society that each style may facilitate, and the problems to which each style may give rise.

Classification of military governments has always been an imprecise business, if only because most of them rule without constitutions, or with constitutions which are not adhered to. One of the most comprehensive attempts at classification was by Finer, who looked at such variables as the presence of absence of civilian ministers, legislatures and political parties (Finer in Kolkowicz and Korbonski, 1982, p. 284). One negative feature, from our point of view, which emerges from this classification is the rejection of the one-party state as a vehicle for right-wing military governments. Of the twelve military one-party states listed by Finer, ten were left-wing in our definition, one was indeterminate and one (Zaire) had dubious claims to be regarded as military. Military governments on the right prefer either to ban parties or to put their weight behind a dominant party in a nominally pluralist system, as in Brazil, Paraguay and much of Central America. This difference presumably reflects the left-wing preference for claims to legitimacy based on a (nominally) mass party which represents the whole nation, as against the right-wing suspicion that parties may become a vehicle for populist demands. If they are to be permitted at all, it is as an electoral vehicle for vanquishing the left-wing foe rather than as a major institutional pillar, especially when more reliable pillars are available in the form of business, bureaucratic and traditional institutions. The main exceptions are the historically distant regimes in Franco's Spain and Peron's Argentina, where the influence of contemporary fascist regimes was present and there was at least an illusion of mass involvement.

Finer used his variables to produce a fourfold classification of military governments based on the extent of involvement of parties, legislatures and armies (Kolkowicz and Korbonski, 1982, p. 301). Perlmutter offers a different method of classification which concentrates more on the interaction between civil and military groups rather than the existence of formal structures. He argues that any classification of military regimes should use four criteria to explain the differences between various types:

A. The nature of the relationship between the military and the civil elites and structures.
B. The scope of the military and civil organisational and institutional autonomy in the military regime.
C. The nature of the political and administrative instruments employed by the military regime to achieve modernisation and legitimacy: bureaucratic structures, communications, political parties, interest groups and . . . the military itself.
D. The classes or groups penetrated by the military regime and the class it seeks to co-opt or collaborate with. (Perlmutter, 1980, p. 104)

Perlmutter arrives at a fivefold classification of corporative, market–bureaucratic, socialist–oligarchic, army–party and tryannical military regimes (ibid., pp. 105–17). This approach has the advantage of being 'functional' as well as incorporating Finer's more 'structural' approach (the interaction between the regime and the wider society, as well as whether parliaments or parties are permitted), but it is too broad for a study restricted to right-wing military regimes. Perlmutter's third and fourth types fall outside the sphere of right-wing politics, and the fifth is said to be found in tropical Africa, where the interests of the rulers and their immediate followers prevail over any coherent ideology, whether of the left or right. The first two, corporatism, 'market–bureaucracy', come closer to the right-wing sphere, but a twofold classification would hardly do justice to the varied forms of right-wing military government. The classification given in Table 3.1 accepts most of Perlmutter's criteria, but with greater emphasis on the basis of authority rather than the structures used, since the names of such structures (political parties, interest groups etc.) may conceal wide differences in their nature between countries. Our classification therefore looks at two dimensions of military government: the power structure and the relationship with civil society. The power structures suggested are personal rule, military authoritarianism, civil–military authoritarianism and limited democracy.

How Can Soldiers Govern?

Table 3.1: Different structures of military government and their relationship with civil society

Power structure	Conditions required	Possible relations with civil society		
		Charismatic Rule	Terror	Clientelism
Personal rule, e.g. Chile, Paraguay.	1. Limited pre-coup contacts between army and civil elites. 2. Weakness of civil elites. 3. Professionalised army with few factional challenges. 4. Skilled individual leader.	Possible in very limited sense.	Likely	Possible at lower levels.
Military authoritarianism, e.g. Argentina 1976–81, Bangladesh, Brazil 1965–8, Greece, Uruguay, Parkistan.	1. Limited pre-coup contacts between army and civil elites. 2. Weakness of civil elites and civil political structures. 3. Lack of civil support for the military. 4. Military rejection of civilian political system as a whole.	No	Likely, especially where civilians offer resistance.	Possible if perceived civilian threat is relatively weak, e.g. Pakistan 1958–68.
Civil–Military Authoritarianism, e.g. Argentina 1966–73, Brazil 1969–80, Bolivia, Central America, South Korea 1972–87.	1. Interdependence between army and civilian groups. 2. Exploitation of a divided army by rival civil groups (Central America). 3. Powerful civilian groups cannot be dislodged completely, (South America).	No.	Likely, but often ineffective.	Possible if military professionalism is low. e.g. Bolivia, Indonesia.
Limited democracy e.g. Brazil 1980–5 Indonesia, Thailand, Turkey, South Korea 1961–71.	1. Experience of pluralist politics before military intervention. 2. Growth of civilian democratic demands with socio-economic change after military intervention. 3. Military search for broader base.	No.	Unlikely.	Possible, but democratic channels provide alternative means of distributing resources.

Table 3.1 Contd...

| Bureaucratic authoritarianism | Possible relations with civil society | | Possible problems |
	Co-option of civilians	Corporatism	
Limited by arbitrary nature of personal rule.	Very limited. Civilians are hired and fired rather than co-opted.	Unlikely	1. Little institutionalised control over civilians 2. Loss of military professionalism. 3. Insecure base.
Possible.	Very limited.	Unlikely.	1. Lack of legitimacy. 2. Loss of military professionalism and increased politicisation of the army. 3. Vulnerability if material benefits cannot be delivered.
Possible if civil institutions are sufficiently developed.	Substantial.	Possible if military institutions have sufficient coherence.	1. Little coherence or continuity. 2. Instability in the absence of either sufficiently developed democratic norms or effective authority.
Unlikely.	Substantial.	Possible, but limited by democratic channels.	1. For the military, demo-cratisation may gather a momentum which they cannot control. 2. For civilians, attempts extend democracy further may provoke military retaliation.

The possible relationships with civil society are those based on charisma, terror, clientelism, bureaucratic authoritarianism, co-option and corporatism. Our tasks are to attempt to explain the forces giving rise to each type of power structure, to examine the likelihood or otherwise of each structure coexisting with particular relationships with society, and to speculate on the implications of each type for the respective roles of civil and military institutions and the problems they may encounter. These structures are, of course, ideal types and in practice there is much overlap between them.

Personal Rule

Extensive personal rule by a military man is difficult to find, but Pinochet's Chile and Stroessner's Paraguay come closer to this model than most (See especially Lewis, 1980, pp. 22–6; Bouzutzky in Malloy and Seligson, 1987, p. 86; Clapham and Philip, 1985, pp. 306–24; Cammack in Randall, 1988, p. 125). Instead of merely presiding over a junta, the ruler hires and fires civil and military subordinates and, where necessary, appeals over their heads to a wider population. To explain the emergence of autocracy is never easy, and the skill and fortune of individual leaders is always one of the unquantifiable ingredients. Beyond that, it is necessary to have an army which has been made docile through effective purges, although this still begs the question of why the army is willing to submit to such treatment. A degree of discipline and cohesion, if not professionalism, is necessary, hence the unlikelihood of personal military rule in Central America for more than very short periods. For the rest, a search for explanations in civil society may be more rewarding. Lewis mentions poverty and lack of experience of democratic government as conducive to dictatorship in Paraguay (1980, pp. 22–7), echoing Finer's observation about low political culture, yet Chile has also experienced personal rule despite greater wealth and experience of pluralist politics. What may be more important is the weakness of civil elites, which are unable either to bargain for a share of power or to make alliances with rival military factions and thus press for a more balanced military government. The civilian weakness may arise because the military have taken over at an early stage in socioeconomic development, as in Paraguay and in non-right-wing governments in Africa and the Middle East, or at the other extreme because a long period of military abstinence from politics, as in Chile, has made for few civil–military alliances and therefore little need to repay civilians with a share of the spoils of office (See especially Philip, 1985, p. 322 on Chile).

I have suggested that a military government's relationship with civil society may be cemented by one or more of six overlapping devices: charismatic rule, terror, clientelism, bureaucratic authoritarianism, co-option and corporatism. The charismatic element is likely to be stronger under personal rule than under the other types of military government, but still of limited significance. Military dictators are seldom loved by their subjects, but people may be keen to keep them in power if they see serious disorder or loss of personal wealth as the only alternative to the strong man. This would help to explain the mandate which was given to General Pinochet by Chilean voters in relatively free referenda before 1988. When charisma is inadequate, the alternative of terror is widely used, especially when links with civilian elites are only tenuous. The absence of such links means both that voluntary compliance with authority is less likely and that there is little to constrain the army from torturing and killing any who stand in its way.

The remaining devices are possible rather than basic features of personal rule. Clientelism, in the sense of groups and individuals obtaining resources through personal links with power holders, may exist at lower levels but has little bearing on major political decisions. Bureaucratic authoritarianism, as we saw in previous chapters, is a difficult concept to apply to the real world, but if we take it to mean that civilian technocrats are given wide powers to re-mould society in the interests of certain types of indigenous and foreign capital, then a personal ruler fearful of populist pressures is unlikely to spurn such technocratic aid provided it does not threaten his own survival or legitimacy. Research is so far limited on the personal links between military leaders and free market economists, but there is clearly some ideological affinity between the discipline of the parade ground and the discipline of the market. Each provides a visible scale of rewards and punishments, and each ensures the protection of those in authority against the challenge of those who prefer distribution to be based on choices expressed through the ballot box or demands articulated from below (see especially Whitehead in Hojman, 1985, pp. 12–15). This is not to argue that free market economics is an inevitable concomitant of right-wing military rule, merely that such economic arrangements can be rationalised easily by soldiers when it is in their interests to do so. But if bureaucratic authoritarianism is taken to mean not merely a loose division of labour between a dictator and technocrats, but a hierarchical order in which the civil and military bureaucracies take decisions which are reinforced through coercion, then the concept of bureaucratic authoritarianism is more difficult to reconcile with personal rule. Links with civil society through co-option or corporatism will be no more than minimal because both concepts assume that civilians have assets to trade which would be useful to the ruler. Certain civilian skills will be necessary in formulating and implementing policy, but the civilians are likely to be hired and fired at the rulers' convenience rather than co-opted as indispensable parts of the political process. Corporatism, too, sits uneasily with personal rule if we take it to mean that semi-autonomous civilian groups are strong enough to bargain for a share in decision-making. We have to go back to Peron in search of such a model, and to a developmental situation, unusual today, in which a military autocrat could co-operate with both organised labour and capital without jeopardising the economy unduly.

The main problem for the personalist regime is the narrowness of its base. In the short term it has the advantage of minimal debts to civilians, and can therefore carry out more sweeping changes without the need to compromise, as in the case of the more thoroughgoing monetarist policy in Chile compared with Argentina and Brazil (Philip, 1985, p. 332), but in the long run reliance on terror or plebiscitary rule prove too loose a structure for controlling events. If the policies of civilians who are hired, rather than co-opted or incorporated into government, prove to be embarrassing, as they did with the economic crisis in Chile in the early 1980s, the civilians can be sacked after the damage has been done. But the damage may be more difficult to prevent than in a regime where there is a greater dialogue between soldiers and civilians on a more equal basis, and where each can make adjustments to avert a potential crisis. On the military side, questions arise about the strain that personal rule places on the army. Perlmutter argues that professionalism depends on the extent to which a military government does *not* rely on the army to retain power (1986, p. 11). This may be a rather narrow view of professionalism, since the professional ethic accepts the legitimacy of military intervention in politics in many countries, but prolonged military government of any sort will cause strains as soldiers in government enjoy privileges not available to soldiers in barracks. These strains may be eased by generous provision for the army, but a pyramidal structure with one ruler at the apex can easily disintegrate if the ruler departs by accident or design, or if he becomes personally unpopular. Prudent rulers may thus seek broader coalitions with civilians to avert such disasters.

Military Authoritarianism

We move on to a system in which decision-making depends on a junta rather than a single military man, but still with minimal civilian involvement. Argentina, Bangladesh, Greece, Pakistan, Uruguay, and possibly Brazil between 1965 and 1968 approximate to this model. As in the case of personal rule, such regimes may be explained in terms of limited pre-coup contacts between the military and civilian elites, for example in Uruguay (Handelman in Drake and Silva, 1986, pp. 205–7) or the weakness of civil elites and civil pre-coup structures, as in Bangladesh and Pakistan (Ahmed in Gardezi and Rashid, 1983, p. 132; Rizvi in Clapham and Philip, 1985, pp. 201–36). This again takes us towards different ends of the developmental spectrum. Remoteness between civil and military elites was a feature of Uruguayan politics in a relatively developed country with a long history of pluralist politics, whereas civil elite weakness was a feature of Pakistani politics. No civilian group had built an effective power base in the short period between independence and the first coup. We should be on our guard in looking for too much uniformity within the military authoritarian category.

Other reasons for military authoritarianism have to do with the attitudes of civilian and military elites towards each other. In Greece and Uruguay the army could find few prominent civilians willing to support them (Danopoulos, 1983, pp. 492–3; Gillespie in O'Donnell *et al.*, 1986, p. 179). The Greek military in turn were contemptuous of the civilian elite and the whole political system, as were their counterparts in Pakistan. Our trawl is again picking up apparently dissimilar countries, but one common feature is the strength and professionalism of the army — one forged under the British Raj and the other in an anti-communist civil war. The coercive power and relative unity thus generated enabled the military authoritarians to survive in the face of civilian hostility.

Of the possible relations between a military authoritarian government and civil society, the collective nature of the junta rules out the possibility of a charismatic following. Bureaucratic authoritarianism, civilian co-option and corporatism are unlikely for the same reasons as under personal rule — civilians are not wanted, or do not want to participate in large numbers. As in the personal rule model, civilians are hired and fired without being closely integrated into the processes of government. This does not mean that their role is unimportant. They may play a significant role in major areas of policy, as with economic policy in Uruguay, but in the absence of a strong power base their survival depends on the goodwill of the military. In areas which the military consider vital for their own survival, such as national security, control of the budget and control over the constitutional powers of such political structures as exist, soldiers remain autonomous. Terror is much more likely, especially where civilian resistance is high, and is extremely effective. The powerful armies of Argentina, Brazil and Uruguay had largely destroyed opposition terrorism by the time they returned to barracks, in contrast to the continuing civil wars being fought by weaker armies in Central America. Where military authoritarianism is due more to civilian weakness than to military strength, the element of organised terror will be less, as in Bangladesh and Pakistan. There is in these countries a possibility of developing a political structure, however ramshackle, which does not rely on either shooting or torturing civilians or bringing them into the political process as junior partners. Clientelism may offer material rewards to favoured civilians without giving them much involvement in national political decisions. In Pakistan clientelism was institutionalised, if that is not a contradiction in terms, through Ayub Khan's creation of Basic Democracies — local authorities dominated largely by landowners, businessmen and contractors — which provided an electoral college for choosing the (military) president. This was an attempt to bypass politicians and political parties which survived for a decade until the downward flow of resources required to lubricate the system began to dry up (Rizvi in Clapham and Philip, 1985, pp. 205–15). A similar, less successful, system was attempted in Bangladesh after its secession from Pakistan (ibid., pp. 230–4).

Regimes of this sort are strong in the short term but vulnerable in the long (or even medium) run. Even if civilian institutions are weak, a military government which bases its authority more on force than legitimacy may face a challenge from subordinate soldiers who want to take power in the way that the existing incumbents did. This may hasten a return to barracks if acceptable civilian successors can be found, but the alienation of these governments from civilian elites may mean that such a move is only a last resort when the alternative is a long period of conflicts with aspiring civilian politicians, some of whom would eventually find allies in an increasingly divided army. Such a handover to civilians was the outcome in Argentina after the Falklands War and Uruguay after the failure of the military government's economic policies. In Greece and Pakistan, the professionalism of the armies was eventually overstrained by unsuccessful military adventures against Turkey and India which provoked internal military as well as civilian revolts. This might support the once-fashionable thesis that pure military governments are weakened not only by the absence of a secure base in civil society but by a lack of political skill, which drives them into dangerous decisions that more skilled civilian politicians would have avoided. I have argued elsewhere that civilian rulers in countries prone to military intervention are themselves not always people with much greater foresight (Pinkney, 1973, pp. 152–66), but military governments do seem to have a tendency to resort to unwinnable wars when others might have resorted to diplomacy.

If a disastrous war can be avoided, there is still the problem of the shallowness of the government's base. The illegitimacy of the government, and its flouting of constitutional norms and human rights, may be overlooked while memories of a less than perfect civilian predecessor are still fresh, and relative prosperity and order are enjoyed, but the government has little fat to sustain it if economic conditions deteriorate or social tensions mount. If soldiers are not forced out of office altogether they may try to secure their position by resorting to civil–military authoritarianism or limited democracy.

Civil–Military Authoritarianism

I am not suggesting a regular sequence of developments from personal rule through military authoritarianism and civil–military authoritarianism to limited democracy. Some military governments may progress in that way (possibly Brazil), but some such as Argentina will shuttle uneasily between the different types, and others, such as Bolivia and the Central American republics, will remain mainly in the civil–military authoritarian groove throughout their lives. Even these will not remain static. Civil–military authoritarianism may fluctuate between arrangements where governments coming to power by force are able to rule only because civil elites sustain them, to arrangements where the formalities of the electoral process produce a government, led sometimes by a recently retired soldier and sometimes by a civilian, which is subject to military veto in major areas of policy.

These forms of government can be explained in terms of an interdependence of the army and civilian groups, not just during the lifetime of a particular government but over a long period, on account of the nature of society. In Bolivia and Central America we have the fragmented boundaries between the military and civil society described in the previous chapter, where both civil and military factions frequently change coalition partners in an attempt to secure a greater degree of power and influence. The army lacks the professionalism, unity, coercive resources or political skill to rule on its own, yet civilian political culture offers no guarantee of governments chosen by free elections resisting unconstitutional overthrow, or even a guarantee that elections will be free. Where socioeconomic development and military professionalism are greater, as in Argentina and Brazil, the civil–military coalition may arise less because of the fragmentation of the army and more because of the resilience of civil institutions, which will not allow personal rule or pure military authoritarianism for more than short periods.

Relations between civil–military authoritarians and civil society will, by definition, be characterised by various subtle links rather than heavy dependence on charisma or terror. This is not to say that extensive terror will not be used, as the experience of Central America makes clear, but such violence is often a reflection of weakness rather than strength. In El Salvador and Guatemala the continuation of guerrilla resistance to government terror suggested something less effective than Stalinist or Maoist rule. The very fact that the military need to share power with civilians suggests that terror is only one instrument of power, and not necessarily the most important.

Where military professionalism is relatively low and the necessity for a civil–military coalition is brought about more by military weakness than civilian strength, clientelism may help to cement military links with society, as in Bolivia (Gamarra in Danopoulos, 1988, pp. 47–78). In any event the co-option of civilians to positions of authority, whether formal or informal, will be more common than in the military authoritarian model where civilians are hired rather than co-opted. Whether the co-option is structured in the form of bureaucratic authoritarianism is a matter of dispute. Few would claim to see anything approaching the existence of such models in Central America but in Brazil, and more especially Argentina, there is evidence of governments moving in the direction of such relationships. Bureaucratic authoritarianism, as noted previously, is seen as a response to a relatively late stage of capitalist development which has not been reached in Central America. If it is to function it requires civil institutions to be sufficiently developed to behave in a bureaucratic manner, just as corporatism requires a degree of cohesion on both civil and military sides if lasting bargains are to be struck. Where there is not even a hint of corporatism or bureaucratic authoritarianism, the civil–military coalition will be built on more shifting foundations.

Civil–military authoritarian regimes generally have a greater longevity than governments of soldiers ruling alone, but continuity of regime type may mask changes of both personnel and degrees of influence. Caught between the two stools of order based on military authority and stability based on a degree of democratic legitimacy, these regimes have the delicate task of satisfying the key elements in both their civil and military constituencies and, in many, the foreign backers who underwrite them. Brazil experimented with varying degrees of terror and civilian participation as power shifted between different military factions, and as civilian attitudes became more hostile with worsening economic conditions. In the less professionalised armies of Central America the power struggle is more naked, but the weakness of civil institutions makes any transition to limited democracy difficult. The weakness of the political system as a whole makes it more vulnerable to foreign influence. United States unwillingness to sustain the worst excesses of authoritarianism, from the election of President Carter onwards, has led to more attempts at civilian government chosen by free election, but the absence of deeply rooted democratic norms means that in practice the coercive power of the army gives it a veto in major areas of policy. This is not so much 'limited democracy' conceded by an army making a calculated retreat, as a temporary abdication of power by the military, who have ample freedom to return if they feel that their interests are threatened.

Limited Democracy

I use the term 'limited democracy' not to describe any attempts to tack pluralist structures on to a military government, or even to describe civilian regimes subject to military veto (which are not 'military governments' in our definition), but to describe systems in which there is a more institutionalised concession of power to pluralist forces. This involves permitting relatively free competitive elections, though generally for the legislature rather than the executive, and with unacceptable individuals and parties disqualified from taking part. Indonesia, Thailand, Turkey and South Korea (from 1961 to 1971) all belongs to this category, while Brazil, with its chequered history of diverse types of military government, has also been through this phase.

If we try to explain the emergence of limited democracy, one clue might lie in the fact that military governments in these countries are (or were) less stridently right-wing than in the countries we have looked at so far. The initial military takeovers in Indonesia, Thailand and South Korea were in countries where there was not yet a strong capitalist class, comparable with South America, wanting to snatch power from rising popular movements, while in Turkey the reforming tradition of Atatürk made the army less conservative than its southern European counterparts in Greece and Spain. Some observers would dispute whether the Indonesian or Turkish military governments were right-wing at all, but I have counted them as such on account of the fierce anti-communism of the Indonesian army, and the Turkish military's growing business interests and emphasis on 'order' rather than social reform.

If a government is less obsessed with rolling back the tide of social welfare, egalitarianism and populism than in the countries we have examined so far, it can more easily risk electoral competition. It may be pressed into doing so in order to obtain a degree of legitimacy if the country has a previous record of pluralist politics, as in Thailand and Turkey, or if socioeconomic changes after military intervention gives rise to pluralist demands, as in South Korea. Indonesia is a more exceptional case in that military intervention came about by government invitation rather than through a coup. The pluralist tradition was much shallower and the decision to permit elections might be seen as an attempt by the government to build a civilian base rather than to respond to popular pressures.

The functioning of limited democratic regimes, like that of civil–military authoritarianism, depends on an interaction between the military and civilians, but in this case the civilians have an electoral as well as a pressure group base. Elements of corporatism may exist, notably in Indonesia, but the common feature is the need to create a party, or harness existing parties, in order to provide a safety valve for public demands without allowing the quasi-democratic process to undermine the government's authority. Paradoxically this does not mean a neat division of labour between soldiers and civilians, but (except in the case of Turkey where civil–military boundaries are more integral) a structure in which the army penetrates civil institutions extensively as an insurance against deviations from military-imposed guidelines. Thus the ruling party in South Korea was dominated by army officers and ex-officers even before limited democracy gave way to authoritarianism (Kim in Bienen and Morrell, 1976, pp. 24–5), over half the Indonesian senior civil service was occupied by military men (MacDougall, 1982, pp. 89–96), and in Brazil over 8,000 retired officers occupied state posts even after the formal ending of military government (Skidmore, 1988, p. 273). At the same time, civilians not only hold elected legislative posts but are co-opted extensively into executive positions.

Limited democracies have the advantage over civil–military authoritarian regimes of a more secure basis of legitimacy, but they face the problem of controlling the pace and direction of democratisation. There is always the danger of the 'wrong' party winning elections, as in Brazil and Turkey, and precipitating a return to civilian rule on conditions which the military would not have chosen. The military may try to minimise the damage by retaining a foot in the door through such devices as the retention of a soldier as president (Turkey), the continued occupation of important public sector posts by soldiers (Brazil) or the retention of a large military element in the construction and operation of civilian coalitions (Thailand) (Thomas in Danopoulos, 1988, pp. 124–5). There is always the danger that the military will lose heavily by trying to impose more stringent conditions than the civilian population is willing to tolerate, and then be banished from political power completely, and possibly be put on trial for their misdemeanours, but soldiers in limited democracies have generally escaped with nothing worse than loss of office. Civilians, like soldiers, have to steer a delicate balance between demanding a greater share of power and risking the displeasure of those in authority by demanding too much. South Korea was a case in point, where the populist demands of the opposition in 1971 frightened the military into suspending pluralist politics.

There is, none the less, a greater element of continuity both within the longer-lived limited democracies (Indonesia, South Korea), and between these regimes and their successors (Brazil, Thailand, Turkey). This may be partly because the army's objectives are more moderate than those of soldiers in authoritarian regimes, but it also reflects a willingness to conciliate rather than repress public opinion. Whereas many military authoritarian regimes end with an ignominious retreat by the military after they have overreached themselves, and many civil–military authoritarian regimes end with uneasy compromises in the absence of either sufficient military force or sufficient public belief in democratic legitimacy, limited democracy provides an easier transition as the scope for democratic participation is extended or contracted incrementally in response to events. The outcome may fall far short of the democratic ideals, but fewer soldiers are likely to fear purges or prosecutions for their misdeeds, and civilians are likely to be able to govern within more clearly understood limitations.

Conclusion

What is the value of our classification? It may be objected that it brings together some strange bedfellows: Greece and Bangladesh, Guatemala and South Korea, Indonesia and Turkey, Brazil and almost everyone. Neither is there any clear correlation between our categories and the self-appointed tasks of the military outlined in Table 2.1. Thus military authoritarianism can be used in attempts to restore traditional values (Greece), to demobilise the masses (South America) or to prevent national disintegration (Bangladesh and Pakistan); civil–military authoritarianism can be used for demobilisation (South America), encouraging state capitalist development (South Korea 1972–87) or containing rising mass movements (Central America). Limited democracy can be used to restore order (Thailand, South Korea 1961–71) or to prevent national disintegration (Indonesia). But this may reflect the ability of different structures to adapt to different tasks in different circumstances. Our classification transcends different degrees of socioeconomic development in narrow quantitative terms, important though these are in explaining the problems and behaviour of military governments, in the belief that it is in highlighting the relationship between the military and the wider society that we can bring out the diverse forms that right-wing military government can take. Greece and Bangladesh would face different problems and experience different styles of government whether they were ruled by soldiers or civilians, on account of their different cultures and levels of development. To emphasise their differences when governed by the military would therefore do no more than draw attention to the obvious. But the fact that both have experienced military authoritarianism rather than other forms of military government gives them certain common problems which mark Greece off from, say, Turkey which is closer than Bangladesh in terms of culture and development, but which experienced a different form of military intervention that made for a different power structure, a different distribution of resources and a different type of transition to civilian rule. If we can focus on the nature of the relationship between the right-wing military government and civil society, rather than the type of society in which the military have intervened, we can more easily examine the problems peculiar to a military government and the resources available to it for tackling them.

PART II
Variations on Right-Wing Themes

The previous chapter made a broad classification of right-wing military governments. It also looked at the argument that, at first sight, there was as much diversity within each category as there was between them, quite apart from the problem that some countries have shuttled between the different categories. But in Table II:1 I suggest that there are important unifying factors within each category. The 'personal rule' and 'military authoritarian' types are grouped together, since they are similar in most respects other than the powers of individual leaders, and these are compared with the 'civil–military authoritarian' and 'limited democracy' types.

Table II.1: Development, pluralism and military strength in countries with different types of right-wing military government

Type of right-wing military regime	Socioeconomic development	Public support for pluralist institutions	Period in which pluralist politics emerged	Military strength and professionalism
Personal rule, military authoritarian	High, except Bangladesh and Pakistan	Strong, except Bangladesh, Pakistan and Paraguay	Bangladesh and Pakistan after 1945, others nineteenth century	High
Civil–military authoritarian	Generally low	Weakest	Mainly nineteenth century, or early twentieth century, except South Korea	Lowest
Limited Democracy	Generally low	Intermediate	Mainly twentieth century	High

Countries under personal rule and military authoritarianism are distinguished by relatively high levels of socioeconomic development (except Bangladesh and Pakistan) and relatively strong public support for pluralist institutions (except in Bangladesh, Pakistan and possibly Paraguay), as evidenced by a history of free competitive elections. Civil–military authoritarian regimes have the lowest degree of support for pluralist institutions, and the lowest level of military strength and professionalism, as evidenced by the frequency of counter-coups and constantly shifting alliances between different civil and military factions. Limited democracies are distinguished mainly by the fact that they achieved independence only after the Second World War, or underwent the transformation from oligarchy to pluralist politics relatively recently. These basic differences may give us clues as to why countries belong to the categories they do. Military authoritarians are faced with the greatest civilian hostility, stemming largely from pluralist traditions which have frequently accompanied development. At the same time they have strong, highly professional armies which can impose their own order. Or, in the exceptional cases of Bangladesh and Pakistan, armies which inherited their professionalism from the imperial power, and were strengthened to meet external threats, have imposed order in the absence of civil institutions able to generate a sufficient degree of legitimacy. In civil–military authoritarian countries, a low degree of support for pluralist institutions and a low level of military professionalism reduces the possibility of either the army ruling alone or civilian groups generating sufficient democratic legitimacy. It is the weakness of both civilian *and* military structures that leads factions within each to seek support in the other.

The limited democracies are a more complicated case. A generally lower level of development than that enjoyed in military authoritarian Greece or South America, combined with a high level of military professionalism, might be expected to produce similar military authoritarian governments, yet armies in these countries have been more self-effacing. As the distinctive variable in the countries is either a brief existence as an independent nation (Indonesia, South Korea) or the late emergence of pluralist politics (the 1920s in Turkey and the 1930s in Thailand), we can speculate that pluralist structures fashioned since the First and Second World Wars may be better equipped to withstand authoritarianism than those which evolved in the more oligarchic nineteenth century. This is contrary to the accepted wisdom that the most deeply rooted democracies are the most resilient, but it may be that if democracy is more of a deliberate creation than an outcome of historical evolution, then some of the democratic values will percolate through to the army, or even originate within it, as in Thailand and Turkey. There may also be a greater determination on the part of civilians to preserve or restore recently acquired rights than in countries where pluralism is perceived more as a device to facilitate competition between old-established elites. This democratic model may not fit Indonesia, though even in that country there was an almost corporatist tradition of seeking a consensus between varied groups. Neither will it fit countries with lowest levels of socioeconomic development, otherwise we might expect to find thriving liberal democracies in Africa, from Cairo to the Cape.

This section tests and illustrates some of the ideas we have developed about the nature of politics in each of our categories of right-wing military government. In each case, we shall examine how clear a pattern there is in the conditions which gave rise to each type, its relationship with civil society and the problems it faces, whether in trying to survive or in trying to establish a more durable form of government. I have selected one personalist regime (Chile), two military authoritarian (Uruguay and Pakistan), three civil–military authoritarian (Guatemala, El Salvador and Bolivia) and three limited democracies (Thailand, Indonesia and Turkey). Any such selection is bound to be somewhat arbitrary. The well-worn examples of Argentina and Brazil have been avoided on the grounds that there is already ample literature on them, as have countries at the opposite extreme which have been explored insufficiently by academics, such as Paraguay and Honduras. Others were excluded because right-wing military government ended at least two decades ago.

Of the countries included, Chile provides a remarkable example of the survival of a personal ruler who was able to reverse the process of popular mobilisation, and Uruguay an example of the installation of a repressive government in the sort of country where all the indicators suggested that it should not have happened. (Greece provides a similar, but more historically distant and less well-documented example.) The case of Pakistan shows that right-wing military authoritarianism can also flourish in a much more backward country, where military rule would normally be associated with praetorianism, if the army has sufficient professional cohesion. Our three civil–military authoritarian countries are a more homogeneous group, with the army in each case an indispensable political actor, yet able to achieve little and eventually preferring to exercise a veto power from the sidelines rather than retaining responsibility for disorder, economic stagnation and unwinnable civil wars. The three limited democracies are the most heterogeneous group, but all have in common a more recent emergence of pluralist politics than the countries of Latin America. Their diversity in other respects illustrates the varied conditions of civil–military relations which may force the military to acknowledge the political rights of citizens: in Turkey the tradition of integral civil–military boundaries which insists on the autonomy of civil institutions, in Thailand the converse situation where the army's penetration of civil institutions is so extensive that it can afford to permit pluralist competition with little fear of losing control, and in Indonesia the army's need to develop a viable political framework in order ro reduce its own burden in a country where civil political structures are fragile. No doubt a case could have been made for including South Korea in preference to Indonesia, but the literature on the former is more sparse, while the latter provides an opportunity to examine one of the right-wing military regimes which has made little progress towards disengagement.

4 Personal Rule and Military Authoritarianism: Chile, Uruguay and Pakistan

Chile: The Ideological Right

Pre-coup Politics

Chile is one of the most socially and economically developed countries to have experienced military government. It lies forty-ninth on Sivard's development ranking, with an adult literacy rate of 89 per cent and 86 per cent of the population employed outside agriculture. By the 1970s import substituting industries were growing in an increasingly interventionist economy, new groups were being incorporated into the political system, and competing political parties ranged widely across the ideological spectrum (Garreton in O'Donnell *et al.*, 1985, pp. 96–7). Unlike most of its neighbours, Chile remained immune to military intervention for nearly three decades after the Second World War. It is not one of Finer's countries of 'low political culture'.

One might have expected these features to provide continued insurance against military intervention, but many of them were to prove signs of weakness as much as strength. Not only did they contribute to intervention, but to the harshness and longevity of the military regime which came to power in 1973. The social, economic, political and military elements are difficult to disentangle from each other. O'Brien comes closest to an economic explanation of military intervention when he speaks of the internationalisation of capital disrupting the alliance between the bourgeoisie and the proletariat, and of United States support for the army and economic destabilisation (in O'Brien and Cammack, 1985, pp. 148–50), all of which might suggest that Chile was being engulfed in similar economic pressures to other South American countries. But in Chile the stakes were higher. The long period of uninterrupted civilian politics, with little fear of a military veto, had allowed the Marxist President Allende to come to power, and this posed a greater threat to the civilian elite and international capitalism than the milder radicalism of neighbouring civilian governments. At the same time the country's apparent success in sustaining pluralist politics masked underlying weaknesses. As in much of South America, an apparently buoyant democratic system rested on a weaker 'sub-system'. Garreton describes the weakness of 'autonomous organisations' in society which were dependent on access to the party system in a country where vigorous party competition at national level was not matched by democratic participation in the wider society. This, it seems, enabled extremist parties to emerge in a way that would not have been possible in a country where parties were more of a reflection of society, and at the same time it left governments with insufficient reserves of legitimacy to tide them over times of crisis or economic depression (Garreton in O'Donnell *et al.*, 1985, pp. 96–7). Here we come close to Eckstein's argument that political stablility depends on a congruence of norms between political and social institutions (1966, pp. 234–6). The lack of congruence in South America may be explained in terms of the 'democracy from above' thesis we have already explored, in which the expansion of state structures precedes the growth of autonomous popular participation. If this is true, it suggests again that Chile is not unique but does everything in a more extreme fashion than its neighbours.

By 1973 Chile had all the ingredients for a political and economic crisis. A government mismanaging the economy and facing hyperinflation was caught between rising mass demands, which it could neither satisfy nor stifle, and growing pressures from economic elites and international capital for a stable market for profitable investment. While the ideal of pluralist politics might enjoy a greater legitimacy than in civil–military authoritarian systems, the actual form it took in Chile in the 1970s enjoyed less support. Increased mobilisation of political forces on both left and right, increased violence and an unwillingness to compromise made the survival of the government unlikely (Valenzuela in Linz and Stepan, 1978, pp. 81–101). With a more passive army the outcome might have been more of the type experienced in the Third French Republic, with one unstable coalition succeeding another, but in the event the army was far from passive.

A long period of previous abstinence from military government did not save the country from prolonged dictatorship, any more than a long record of pluralism and economic development. In institutional terms the army appeared to have fewer links with civilian elites than in countries subject to more frequent military intervention, although political order depended on something more than a benevolent police force. Army officers held many offices of state, up to cabinet level, and the military exercised extensive control over Emergency Zones as disorder worsened, but this was a relatively recent development after decades of 'pure' civilian government (North, 1976, pp. 73–97). In terms of social position, however, most of the officer corps saw its material interests as bound up with the middle class in opposition to a Marxist government, and with the need to restore law and order at a time when the government seemed unable to do so. Both self-interest and the fulfilment of a professional role thus pointed to military intervention, but there were still many officers who wanted to maintain the non-political tradition. In the event the political climate proved too hostile for military neutrality. The government went out of its way to meet the demands of the army for more pay and equipment (Valenzuela in Linz and Stepan, 1978, pp. 81–105), but at a time when opposition parties, employers, the professions and even some sections of the labour movement were showing little respect for the rule of law and many groups were urging the army to intervene (North, 1976, p. 97;

O'Brien in O'Brien and Cammack, 1985, p. 150), a military takeover was hardly unexpected.

Whether the causes of intervention were primarily economic, social, political or military is difficult to say. At the extremes we have O'Brien's argument about the influence of international capital in a changing economy and Valenzuela's argument that a 'fundamentally political' crisis preceded the socioeconomic crisis (in Linz and Stepan, 1978, p. 106). Industrialisation in a country facing a highly competitive world economy puts a strain on most nations that undergo it, and in many it has led to the military intervening on the side of capitalism and order, but the insecure social foundations of the Chilean polity and the behaviour of the political actors undoubtedly hastened the intervention. The capacity of the political system was tested beyond the limits to which more prudent actors would have put it, and an army with an impressive record of abstention from politics took the law into its own hands.

Military Ideology, Interests and Objectives

If the occurrence of military intervention was not unexpected, the extremism of the military government took many by surprise. Philip offers a clue to many of the events in Chile when he argues that much of the behaviour of the military regime is explicable in terms of the previous near-absence of military government (1985, p. 322). An army closer to the centre of the political system might have intervened earlier, but with a lighter touch and with an acceptance that politics is the art of compromise. But for the Chilean army politics was more a matter of blacks and whites. It did not intervene to pursue short-term personal or corporate demands, as in much of Central America and Africa, because it was already strong enough to extract resources from civilian governments, but the emergence of popular movements and Marxism were another matter. If the political system was unable to contain these forces, then parties, elections and pressure group activities had to be suppressed altogether. Loveman describes the ideology as anti-Marxist, and drawing on Christian and Hispanic traditions, with an emphasis on God, Fatherland and Family (1988, pp. 260–4), while North and Garreton emphasise the influence of a long period outside politics in maintaining a high level of professionalism, and beliefs in order, hierarchy and discipline (North, 1976, pp. 74–9, 98; Garreton in O'Donnell *et al.*, 1985, p. 97). Officers taking power in other parts of the world may share some of these beliefs, but either internal disunity or civilian resistance force them to behave more like politicians and less like soldiers. In Chile the army enjoyed the professionalism and resources that one finds in most South American countries, but it also had fewer inhibitions about suppressing opponents whose beliefs were outside the normal orbit of South American politics and, especially in its early years, it met with relatively little resistance from civilian elites, who were satisfied with any alternative to the Allende regime.

In terms of actual policies, the ideology pointed not only to the demobilisation of most pluralist institutions, but to an uninhibited free market economic policy which Garreton suggests fitted well with notions of hierarchy and discipline (Garreton in O'Donnell *et al.*, 1985, p. 100). We come back to the parallel between the discipline of the parade ground and the discipline of the market.

Military Strengths and Weaknesses

The longevity of the military government is remarkable by any standards, and apparent handicaps have often turned out to be strengths. Political in-experience also implied an absence of debts to civilians. A rigid adherence to one economic dogma for eight years, for all the hardship it caused, crippled many alternative centres of power, and personal rule, which might have left the regime vulnerable to the whims of an assassin's bullet or the plotting of junior officers, helped to maintain an effective hierarchy under General Pinochet's leadership when other military governments were falling victim to factional struggle. There were also less ambiguous advantages such as the pro-fessionalism of the army and lack of effective civilian resistance in the early years. The individual skill of General Pinochet is difficult to assess, but his tenacity stands in contrast to the rapid turnover of military rulers in Argentina and Brazil. He was shrewd enough to ensure the progressive removal of many of his peers, and to control promotion and keep a close watch on the security service (Garreton in O'Donnell *et al.*, 1985, pp. 100–3), and to legitimise his rule by means of referenda (Bouzutsky in Malloy and Seligson, 1987, p. 86) without allowing mass participation in such activities to stray into competitive politics. The choice, as in the early Gaullist referenda, may have been framed as a limited one between the General and chaos, but in both cases the choice was a free one and the electorate was willing to give the General the benefit of the doubt.

The weaknesses were those inherent to most of the military regimes which give little scope to civilians: political inexperience, dogmatism and a greater reliance on repression than co-operation. Plebiscitary legitimacy and reminders of the horrors of the previous civilian government cannot sustain a military government indefinitely. Enthusiasm for pluralist politics may have been blunted by the experience of the early 1970s, but Chile was still a country with a long democratic tradition which might reassert itself if the performance of the military government were found wanting. We must therefore turn to the areas in which a limited number of civilians were involved in policy-making, and examine the impact of this on the polity.

The Military and Civilians Elites

The paradox of one of the Latin American countries most steeped in pluralist politics departing furthest from pluralism continues when we look at the recruitment of civilians to governmental posts. After large numbers of right-of-centre politicians had been urging the military to intervene, one might have expected the military government to reciprocate by building a broad civil–military coalition. Yet few civilian politicians were appointed in the first eight years and power passed to monetarist economists unaffectionately known as the 'Chicago Boys' after their Alma Mater. There was no obvious reason for a prejudice against right-wing politicians, though some soldiers blamed the rise of President Allende on the inadequate performance of his Christian Democratic predecessors (O'Brien in O'Brien and Cammack, 1985, p. 176). But right-wing politicians needed the army more than the army needed them, and it suited the army to hire technocrats with no independent power base rather than share power with politicians, as weaker military governments frequently have to do. The Chicago Boys had enjoyed influences in the quality press before the coup (O'Brien in O'Brien and Cammack, 1985, pp. 145–7) and their ideas appealed to the military on practical as well as philosophical grounds. As Whitehead points out, their policy offered a clear system of rewards and punishments, with the latter falling mainly on the enemy, and a redistribution of resources from vanquished to victor (Whitehead in Hojman, 1985, pp. 12–15).

The narrowness of the civilian support base casts some doubt on whether the military government represented the 'ruling elite' or 'ruling class'. Bouzutzky suggests that the attraction of appointing technocrats was that they would not act from 'narrow class or partisan interests' (Bouzutzky in Malloy and Seligson, 1987, pp. 68), and O'Brien emphasises their aims of integrating Chile into the world capitalist economy and supporting multinational corporations (O'Brien and Cammack, 1985, pp. 145–7). While some elites benefited from such policies, others, especially those in manufacturing industry exposed to foreign competition and those in a shrinking state bureaucracy, did not. The many groups previously dependent on access to the party system for political rewards were now cast adrift.

The unambiguously right-wing social and economic policies are well documented, quite apart from the number of tortures, executions, imprisonments and disappearances which can never be recorded. Of 479 public enterprises, 455 were denationalised; health care, pension funds and education were increasingly privatised; the role of the state in investment and business regulation was reduced; the economy was opened increasingly to foreign competition, and long-established labour and welfare laws were repealed. By 1983 real wages were 14 per cent lower than in 1970, and unemployment was rising. The number of products subject to price control fell from 4,000 to 8, and social expenditure fell by 20 per cent between 1970 and 1982 (Bouzutzky in Malloy and Seligson, 1987, pp. 67–78; Loveman, 1988, pp. 267–9; Sanders in Handelman and Sanders, 1981, pp. 10–11; O'Brien in O'Brien and Cammack, 1985, pp. 169–75).

By 1982 the monetarist policies, especially the overvaluation of the currency and the reduction in tariffs, were harming not only the poor but much of the business community. Gross domestic product fell by nearly 20 per cent in a year and many businesses went bankrupt. Many policies were now reversed. Dishonest financiers were arrested, tariffs were increased and exchange rates adjusted. Public works programmes and housing subsidies were introduced (O'Brien in O'Brien and Cammack, 1985, pp. 154–60). By 1988 the country had enjoyed an annual 5 per cent growth rate over four years, although the wealthy continued to benefit disproportionately. The average income was still 15 per cent lower than in 1970 and the minimum wage was 40 per cent lower than in 1981 (Coad, 1988, p. 14).

The changes of economic direction were accompanied by changes of political direction. The whole cabinet resigned in 1982 and the Chicago Boys departed. Pinochet appointed a new cabinet designed to rally traditional right-wing support (Garreton in O'Donnell _et al.,_ 1985, pp. 113–14), but the regime remained a personalist one, dependent on repression tempered by referenda. O'Brien argues that the armed forces had been less prepared for power than their counterparts in the rest of Latin America and lacked training in economic management. They had therefore been happy to leave economic policy in the hands of the Chicago Boys, while enjoying the wealth created by this policy and by generous budgetary allocations (O'Brien and Cammack, 1985, pp. 177–8). When crises threatened the political as well as the economic sphere, Pinochet relied on the advice of close personal advisers rather than the military junta, which acted as little more than a weak legislative body (Garreton in O'Donnell _et al.,_ 1985, p. 105). The regime thus lacked the characteristics both of the bureaucratic authoritarian model, since neither the civil nor the military bureaucrats played a prominent part in policy-making, and of any corporatist model, since much of its effort was devoted to dismantling social and political organisations rather than incorporating them in governments (see especially Bouzutzky in Malloy and Seligson, 1987, pp. 86–7). The division of labour between military leaders concerned with policies designed to secure stability and demobilisation, and technocrats concerned with economic policy was wider than under most military regimes. The abstinence of most of the senior military ranks from politics had the advantage of helping to leave military professionalism intact and thus prolong the life of the regime, but a price had to be paid in terms of lack of control over policy, which could have been fatal if the civilian opposition had been more united. After the excesses of the Chicago Boys had been modified, Pinochet could claim a substantial degree of success by his own standards in achieving stability, eliminating the threat from the extreme left and reshaping the economy. There seemed to be little left for him to do by 1988 beyond offering the electorate 'less of the same', but the virtual exclusion of civilian politicians from government for fifteen years rendered any transition to a like-minded civilian government difficult. Pinochet preferred to offer himself for another eight-year term in a straight 'Yes' or 'No' plebiscite. In view of the suffering that much of the population had endured it was either a tribute to his own personal following or a commentary on the ineffectiveness of the opposition that he lost by a margin of only 11 per cent. But defeat is still defeat, and the Chilean polity was left to negotiate one of the most difficult transfers of power — from a dictator, reluctant to depart and supported by the army, to civilians who might seek to reverse his policies and avenge his misdeeds.

Uruguay: The Isolated Right

Pre-coup Politics

Uruguay had even less reason than Chile to expect to be visited by right-wing military intervention in 1973. It enjoys a higher per capita income and an adult literacy rate of over 90 per cent, and over 85 per cent of the population is employed outside agriculture. Its history of pluralist politics is at least as long as Chile's, and more stable. There was no obvious threat from extremist parties, and both inter- and intra-party competition were institutionalised within a two-party system. The population was more homogeneously European than in Chile, political participation had reached higher levels earlier and wealth was distributed relatively evenly. To explain the 1973 coup in terms of a poor economic performance and the rise of an urban guerrilla movement, as most of the literature does (see especially Gillespie in O'Donnell *et al.*, 1985, pp. 173–7; McDonald, 1985, p. 57; McDonald, 1975, pp. 27–9; Philip, 1985, pp. 344–6; Finch in O'Brien and Cammack, 1985, pp. 89–90), seems at first sight to be using explanations more appropriate to a much more backward country. Even if we reject the notion of 'high political culture' as a barrier to military intervention as an oversimplification, one might still have expected relative wealth, ethnic homogeneity and institution-alised competition between moderate parties and factions to have preserved this 'Switzerland of South America'. Admittedly the economic failure and terrorism were more than the minor annoyance that they have been in much of Western Europe. Real incomes had been falling since the 1960s, inflation was approaching 100 per cent a year (Philip, 1985, pp. 344–6; Finch in O'Brien and Cammack, 1985, p. 89) and the threat of the Tupamaros guerrillas was considered serious enough to stimulate a near doubling of the armed forces' share of the budget in the five years before the 1973 coup (Handelman in Handelman and Sanders, 1981, p. 219), but Uruguay was no banana republic facing economic ruin or civil war.

It may be that a staid political system which only permits competition between moderate parties can sow the seeds of instability almost as much as the Chilean system which gave free rein to extremists. If the traditional parties cannot arrest economic decline and the social problems to which it gives rise, yet the system cannot accommodate those who advocate radical remedies, extra-constitutional outlets are likely to be sought. On the left the Tupamaros attracted alienated middle-class youth, and on the right the army reacted (or probably over-reacted) by pressing for repression which was ultimately to destroy the whole democratic edifice. According to McDonald:

> Uruguay's democratic heritage was the strongest hallmark of its traditions and culture, but the apparent acquiescence, if not outright support, of public opinion for the military's actions suggests that, in the face of daily challenges to individual economic and personal security, political commitments can run a poor second. (1975, p. 42)

Not only did consensus politics seem dysfunctional in the face of the twin threats to economic and personal security but the other alleged safeguard of pluralist politics, integral civil–military boundaries, may also have hastened its demise. As in Chile, a long period of military abstinence from politics left the army with few guidelines on how to interact with civilians in dealing with disorder. In social as well as political terms, army officers were an out-group, coming mainly from rural middle-class families with few social ties with the urban elite. Instead of co-operating with politicians, the army took the law into its own hands. Ministerial appointments were vetoed, Congress was suspended, terrorism was met with a response out of proportion to its magnitude, until the gradual erosion of civil authority culminated in the establishment of a military government.

Military Ideology, Interests and Objectives

The more consensual nature of Uruguayan politics, in comparison with Chile, was reflected in the officer corps' ideological boundaries. The long tradition of liberalism in politics and statism in economics precluded the extreme policies followed in Chile (Gillespie in O'Donnell *et al.*, 1985, p. 177), and immediate objectives of reducing inflation, stimulating economic growth and competition, and seeking greater efficiency in the public sector (ibid., p. 177; Finch in O'Brien and Cammack, 1985, p. 93) might seem more pragmatic than right-wing. Some officers even admired the left-wing military government in Peru (McDonald, 1974, pp. 28–9) but the pre-coup crusade against terrorism and ineffective reformist government had already put the right in command, and after the coup many moderate and left-wing officers were purged (Philip, 1985, p. 249; Handelman in Handelman and Sanders, 1981, p. 233). The ideology was less stridently right-wing than in Chile, but men from the rural middle class with few political allies, attempting to grapple with urban terrorism and to manage an economy which had grown inefficient on political patronage in an era of growing world competition, had little alternative but to go at least some way along the road of free market economics and political demobilisation, and to seek support from multinational capital.

Military Strengths and Weaknesses: Relations with Civilian Elites

In quantitative terms the army could not complain of impoverishment. The armed forces' share of the national budget in the five years before the coup grew from 13.9 per cent to 26.2 per cent, and to over 40 per cent five years later — the highest proportion in Latin America (Handelman in Handelman and Sanders, 1981, p. 219). The army also enjoyed the advantage of professionalism common to most long-established South American armies. But in qualitative terms the weaknesses were clear. There was no obvious justification for seizing power beyond the dubious one of combating the almost-defeated Tupamaros, and this lack of legitimacy was a handicap in a country where the only previous 'military' rulers had come to power via party politics rather than coups. Add to this the social isolation and political inexperience of the officers, and it is not surprising that they relied heavily on repression rather than building a civil–military coalition. Human rights groups calculated that the number of imprisonments under military government was the highest in the region (Gillespie in O'Donnell, *et al.*, 1985, pp. 176–7). In the short term there were civilian elites, especially in the financial sector, who stood to benefit from the repression of trade unions and terrorists, and the exposure of the economy to multinational corporations, but the nexus was based on material benefit rather than any sense of loyalty to this form of government.

Bureaucratic authoritarianism, corporatism and clientelism are again difficult to detect, on account of the remoteness of the army. As in Chile, the hiring of civilian technocrats was preferred to a partnership with politicians, most of whom were disqualified from office on the grounds of either alleged left-wing extremism or involvement in failed regimes. But the more moderate attitude of the Uruguayan military to social welfare and the mixed economy left the technocrats with less clear terms of reference and led to frequent disagreements over economic policy (Gillespie in O'Donnell *et al.*, 1985, p. 177).

The main policy outcomes, as one might expect, indicated a military government of the pragmatic right rather than the ideological right. Landowners, whose social links with the military we have noted, were able to obain favours on matters such as prices, tax rates, credit terms, subsidies, tariffs and exchange rates. Sectors such as construction, banking and commerce expanded, but the state continued to invest in infrastructural projects (Finch in O'Brien and Cammack, 1985, pp. 89–93). Trade unions were crushed and real wages in 1981 were at two-thirds the level of the eve of the coup, despite a period of sustained economic growth (Gillespie in O'Donnell *et al.*, 1985, pp. 178–9). Political repression involved not only a South American record for the number of imprisonments but the banning of 15,000 people from political activity in the proposed new constitution. Members of 'traditional' parties were merely disqualified from standing for political office but those on the left were deprived of the vote (ibid., pp. 176–9). But neither the mixed economy nor political pluralism were destroyed beyond recognition, as in Chile, if only because the military were not strong enough to put anything in their place.

The Military, Society and Withdrawal

Economic recession and rising oil prices in the late 1970s and early 1980s left the government without even material benefits to compensate for its shallow legitimacy. Lacking any effective civilian power base and out of favour with the United States on account of its violation of human rights, it had to seek a return to civilian rule on the best terms it could. The military envisaged a shift to what we have called 'limited democracy': a constitution which would have given them ample powers of veto, and a single presidential candidate approved by both main parties, but they now had to pay the price for freezing parties

out of politics over the past seven years. All parties combined to support a
'No' vote in the 1980 referendum on the constitution, which was rejected by
57 per cent of the electorate (Clapham and Philip, 1985, pp. 349–50). Voters
might not be enthusiastic about the return of politicians who had failed to
produce economic benefits or curb terrorism, but they could not be
frightened by arguments about Marxism as the only alternative to the
military, as in Chile. If a 'No' vote hastened the departure of rulers relying on
repression without delivering any tangible benefits, and their replacement by
civilians who were politically inept but at least respected people's right to civil
liberties and democratic choice, the latter seemed a more attractive
proposition.

The next four years saw the continued downward slide of the military, just
as the three years before the coup had seen a similar slide by civilian rulers,
with each gaining momentum as it progressed. Politicians deemed to be left-
wing continued to be banned from contesting elections, but the presidential
primary elections in the main parties in 1981 were both won by anti-military
candidates (Gillespie in O'Donnell *et al.*, 1985, pp. 180–2). A formal
agreement between the military and leading politicians was reached over such
matters as the method of choosing military commanders, the role of the
National Security Council, judicial review of government actions and the
right of parliament to declare a state of insurrection (ibid., p. 190), all of which
suggest both a recognition by the military of the need for orderly withdrawal
and a recognition by politicians that the future role of the army could not be
ignored. This spirit of compromise continued until the 1984 election, which
was won by President Sanguinetti who was a conservative but had distanced
himself from the military and had campaigned for a 'No' vote in the
referendum. Philip suggests that the choice reflected a belief that such a figure
would be most likely to facilitate a smooth return to civilian rule, without
antagonising the army by calling it to account for its behaviour in power
(Philip, 1985, p. 352). This may be crediting voters with undue rationality, but
their choice had such an effect. Uruguay emerged like a time traveller who had
departed on a series of improbable adventures, only to return to all the
familiar, largely unchanged surroundings. The two main parties were there
again, the left was eclipsed and the Colorado Party won by a similar margin
in 1984 to that which it had gained in 1971 before the start of the odyssey.

It would be tempting to see the military interregnum as an aberration in an
otherwise pluralist polity, but the soldiers who took power and held it for
eleven years cannot be dismissed as mere adventurers who were fortunate
enough to catch civilian politicians off guard. Uruguay suffered similar, if less
extreme, problems to its Southern Cone neighbours in terms of economic
dislocation and terrorism, which a pluralist system seemed unable to control.
The extent of the problems and successful intervention of armies in
neighbouring countries always made military intervention a plausible
outcome, just as the failure of soldiers to meet expectations, and the steps of
their counterparts towards withdrawal in Argentina and Brazil, influenced
the return to barracks in Uruguay. But the actual nature of military
government and the survival (or reclamation?) of much more of the pre-coup
landscape in Uruguay than elsewhere, suggested the importance of politics

rather than economics. The moderate and competitive nature of the pre-coup system left the military with fewer bogeymen to invoke whether in justifying their seizure of power or in refusing to return it. The unwillingness of any significant civilian group to sustain the government explains its resort to brutality, but it also explains its vulnerability when economic conditions worsened. Pure military authoritarianism could not survive, but there was no room on the political spectrum for an army-created party. Where else could Uruguay go but back to 1971?

Pakistan: The Unchallengeable Right

Pakistan is remote from Chile and Uruguay in socioeconomic as well as geographic terms. It lies 123rd on Sivard's indicators of development, with nearly three-quarters of its population illiterate and over half still employed in agriculture. Its per capita income is only one-seventh that of Chile. One might expect military intervention in such a country to be closer to the tropical African than the South American model, with soldiers nursing narrow personal and occupational grievances displacing civilians and then making only minimal changes to the distribution of patronage and resources, rather than making radical right-wing changes to strengthen established elites and international capitalism. Yet the right-wing credentials of Pakistan's two military regimes are not in dispute. General Ayub Khan's government (1958–68), for all its contribution to reduced corruption, cleaner cities, more efficient public utilities and economic growth, presided over a country in which the gap between rich and poor became wider and workers' right remained precarious (Rizvi in Clapham and Philip, 1985, pp. 211–12; Tahir-Kheli, 1980, p. 642). Ayub was ousted not by a palace revolution but by demonstrations supported by students, workers, lawyers and much of the lower middle class (Tahir-Kheli, 1980, p. 644). The military returned to barracks in 1971 after the failure to prevent the secession of Bangladesh, only to remove President Bhutto and return to power under General Zia in 1977. Bhutto's policies of concessions to the Soviet Union, nationalisation and land reforms were now replaced by more orthodox right-wing policies, United States military assistance and the detention or execution of left-wing politicians, including Bhutto himself.

One significant difference between Pakistan and other countries in a comparable state of 'underdevelopment' is the size and professionalism of its army. The army numbers nearly half a million, and 7 per cent of the gross national product is devoted to defence. Of the twenty-four least developed countries under military government, this figure is surpassed only by South Yemen, Mauretania, Ethiopia and Somalia (SIPRI, 1987 pp. 109–12). The size of the army is explicable in terms of Pakistan's strategic position, and the commitments it took on in fighting against India, Bangladesh and the Soviet Union. The professionalism can be attributed partly to experience of the British Raj, but it is still remarkable that it has endured after two turbulent periods of military government.

Pre-coup Politics and the Background to Military Intervention

Attempts to analyse military government in Pakistan often reflect its ambivalent position as a military giant and economic pygmy. Should it be treated as a politically backward country in which fragile political structures, deficient in public legitimacy, competence or integrity, inevitably capitulate to the first show of organised military force (the 'tropical African model'), or as a country in which a highly professional army seeks to defend the elite interests of its members and its allies (the 'South American model')? The military takeovers of both 1958 and 1977 have been explained in both terms.

Tahir-Kheli explains the emergence of Ayub Khan in 1958 in terms of corruption and the weakness of civil institutions (1980, p. 412), and attributes Zia's takeover to the isolation of Bhutto as a dictator following the chaos precipitated by a rigged election. Dyer and Keegan also offer African-type explanations. Political institutions in 1958 were weak and immature, and Pakistan was short of competent politicians and administrators, with parliamentry democracy resting uneasily on MPs elected indirectly by long-defunct provincial assemblies (Dyer and Keegan in Keegan, 1983, p. 441), while in 1977 the country was threatened with civil war over the disputed election, and senior officers intervened in the realisation of the need to re-establish authority over middle-ranking and junior officers who were being used by Bhutto to quell civil unrest (ibid., pp. 455–6). Rizvi, in contrast, sees Ayub Khan's takeover less as the result of the (admitted) failure of parliamentry democracy than the desire of civil–military elites and unrepresentative politicians to keep out 'representative elites' (Clapham and Philip, 1985, pp. 201–4) while Ahmed sees the 1977 coup as a reaction against Bhutto's left-wing policies (Gardezi and Rashid, 1983, p. 95). It was: 'Undertaken to transform the state apparatus in such a manner that the ultra-right shall now be propelled into a hegemonic position in all basic structures of authority' (ibid., p. 120).

Seekers of middle-of-the-road explanations might detect flaws on both sides of the argument. The African-type explanation of weak political structures has much plausibility in a country which gained independence in violent circum-stances in 1947 and had not experienced a directly elected parliament when the military first took over in 1958. But, as in Burma and Indonesia, the takeover was at the invitation of a civilian government unable to maintain order — a process unusual outside Asia, which might suggest both a civilian modesty regarding their own competence not found in Latin America, and a recognition of the potential effectiveness of the army seldom found in Africa. Yet if Pakistan is so unused to free competitive elections, one wonders whether the response to Bhutto's victory in 1977 is attributable to the fact that the rules were not scrupulously adhered to (which was hardly unexpected), or to the fact that the election was won by an unacceptable left-wing government. If the latter argument holds, we are still left with the question of whether the army was defending some broader coalition of right-wing interests, as it frequently is in South America, or merely expressing a distaste for policies which put a strain on the army's role as the guardian of law and order. To pursue these questions we need to look more closely at the nature of civil and military institutions.

Military Interests, Strengths and Weaknesses

Attempting to discover whether military leaders in Pakistan have any clear ideology is no easier than in any other country. Ayub Khan laid much emphasis on national unity, in contrast to the allegedly divisive concerns of party politicians (1967, pp. 49, 221), while the Zia regime relied increasingly on appeals to nationalism and national security during the war in Afghanistan, and to Islamic fundamentalism. Such ideological positions are not inherently right-wing, as the experience of Libya shows, but the main threats to the stability of the government were seen to come from the left, both from the Soviet invasion of Afghanistan, and from populist politicians and agitators who had undermined Ayub and supported Bhutto. Conservative alliances were therefore cemented with the United States, and business and religious leaders, to provide alternative bases of support. But Ahmed suggests that the Zia government's main interest was the pursuit of its own hegemony rather than to act as an instrument of the big bourgeoisie. It would, he argued, be willing to make alliances with other groups should the need arise (Ahmed in Gardezi and Rashid, 1983, p. 126).

The army's strength, we have suggested, lay in its size and professionalism. The professionalism is remarkable when one considers the strains imposed by two periods of military government and by military defeats at the hands of India and Bangladesh. It can be explained partly by the actual style of military government which, despite heavy reliance on martial law, preventive detention and the suppression of party politics, did not involve undue military penetration of the political/administrative structure.

> Had [the army] got directly involved in the civil administration, the effect would have been a further demoralisation and disintegration of civil authority. *It would also have made the withdrawal of the army from civilian life to their normal sphere of work difficult.* (Ayub Khan, 1967, p. 77; emphasis added)

Both Ayub and Zia preferred to allocate most top positions to civilians, though not those with strong power bases of their own. As in Chile and Uruguay, the relationship was a 'hiring and firing' one, rather than one of partnership. Military authoritarianism was thus retained at a minimal cost to professionalism, and the chain of command held together. This was to the benefit of the army as an institution. Whether it has been an advantage to the political process is another matter. As Danopoulos suggests in analysing the Greek experience, 'military professionalism emphasises traditional values such as stability, hierarchy and order' which may not travel well in the less structured world of politics (Danopoulos, 1983, p. 494). If soldiers had allowed themselves to become more political, and come to terms with the representatives of a wider public opinion, the army's integrity might have suffered, but the country might have lurched less uneasily between military authoritarianism and a stunted form of pluralist politics in which violence and extremism were seldom far below the surface.

The Military and Civilian Elites

The distaste of Pakistani soldiers for politicians with popular bases of support has led to a search for other types of civilian ally. Ayub Khan's cabinet comprised non-political civilians and only four generals (Dyer and Keegan in Keegan, 1983, p. 444), and the Civil Service, the other major bulwark, of the British Raj, came back into prominence (Rizvi in Clapham and Philip, 1985, p. 204). Here we have the tempting model of the re-creation of imperial rule under civil and military bureaucrats, unsullied by ambitious politicians or corrupt businessmen, but as Ayub Khan conceded:

> Having suffered through the perfidy of the so-called political parties, I was hoping that we would be able to run our politics without the party system. But we needed a disciplined body in Parliament and links with the people outside. (Ayub Khan, 1967, p. 221)

Perhaps to minimise the politicisation of the army, Ayub allowed the re-formation of the Muslim League in preference to creating a military party. He also created a system of local basic democracies which were to provide an electoral college for indirect presidential elections in the hope of bypassing the urban middle class. Yet neither move provided an adequate means of bridging the gap between elites and the masses. The Muslim league attracted few political heavyweights (Rizvi in Clapham and Philip, 1985, p. 209). Membership of a military-backed party may offer few openings at the top while the military are in command and may prove an embarrassment once they fall from grace. The basic democracies, instead of coming under the control of pliable village elders as the government had hoped, often fell into the hands of corrupt landlords and businessmen (ibid,. p. 205; Maniruzzaman, 1971, pp. 225–8). In the short term this helped to preserve a clientelistic system for the distribution of resources which may have strengthened the government's base, but resources began to dry up with the outbreak of war with India. The regime began to face the familiar problem for military governments that if it could claim neither democratic legitimacy nor the credit for material prosperity, then it would either have to find ways of civilianising itself or make a dignified retreat to barracks. Discontent fuelled by autocracy, corruption and nepotism led to student and religious demonstrations against the government in 1968, and to Ayub Khan's handover to General Yahya Khan. Yahya offered himself for re-election in 1970, and the result produced an opposition majority in East Pakistan which then fought and won a secessionist war. With military defeat now added to the army's other sins, Yahya handed power over to a civilian government under one of his former ministers, Zhulfikar Ali Bhutto.

When military government was restored under General Zia, the option of relying on the civil bureaucracy was less attractive, as much of it had been politicised by Bhutto (Rizvi in Clapham and Philip, 1985, p. 129). Zia's original cabinet of generals was replaced by an all-civilian one in 1978, mainly from conservative Islamic parties which had together received less than 15 per cent of the vote in the previous election (Ahmed in Gardezi and Rashid, 1983.

p. 120). If mass politics was still unacceptable, a populist appeal to Islamic fundamentalism might yet give the government a base of support, especially in view of events in neighbouring Muslim countries.

The role of business elites, which figured more prominently under South American military authoritarian regimes, was less significant in Pakistan. We come back to the paradox of a developed army and an underdeveloped economy. As Ahmed points out, Pakistan is more important to the West for its strategic position than as a source of investment (Ahmed in Gardezi and Rashid, 1983, p. 132), so the country's politics has not been characterised by any obvious involvement of Chicago Boys serving the interests of banks, merchants or international capital, although trade-offs between politicians and local businessmen have followed a pattern familiar in Third World politics. This economic power vacuum might seem to strengthen the position of military governments, but it raises problems as to the sort of base on which a political system can build if military authoritarianism becomes insufficient. The military giant may become a lonely figure.

The Military, Society and Withdrawal

Unable to find anyone his own size at elite level, the military giant has had few inhibitions about using his strength against the wider society when occasion has demanded it. Ayub Khan relied on martial law for long periods; Zia relied on it for the first seven years of his rule, together with military courts, public floggings and the detention of between 20,000 and 100,000 political prisoners. During those years of terror there seemed to be few limits to the government's powers, and not even the execution of Bhutto produced a rebellion (Ahmed in Gardezi and Rashid, 1983, pp. 95, 130, 134). Ayub had attempted to secure popular legitimacy not only through basic democracies but by offering himself as an unopposed presidential candidate in 1960, when he won 90 per cent of the vote. In 1965 he won only 64 per cent of the vote — the sort of result that reflects badly on a government in indicating both its unpopularity and its inability to rig the result convincingly (Gauhar, 1985, p. 110). Zia, too, tried to win popular legitimacy without running the risk of parties mobilising mass opposition. A referendum to approve Islamic legal reforms was approved by 98 per cent of the electorate, and a non-party election to the legislature was held in 1985 at a time when most party leaders were in detention or exile.

Yet we have seen that the most authoritarian government is vulnerable to worsening economic conditions, and may look less self-assured once a few groups dare to challenge it. Pakistan, as a largely rural, illiterate, Muslim country, in which political competition has been permitted for only brief periods, had not provided an ideal setting for political parties or pressure groups to articulate mass public opinion, but in the end both military governments were toppled by popular pressures rather than palace revolutions. The Ayub government was caught in the cross-currents of demands for the constitutional acceptance of Muslim fundamentalism, for pluralist democracy and regional autonomy (Gauhar, 1985, pp. 126–9), and when concessions to democracy produced a secessionist majority in the East, the military government realised that it was time to go. The downfall of the second military government seems, at first sight, to be more the product of the activities of narrower groups. The 1985 constitution produced not only an elected legislature but a civilian prime minister and cabinet to control day-to-day policy, sharing power uneasily with President Zia. Pakistan appeared to be crossing the threshold from military authoritarianism to limited democracy, in the realisation of the need to avoid the isolation from the population which the Ayub government suffered. In June 1988 Zia dismissed the cabinet and dissolved parliament, mainly on account of their 'interference' with military affairs, especially in connection with the war in Afghanistan. Zia's legitimacy now depended on securing another favourable parliamentary election result but, before the polls could be held, he and several other leading army officers were killed in an air crash, apparently as a result of sabotage. The caretaker military government could hardly cancel the election without the risk of widespread violence, and was not strong enough to insist on another non-party contest. Once the party battle lines were drawn, the main challenge came from the Pakistan People's Party (PPP) under the leadership of Benazir Bhutto, the daughter of the executed president. The military authorities made her challenge difficult through their control of the media, and a last-minute decision that voters should produce identity cards (which many did not possess) at polling stations, but the PPP still emerged as the largest single party. The events precipitating the election had been largely the result of manoeuvrings at elite level — the dismissal of a prime minister, the assassination of a president and the return of an exiled opponent to demand party competition — but the actual holding of the election enabled mass public opinion to pass judgement on the military government. Authoritarianism, terror and growing poverty at a time when more resources were being devoted to the war in Afghanistan, were among the issues on which dissatisfaction with the regime was expressed (See especially Ali, 1988, p. 23).

It would be tempting to draw parallels with the Uruguayan experience of returning to the politics of the early 1970s, with the same party returned as in the pre-coup election, but whereas military intervention in the relatively developed Uruguayan polity seemed like an aberration, military rule in Pakistan has been the norm, and the area of civilian government policy subject to military veto is likely to be wider. The PPP itself had become a more moderate party by 1988, more willing to give candidatures to landlords, industrialists and religious leaders who could deliver votes, and to make concessions to the demands of the World Bank, the International Monetary Fund, United States foreign policy and the army itself (See especially Brown, 1988, p. 9; Noman, 1989, p. 40). The ghosts of Ayub Khan and Zia might have been well satisfied with the outcome. The army had retreated in 1971 with its public reputation dented, but its hierarchy and professionalism still intact. In 1988 the withdrawal seemed even more orderly, in spite of the death of the leader, and could be seen as the culmination of a longer process. Once the radical left had been destroyed through crude authoritarianism, limited democracy was introduced to bolster the regime's legitimacy without undermining its authority. As pressure build up for wider electoral participation, the concessions to legalised parties were made, but with sufficient manipulation of the electoral process to prevent an always probable defeat from being turned into a rout. Power passed to a moderate party which acknowledged the need not to pursue any policies that might precipitate another coup. In terms of the dangers inherent in military authoritarianism that were noted in Table 3.1, the military had largely avoided losing their legitimacy or their professionalism. They had delivered little in terms of material benefits, but their own skills and the weaknesses of the Pakistani political structure ensured that they paid a relatively modest price for such a failure.

5 Civil–Military Authoritarianism: Guatemala, El Salvador and Bolivia

Introduction

Our countries with civil–military authoritarian government — Guatemala, El Salvador and Bolivia — are much less developed than Chile or Uruguay, though much more developed than the deviant case of Pakistan. They occupy the 86th, 88th and 84th positions respectively in Sivard's ranking. The percentage of their labour forces employed outside agriculture varies from 46 in Guatemala to 60 in El Salvador, and adult literacy varies from 46 per cent in Guatemala to 63 per cent in Bolivia. They could not be described as 'industrialised' countries, yet they have moved beyond the stage of dependence on a few major plantation crops or minerals. In Guatemala, for example, Black has described the way in which an elite dominated by coffee barons was displaced by a broader one based on cotton, banking, manufacturing industry, rubber and sugar, and linked to multinational corporations (Black *et al.*, 1984, p. 17). In the absence of external political pressures these countries might conceivably have followed a similar path to that of their wealthier South American neighbours in the nineteenth century, with rival oligarchies using armies to advance their interests, but with soldiers kept in a subordinate role. But unlike nineteenth-century South America, the armies of post-1945 Central America and Bolivia were not merely the bodyguards of indigenous elites. They emerged, as we saw in Chapter 2, as part of the repressive apparatus of landed elites in plantation economies, but under the simultaneous influences of the Cold War and post-war socio-economic changes which gave rise to larger, more articulate middle and working classes, the role of the military became more complex and extensive. The Cold War provided a pretext for the United States to aid the growth of armies as a bulwark against the perceived communist threat, and this threat acquired new manifestations with the revolutions in Cuba and Nicaragua. Socioeconomic development, as in other parts of the world, led to new groups demanding greater participation in politics and a larger share of the nation's wealth. The conflicts generated by such demands are seldom easy to resolve, but they were made more difficult in these countries by the long tradition of elites employing troops to defend their privileges. When the United States now came to the aid of the elites and strengthened their armies, there was little inducement to seek accommodation with non-elites. The underprivileged, for their part, could take comfort from the violent overthrow of right-wing dictatorships in Cuba and Nicaragua, and seek a solution through guerrilla warfare. Violent conflict thus had a cumulative effect, with repression, economic exploitation and fraudulent elections persuading non-elites that violence was inevitable in the absence of a democratic process, and increases in violence provoking further repression.

One might expect armies in such a situation to hold all the trump cards and to have no need of coalitions with civilians, but the armies suffered at least two weaknesses. Firstly, they could not easily claim a legitimate right to rule alone in countries with a long independent history where civilian rule and contested elections, albeit of an oligarchic type, had become the norm by the second half of the twentieth century. Secondly, the sheer length of continuous military involvement in government from the 1950s onwards, in contrast to the late intervention in Chile and the brief interregnum in Uruguay, politicised the armies by diverting them into such activities as plundering the national coffers, exploiting civilian conflicts and taking control of anti-guerrilla warfare, with the result that military professionalism suffered. Once military leaders lose the asset of a disciplined coercive hierarchy under their command, they are less well equipped to govern, and may therefore require civilian allies. This is not to argue that professionalism was ever high, but its growth was stunted by the fact that the army had moved in to fill a power vacuum in the absence of effective civil authority, and was attempting to perform a multiplicity of roles which militated against the narrower role of providing a disciplined force with its own distinctive values.

Guatemala: The Retreat from Reformism

Pre-Coup Politics

Civil–military authoritarian regimes, unlike the military authoritarianism type, do not normally begin with a 'big bang'. It is therefore more difficult to say when military government began in Guatemala, but 1954 is normally taken as the major watershed. The government had been led by a colonel for the previous four years, but it had been a reforming government which had pursued an independent foreign policy, redistributed land and increased working-class mobilisation (Black *et al.*, 1984, p. 13; Painter, 1987, p. 63). That the military should be involved in such a government reminds us that soliders are less overwhelmingly right-wing in Central America than in the more developed South. Huntington's 'soldier as a radical' in a world of oligarchy (Huntington, 1968, p. 221) survived, although many of these radicals later threw in their lot with the anti-government gurrillas.

The politically naive might have expected the 1950 government to usher in an era of democratic development and economic advancement comparable with New Zealand or Australia, but Guatemala's political roots were different. A long tradition of competitive politics existed but the rules of the competition resembled all-wrestling rather than cricket, with the heavyweights frequently deciding who had won an electoral contest, no matter what the tally of votes might suggest to the contrary. Authoritarianism tempered by coups and fraudulent elections was not alien to Guatemalan political culture, and even those who deplored such arrangements could do little in the face of American-supported troops. It was against this background that an invasion by exiles occurred in 1954, supported by an American government fearful of the impact of a left-wing government at the height of the Cold War, and of the threats to business interests such as the United Fruit Company. This invasion was followed by three decades of civil–military authoritarianism, most of it unmistakably right-wing.

Military Ideology, Interests and Objectives

The search for an explicit military ideology in Guatemala is even more difficult than in South America. There was a strident anti-communism which was fuelled by the rise of a guerrilla movement and events in Cuba and Nicaragua, but crude kleptocracy was more evident than any commitment to the ideals of Friedman or Hayek. Policies were right-wing not only in the sense of attempting to crush guerrilla movements which claimed to articulate the interests of the poor, but in halting the modest mobilisation of the early 1950s and preserving one of the most economically unequal societies in the world. In 1970 the wealthiest 20 per cent of the population received 73 per cent of the nation's income, as compared with the 38 per cent received by the wealthiest 20 per cent in egalitarian Denmark (Seligson in Malloy and Seligson, 1987, p. 177). The land redistributions were quickly reversed and leaders of popular movements were killed or exiled (Black *et al.*, 1984, p. 17). Even largely moderate groups such as teachers, trade union leaders, priests, journalists, Christian Democrats and Social Democrats were denied effective political participation (Simons, 1981, p. 98).

Beyond a desire to suppress communism or popular participation, however, there was limited unity of purpose. It would be difficult to imagine any military government in Guatemala setting out 'a series of clearly-defined political, social and economic objectives and strategies' in the way that the Argentine military rulers did in 1976 (Pion-Berlin, 1985, p. 57). The objectives in Argentina included a 'phased restoration of "proper moral values", national security, economic efficiency and "authentic representative democracy"' (ibid., p. 57). A search for national security was implicit in the anti-guerrilla war, although guerrilla activities were themselves largely provoked by the military, but there was never much interest in moral values or 'economic efficiency' in the sense of relying on the discipline of the market. Free market economics would not easily have been compatible with the use of state intervention to enrich soldiers and their clients in business; and 'authentic representative democracy', if soldiers believed in such a concept, was no more than a distant ideal which could only be pursued if one could ensure that entrenched military and business interests were not challenged. The absence of any clear common objectives may not have been a major handicap in the short term, when military governments can often rely mainly on coercion, but in the long run lack of unity of purpose proved expensive. Handy describes the way in which factions in a heterogeneous army revolved around parties, the pursuit of personal advantage and differences over the scope of brutal military operations. The rifts became deeper after 1982 with divisions between the more conservative older officers and younger officers who 'rhetorically' advocated a type of rural development as an alternative to coercion (Handy, 1984, p. 255).

Military Strengths and Weaknesses

There were three main dimensions of military strength which influenced the effectiveness of the army in ruling Guatemala: coercive, economic and professional. The coercive element seemed unchallengeable in the early stages, with fledgling mass movements crushed and the United States government underwriting right-wing regimes. As guerrilla resistance grew, so did the defence budget, which rose from 10 per cent to 22 per cent of the national budget in the final decade of military rule (Painter, 1987, pp. 48–50). But the effectiveness of coercion depended on the unity of the army and the continued willingness of the United States to support it, and both of these came under pressure by the 1980s.

We have already hinted at the complex relationship between the success of the military in the pursuit of personal and corporate wealth, and effectiveness of the military as rulers. The Midas touch of soldiers in transforming both public and private assets into their own property was remarkable by any standards. The army acquired an interest in forty autonomous state enterprises (Painter, 1987, p. 47); the armed forces owned their own bank and investment fund, and launched several industrial projects, while top military leaders became extensive landowners (Simons, 1981, pp. 97–8). There were few constraints on the use of corruption as a means of self-enrichment (Painter, 1987, p. 47; Handy, 1984, p. 157). The soldiers did not suffer the same fate as King Midas, but it is arguable that this pursuit of wealth made for friction both within the army, where some groups were dissatisfied with their share of the spoils, and between the army and the business community which was being drained by the demands of the army for personal enrichment and for waging the civil war. Bt the 1970s, according to Handy, escalating military involvement in politics and business had divided the military into competing cliques linked to civilian political parties. By the early 1980s the military high command had disintegrated 'into a constantly quarrelling body of competing interests held together, if at all, by a vague sense of military loyalty and the intensity of the brutal civil war' (Handy, 1984, p. 165). This description raises questions about the degree of professionalism in the Guatemalan army. It had always been limited, compared with South America, by the way in which it had been exploited by rival civilian groups. This inhibited its ability to develop its own distinctive values and ideology. Yet one might have expected a long period of military rule, in a country where civil institutions were weak, to help the army develop a greater sense of identity. Handy acknowledges the strength of the army in the 1960s, in contrast to the 1970s and 1980s, as the most effective and cohesive organisation in Guatemala, benefiting from greater technical competence and a better-educated officer corps (Handy, 1984, p. 156). With greater self-restraint, a more professional army might have evolved which could either have restored civilian rule on its own terms or legitimised its own rule, but the underlying social and economic conditions were hostile to such developments. We return to the point that economic development had not reached the stage, as in much of South America, where the officer corps and business elites were largely mutually reinforcing, and where unity in the face of substantial mass movements was an article of faith. In Guatemala, the pre-1954 tradition of the soldier as the champion of development was never completely extinguished. It continued partly through defections to the guerrillas, and the purge which caused the deaths of over 300 middle-ranking officers between 1978 and 1982 was indicative of the fear of continued resistance to the leadership (Painter, 1987, p. 68). There were still young officers in the regular army who believed that repression alone would be self-defeating. These officers supported General Montt's counter-coup in 1982 which brought relatively junior officers into top advisory positions. By their nature such deviations from hierarchy are going to intensify conflict in an institution where hierarchy is highly prized, and the senior officers restored much of their authority in 1983 after threats of disobedience, before a more brutal, conservative regime was established under General Mejia (Handy, 1984, pp. 272–4). But by then the army's divisions were clear, and divided armies find it difficult to resist demands for civilian rule.

The Army and Civil Elites

'Civil–military authoritarianism' does not necessarily imply a balanced coalition government of soldiers and civilians, although both groups will be included. There is a long Central American tradition of a division of labour in which civilian elites employ soldiers to defend their interests without the elites necessarily taking part in government. One could argue that military rule in Guatemala was a modern extension of this process, with soldiers restricting popular mobilisation through edicts from the presidential palace, as well as harassing the guerrillas who threatened public order. The regimes between 1953 and 1984 were civil–military, rather than purely military, in the sense that civil elites exercised a veto power not found in Chile, Uruguay or Pakistan. Failure to observe the conventions of consultation with civilians could bring its own punishments. The selection of a presidential candidate in 1982 without consulting right-wing parties or the officer corps was a major reason for the counter-coup of that year (Dunkerley in Clapham and Philip, 1985, p. 186). The army lacked the will, given its incoherent ideology, and the ability, given its limited professionalism, to alter the economic structure radically on the Chilean or Uruguayan models. It merely exploited the existing structure as best it could. Black speaks of a 'corporate' relationship with powerful private interests, but with the middle-class professions, the church and trade unions excluded, but he never defines the term (Black *et al.*, 1984, pp. 48, 130). One can question whether civil or military institutions enjoyed sufficient coherence for a formal corporate structure to emerge, and whether corporatism is easily compatible with widespread corruption, but the unwritten understanding that the army would use its might to protect indigenous and foreign business interests, while the latter generated extensive wealth to supplement soldiers' pay packets, survived as long as economic conditions allowed capitalist growth, military expenditure and corruption to flourish side by side.

By the 1980s a combination of worsening world economic conditions and military mismanagement brought a halt to capitalist growth. Between 1980 and 1985, half the economic growth of the previous thirty years had been lost, and per capita gross domestic product fell to the 1971 level (Painter, 1987, p. 50). Black argues that self-enrichment had been pursued at the expense of bourgeois consensus (Black *et al.*, 1984, pp. 53–4), so that there was little to sustain the military once it could no longer reward the civilian elite. In 1983 the government tried to impose a new 10 per cent value added tax to meet the rising cost of the civil war. The main business federation responded by attacking the military's interests in state enterprises and public works projects. A visit by the International Monetary Fund in 1984 led to proposals for increased tariffs and higher interest rates. The business federation immediately demanded the withdrawal of these proposals, and threatened to paralyse production and transport, and to withdraw from any dialogue with the government. As a result the government withdrew its proposals and the Minister of Finance and three other ministers resigned (Painter, 1986, pp. 829, 831–2). Lacking any base in the wider population, and lacking foreign support on account of their human rights record, the military were in no position to make enemies in the business elite as well.

Military Relations with the Wider Society

We have noted the suppression of radical and working-class movements throughout the period of military government. According to Amnesty International 140,000 Guatemalans disappeared or were murdered between 1966 and 1986. The security forces not only waged a civil war but acted as death squads to eliminate selected opponents of the regime (Reed, 1988, p. 7). Yet political parties, competitive elections and an elected legislature were permitted, in contrast to Chile, Uruguay and Pakistan, even though the choice of parties was severely restricted and the method of counting votes dubious. Why should these trimmings of democracy have been preserved? The desire to impress the United States was no doubt one factor, since apologists abroad could always argue that fraudulent competitive elections were better than no elections, and that, given time, the constitutional machinery might allow voters a genuine choice, in contrast to the non-competitive system in Cuba which might spread to Guatemala if support for the military was withdrawn and the guerrillas took power. Such arguments might also have made some impression on moderate members of the indigenous elite, but whether going through the motions of democracy made much impression on the wider population is more doubtful. Voting was compulsory, but by 1978 only 31 per cent of the registered electorate voted (Handy, 1984, p. 176). There were several points at which the moderate left were willing to compromise with the army by supporting moderate presidential candidates, notably in 1958 and 1974 (Painter, 1987, p. 64; Simons, 1981, p. 95), but the military always ensured that they won the count no matter who won the vote. In that way, opportunities to build a more broadly based polity were spurned, and the military left with fewer and fewer allies or potential allies.

The democratic facade might also be seen as a continuation of a long-standing competitive oligarchic tradition in which the masses did not expect any significant involvement. The Guatemalan elite, whether civil or military, may have been more confident of its ability to rig elections than the rulers of Chile or Uruguay or even Pakistan, where groups wanting to challenge the government were better organised. Yet by the 1980s the Guatemalan political system was more complicated than an old-fashioned oligarchy. Mass movements had only been kept down by considerable repression and through an alliance between the wielders of coercive and economic power. As the alliance became more fragile in the 1980s, a military government which had no alternative mass base to turn to had little option but to seek an orderly withdrawal from politics on the best terms it could.

The Military and Withdrawal

It was perhaps unremarkable that a military government unable to win a civil war, halt economic decline, retain internal cohesion or attract civilian support should seek an exit from government. What was remarkable was that the military managed to withdraw on such favourable terms, with no prosecutions for its past deeds and a civilian successor which made few departures from previous policy.

Both internal and external explanations can be offered for the availability and electability of an acceptable right-of-centre successor. As an internal explanation, Mazzellia argues that once most of the leaders of progressive political groups had been killed or exiled, more moderate civilian leaders became more prominent (Mazzellia in Danopoulos, 1988, p. 166). One could also argue that defections to the guerrillas reduced the progressive democratic element still further, but such arguments imply the existence of a finite supply of such politicians, which is not generally borne out by experience. A more practical explanation would be that the military, for all their weaknesses, would still not have allowed a left-of-centre party to win.

External pressure came mainly from the United States. Defeat in the Vietnam War had made American presidents and congresses more wary about underwriting right-wing military dictators waging civil wars, and the election of President Carter in 1976 had given greater emphasis to support for human rights, rather than a crude anti-communism, as a condition of continued aid. This policy was never entirely reversed by President Reagan after 1980 (Seligson in Malloy and Seligson, 1987, p. 187; Painter, 1987, pp. 79–80), and by that time there was a growing human rights lobby which Congress could not easily ignore.

These internal and external pressures left both the army and civilian politicians with little room for manoeuvre. A left-wing civilian government would not have been acceptable to the military leadership or the White House, and civilian elites no doubt realised the futility of pursuing such an alternative, which could only have led to prolonged rule by a divided army relying increasingly on coercion. There is no reason why the army should not have resorted to this if all else failed, but it preferred the moderate civilian option so that it could return to barracks (and the civil war battlefield) and attempt to restore its cohesion and reputation. The leading candidates in the 1984 presidential election agreed that there would be no banking or agrarian reforms, no nationalisation, and no prosecutions for human rights violations (Painter, 1986, p. 834). Civilian government thus had a broad appeal across the elite spectrum. It offered no serious threat to the army, yet offered the prospect of the first instalment of something closer to liberal democracy after three decades of repression.

El Salvador: The Right versus the Impotent Left

Pre-Coup Politics

There are many parallels in the political development of El Salvador and Guatemala. In both, an army originally used as the bodyguard of the plantation elite moved to the centre of the stage and fought a long, inconclusive war against social groups which had been denied political participation. In both, military governments were right-wing mainly in the sense of preserving existing political and economic inequalities rather than making radical reversals of left-wing policies. And in both the failure of the military to win a civil war, despite massive repression, or to build a legitimate civilian base, exacerbated divisions within the army, made the governments a growing embarrassment to their American allies and ultimately precipitated their return to barracks.

There were, however, two significant differences. Economically, the rural elites in El Salvador had enjoyed the advantage of drawing their labour from the most densely populated country in Central America, and this buyers' market had enabled them to hire labour on favourable terms in the nineteenth and early twentieth centuries, with less need for military repression than in Guatemala (Dunkerley in Clapham and Philip, 1985, pp. 188–9); and politically El Salvador had not experienced a reforming government comparable with that in Guatemala before 1954. Both these factors affected military relations with civilian elites and the wider population. (They may also have led to the relative neglect of El Salvador as a research site, since researchers are often more attracted by the drama of a 'revolutionary' government cut down in its prime, as in Spain, Guatemala or (mistakenly) Ghana, than by a long diet of right-wing repression.)

In the absence of even a brief period of reforming civilian government, elites and masses were both more inclined to use violence in preference to the ballot box. The starting point of modern military government is normally taken as 1932, twenty-two years earlier than in Guatemala, when the army took power after massacring 10–20,000 peasants to put down a communist-backed uprising. Smaller uprisings in 1944 and 1961 were similarly crushed (Millett, 1981, p. 20). The size of the population may have given the elite an economic advantage in hiring labour, but it also put it at a disadvantage when the weight of numbers was turned against it in peasants' revolts, and this made the civilians elite increasingly dependent on the firepower of the army, which remained in power alone or in co-operation with civilians for over fifty years.

Military Ideology, Interests and Objectives

The unbroken period of military government was not, however, one of unchecked dictatorship. As in Guatemala, right-wing military leaders had problems in retaining their authority over officers whose political attitudes were more heterogeneous, in bargaining with civilian elites who retained strong economic power bases, and in trimming their sails to the changing winds from the United States which could grant or withhold the resources required for repression.

Karl suggests that by the 1980s the army was divided into three main groups: the ultra-right linked to the coffee growers and opposed to reform, the 'apolitical' military technocrats trained by the United States army and 'nationalists' favouring widespread reform (Karl in Drake and Silva, 1986, p. 22). There were a few occasions when the more moderate elements came to the surface, with middle-ranking and junior officers rebelling in a way not found in the more professional armies of the military authoritarian regimes. In 1972 some junior officers joined Christian Democrats and Social Democrats in protesting (unsuccessfully) against the fraudulent conduct of an election (Dunkerley in Clapham and Philip, 1985, pp. 189–90) and in 1979 a group of young colonels overthrew their superiors and installed a short-lived government which included moderate officers, businessmen, social democratic civilians and even the leader of the Communist Party (Millett, 1981, p. 71), but such events were the exception to predominantly right-wing rule. Soldiers with left-wing convictions had the alternative of joining the guerrillas, and there was little middle ground in a country with extremes of wealth and poverty and no free elections. Military government did not even have to be justified or apologised for, as in the countries where military intervention is more of a novelty. It had become the normal form of government, standing between relative stability and violent revolution.

Military Strengths and Weaknesses

Fifty years of unbroken rule may have persuaded soldiers of their own legitimacy in government, but it was a claim which was not accepted so readily in other sections of society. The pressures at work in Guatemala were also evident in El Salvador, including external events such as the impact of the Cuban and Nicaraguan revolutions, the reluctance of the United States government to support the continued violation of human rights, and the internal pressure of a growing guerrilla movement demanding what it saw as political rights and social justice. The army's strength in its first four decades in power had been its ability to use force to preserve an elite which would otherwise have had difficulty in surviving. Its weakness was that in the final decade, when there was a greater balance between government and opposition in the possession of force, it lacked the ability, and frequently the willingness, to build any consensus to resolve armed conflict. No civilian government would have found this easy, but civilians acknowledging their lack of weapons of coercion might at least have attempted to build bridges by other means.

The reforming government of 1979 ended after a few months when some senior military officers refused to obey it, and the Carter administration lent it insufficient support. It was followed over the next three years by military-dominated regimes of varying political orientations. At first they seemed to have much in their favour. They enjoyed strong American support as a clear alternative to the previous repression, and attempted to build broader public support by promising to end official terrorism, retiring several of the officers responsible for it, and attempting a policy of land redistribution. Many businessmen were willing to support them in the belief that at least the appearance of reform was necessary as an insurance against more radical change. But in the end the gap between extreme ideologies and polarised social groups proved unbridgeable. Landowners and the upper class opposed any accommodation with the left. Guerrilla warfare therefore continued, and this gave hardline officers an opportunity to increase their influence and their share of the places in the junta, which moved steadily to the right. For all their well-meaning efforts, the governments delivered little to win the gratitude of the masses. Between 1979 and 1983 real wages fell by 65 per cent and consumption by 50 per cent (Millett, 1981, pp. 71–3; Karl in Drake and Silva, 1986, p.21).

The immediate outcome was the removal of President Durate, the installation of a more right-wing government and what Karl calls the restoration of the alliance between the army and the traditional elite (Karl in Drake and Silva, 1986, p. 13). Dunkerley suggests that the United States' intervention in 1980 had bolstered the army but also hastened its withdrawal, and that the 'breakdown of the political system' had become irreversible (Dunkerley in Clapham and Philip, 1985, pp. 171–7). One could question whether armed repression backed by economic interests and foreign arms should be dignified by the term 'political system', but there was clearly no going back to such arrangements now that force was increasingly being met with force, and American donors were more discriminating. Neither was there any prospect of even a moderate left-wing government, but right-wing rule could at least be given greater legitimacy, and unpopular soldiers the opportunity to retreat from government by holding a non-fraudulent election. In the first instance this was done through a constituent assembly choosing President Magana in 1982. This did not produce radical changes of policy, but it left the door open to further democratisation in 1984 with the direct election of President Durate, a Christian Democrat who had headed the moderate government of 1980–2 and who was not the army's first preference. Civil–military authoritarianism at last gave way to civilian government.

The Army, Civilian Elites and the Wider Society

It is difficult to conceive of any military government ruling El Salvador without acknowledging the substantial veto powers of civilian elites, or vice versa. For long periods the veto power remained dormant because soldiers had little wish to offend the landed interest, but when reforms were attempted after 1979 the brake on radical policies was clear enough. The brake could generally be operated by civilians appealing to sympathetic officers to oust their more radical colleagues, and the fragmented 'non-professional' nature of the army made such intrigue relatively easy. At the more 'structural' level of politics there was a nominal democracy, with Christian Democrats and even Social Democrats permitted to contest elections (Dunkerley in Clapham and Philip, 1985, pp. 189–90), though the government's control of the count ensured (until 1984) that they did not win them. Such a permissive atmosphere might reflect the confidence of soldiers who had held power for fifty years, but it might also reflect the greater tradition of civilian autonomy compared with Guatemala. There was, however, a certain convergence between the countries in the later years as civil and military elites made common cause against rising terrorism.

On military relations with society there is little to be said. Managed elections offered a limited opportunity for mass participation, yet no military government made any real effort to build a popular base. By the 1980s the masses were either indifferent to the formal political process or were actively supporting the guerrillas.

The Military and Withdrawal

As in Guatemala, there was a remarkably smooth transition to pluralist civilian politics after a prolonged period of civil–military authoritarianism, there were similar pressures of American impatience and an army with a tarnished reputation waging an unwinnable civil war. But the fine detail was different. While the Guatemalan presidential candidates had had to agree publicly to renounce any mildly left-of-centre policies, the El Salvador parties showed greater autonomy in agreeing to a transitional right-of-centre coalition in 1982, albeit in consultation with the military (Karl in Drake and Silva, 1986, p. 19), and then producing a result which was much less convenient for the military than that in Guatemala. But subsequent events helped to emphasise the paradox of civilian groups which appeared to be more differentiated from the military than in Guatemala, but which were not necessarily more independent of it. President Durate and his supporters might have wished for a greater departure from previous politics than his Guatemalan counterpart but his actual room for manoeuvre was, if anything, even less. This was partly due to Durate's failing health, but it may also be a reflection of a stronger, less divided army in a country where experience of pluralist politics is even more limited. The civil war, which largely accounted for the army's formal withdrawal from government, has also provided a justification for its continued control of large areas of the country. In addition the backdrop of war gave the extreme right-wing Arena Party an issue to exploit in the 1989 election, when voters expressed a preference for its hardline policies over the apparent ineffectiveness of the Christian Democrats.

Bolivia: The Incoherent Right

Bolivia has many features which make it politically closer to Central America than to its immediate South American neighbours. As in Guatemala, an experiment in left-wing populism gave way to a long period of mainly right-wing civil–military authoritarianism which ended after a series of fraudulent elections had undermined the army's legitimacy, and the economic performance of the military rulers had offered no alternative consolation in terms of material well-being. A major difference compared with Guatemala and El Salvador lies in the lack of clear structural differentiation. Social groups, political parties and even the army itself often appear as loose aggregates whose members are linked to other groups through frequently changing clientelistic ties. Indeed the word 'clientelism' is as inseparable from studies of Bolivian politics as 'stability' in relation to Sweden or 'violence' in relation to Uganda. The reasons are not explained satisfactorily in much of the literature, but the survival of such an arrangement may be related to the gap between Bolivia's political reach and its economic grasp.

Pre-Coup Politics

The revolutionary government which came to power in 1952 gave weapons to workers and peasants, and nearly destroyed the armed forces (Whitehead in O'Donnell *et al.*, 1986, pp. 53–4). The government introduced universal suffrage, made extensive land reforms and expanded the public sector substantially. Yet Malloy describes the relationship between the government and society as clientelistic. This clientelism weakened the ability of groups to form on a horizontal, class-type basis or to develop a coherent ideological position. It became increasingly difficult to deliver benefits to some groups without upsetting others. In the economic sphere, no sector developed based on import substitution, and there was therefore no significant national bourgeoisie to provide the drive for the 'state capitalist economic model' (Malloy, 1977, pp. 455–76). This apparent attempt to develop a socialist political structure without the concomitant social and economic changes left the government vulnerable, and the economic disintegration and political disorder of the early 1960s culminated in a right-wing coup in 1964.

Military Ideology, Interests, Strengths and Weaknesses

The military governments in power between 1964 and 1982 were mainly right-wing, except for a brief interlude between 1969 and 1971, but what they were against was clearer than what they were for. The 1964 and 1971 governments reduced the status of organised labour by reducing both its share of the nation's wealth and its degree of political participation, and ensured that left-wing parties did not compete on equal terms with those of the right. The governments' main allies were the urban middle class and professional groups (Malloy and Gamarra in Malloy and Seligson, 1987, pp. 97–9; Mitchell, 1981, p. 76; Malloy, 1977, p. 480). Yet there was little ideological coherence beyond a dislike of labour and the left. The army, which had nearly disintegrated under the populist government in the 1950s, never developed a sense of professionalism comparable with that of Bolivia's South American neighbours, and the officer corps has been described by such terms as 'incoherent' (Malloy and Gamarra in Malloy and Seligson, 1987, p. 99), 'fragmented' (Mitchell, 1981, p. 78), 'lacking in corporate identity' (Malloy, 1977, 478) and 'socially and politically mixed' and therefore unable to achieve stability (Whitehead in O'Donnell *et al.*, 1986, p. 54). Most of the military governments were clearly right-wing in the sense of increasing social and political inequality, but not in the free market Chilean sense. Much of the elaborate pre-coup state structure was left intact, though not generally for the benefit of those for whom it had been intended. In the absence of any clear sense of professional integrity, officers used the structure to plunder the state coffers in a way comparable with their Guatlemalan counterparts, and profited increasingly from the narcotics trade (Mitchell, 1981, p. 76). Yet the heterogeneity of the officer corps meant that there was no consistency of policy, and the fortunes of intra-military conflict could occasionally bring left-wing officers to power. Influenced by events in Peru, a more populist government came to power in 1969 which nationalised American oil interests and lifted much of the repression of labour, but the government lacked any firm base and was removed in 1971 by a coalition of military factions, civilian out-groups and private economic interests (Malloy and Gamarra in Malloy and Seligson, 1987, pp. 97–9; Malloy, 1977, p. 480).

The Army, Civilian Elites and the Wider Society

Bolivia conformed to the civil–military authoritarian model in that competitive, though fraudulent, elections were held throughout the period of military government. A newly created military party was elected after two years of military government, but Malloy and Gamarra describe it as no more than a personalist clique, with military force as the real basis of executive but state power (Malloy and Seligson, 1987, p. 97). But military force was itself an elusive commodity in a divided army attempting to rule a divided society. Governmental effectiveness, or even survival, still depended on the manipulation of patron–client networks (Malloy and Gamarra in Malloy and Seligson, 1987, p. 98). This required substantial civilian involvement in the political process, and the 1970s saw a long period of power-sharing between parties at ministerial level (Whitehead in O'Donnell *et al.*, 1986, p. 54). The government became more explicitly military by 1980 after a series of elections had produced votes (though not counts) which displeased the military leadership (ibid., p. 56). The brutality of this government suggested a shift from the traditional incoherent Bolivian model to the more businesslike repression of the Southern Cone (Mitchell, 1981, pp. 75–7), yet the tenure of the government was much shorter than those of Argentina and Chile.

The Military and Withdrawal

In the end the army lacked the coherence to survive public censure for its election-rigging, its blatant corruption and its inability to avert economic collapse in an economy heavily dependent on mineral exports (Mitchell, 1981, p. 78; Gamarra in Danopoulos, 1988, pp. 66–72). If the options of election-rigging and coercion were exhausted, the military had little alternative but to acknowledge that their prestige would fall even further unless they withdrew. When a left-wing presidential candidate won the vote in the 1982 election, it seemed prudent to allow him to win the count as well, and allow him to bear the burden of the economic crisis to come. This he did with a vengeance, with the annual rate of inflation reaching 20,000 per cent before another election in 1985 gave power to President Paz, who led a right-wing government which imposed an austerity programme that fell heavily on the poor (Gamarra in Danopoulos, 1988, p. 74).

What, then, had right-wing military government achieved, and did withdrawal leave the army adequately intact to pursue or defend its perceived interests? Such questions are more difficult to answer in the case of Bolivia than in most of the countries we have examined so far. The achievements of most post-war Bolivian governments, civil or military, have been fairly modest in the face of a socioeconomic structure which does not rest easily with any attempt to execute coherent policies. As the army is itself part of that structure, with all the factionalism and lack of professionalism that it implies, it is difficult to speak of military interests. Yet for most of the period of military government there was the common thread of protecting the elite and curbing mass movements. For all the economic disasters of the period, some modest success could be claimed in pursuit of that objective, and without provoking the large-scale civil wars incurred in Guatemala and El Salvador.

6 Limited Democracy: Thailand, Indonesia and Turkey

Introduction

We move now to the frontiers of right-wing military government, and the reader must judge how far the recent governments in Thailand, Indonesia and Turkey have been right-wing or military. In none of these countries has there been a polarisation comparable with Latin America between clearly differentiated elites and emerging mass movements, in which the army has generally intervened on the side of the elite, but all live in the shadow of neighbouring communist states which are, or have been, perceived as a threat. (In the case of Indonesia the shadow may be a very long one, but the fear of indigenous communist collaboration with China has been real enough.) There may thus be a right-wing strand in military thinking to the extent that left-wing politicians are seen as allies of a potential foreign aggressor, but there is not the same feeling as in Latin America of a need to close ranks against working-class movements in general, if only because such movements, if they exist at all, are merely one element in the competition for power and influence rather than the main challengers to authority.

Thailand and Turkey both have much longer histories as independent nations than the Latin American republics, and have therefore had more time for legitimate patterns of authority to evolve and less need for authority based on coercion. Whereas in Latin America military intervention was a feature of politics from the start, with frequent periods of Caudillo rule, Thailand and Turkey had long-established civilian monarchies, with armies playing a subordinate role. When they did eventually intervene, it was as 'modernisers' who saw the importation of Western social and political structures (at least on paper) as part of the process of modernisation, but this modernisation did not, for the most part, imply the elimination of well-established civilian elites, which had evolved without any great dependence on the military, and which it would have required a revolution, rather than a mere coup, to displace. There was thus little alternative to regimes based on civil–military co-operation. Since the initial reforming military governments were to some extent controlling the pace at which new groups demanding increased participation emerged, unlike the Latin American regimes which were merely responding to such changes, it was easier to make concessions to pluralist politics, especially when the civilian elites still had substantial power bases which could be mobilised for electoral support to prevent any sweeping working-class victory. Subsequent military governments were more right-wing than the initial ones (further supporting the Huntington thesis of soldiers becoming more conservative as society develops) but by that time experience of pluralist politics made it difficult to dispense with relatively free, competitive elections.

Indonesia is a great deal more difficult to place in any one category. It is much less developed than Thailand or Turkey, which occupy similar positions on Sivard's scale to our countries with civil–military authoritarian regimes, and is therefore not an obvious candidate for right-wing military government, but the perceived communist threat and the experience of inefficient state economic intervention under President Sukarno pointed the army (though not always consistently) in the direction of a pro-Western foreign policy and a larger role for private enterprise. The limited democratic element might be explained partly in terms of the sheer size of the country, with a population of over 150 million spread over several islands. No military government has ever had the skill or resources to rule a country of that size alone. President Sukarno had failed to impose autocratic civilian rule effectively, and the army had little alternative but to build a legitimate base on a semi-competitive system.

Thailand: The Bureaucratic Right

Pre-Coup Politics

'Bureaucratic' is a word frequently used to describe Thai politics, comparable with the adjective 'clientelistic' in Bolivia. Bureaucracy tends to flourish where the intensity of conflict in the political system is low, and this has been the case for much of Thailand's history. Lissak explains the lack of politicisation in terms of historical continuity. Thailand did not experience the dislocation of the arrival or departure or a colonial power, did not suffer the humiliation of defeat in war, or the consequent social and political ferment among non-elites, and did not have any seriously frustrated social groups (Lissak in Schriffrin, 1976, p. 160). But the cost of being a tranquil backwater in world politics was one of relative social and economic stagnation, which left those who had some contact with the outside world dissatisfied with their lot, including 'commoner' army officers who had been held back by an all-powerful monarch.

By 1932 worsening economic conditions were forcing the king to reduce expenditure on the civil and military bureaucracies, at a time when their members were growing in self-confidence and demanding a European-style constitution (Hoadley, 1975, pp. 13–14). This precipitated the first military coup and the emergence of a civil–military coalition (but with the monarchy retained) which broadened political participation beyond the aristocracy. The government was ousted in 1944 on account of its co-operation with the Japanese, and a weak civilian government survived until 1948. For the next four decades the pattern was one of civil–military coalitions, brought to power sometimes by coups, sometimes by free elections in which soldiers were significant participants, and sometimes by less-than-free elections. Military intervention in Thailand was not, then, a response to serious social, economic or political dislocation in the way that it was in the other countries we have studied. It was closer to the tropical African model of an intra-elite revolt which challenged the competence of the incumbent rulers or their distribution of rewards, rather than an attempt to ward off a perceived left-wing threat or national disintegration, although the left-wing threat did become greater after the military had taken power.

Military Ideology, Interests and Objectives

'The Thai officer corps . . . still adheres to the image of the conservative officer loyal to the corporate interests of the military and especially to certain cliques within it' (Lissak in Schriffrin, 1976, p. 170).

One might have expected a coup by Western-educated officers against an aristocratic government to produce a radical military government comparable with Nasser's Egypt. Rhetoric about 'development' has certainly been one strand in military ideology (Chaloemtiarana, 1979, p. 1; Hoadley, 1975, p. 27), and the military have initiated development projects which would not have found favour on the South American right, but development and modernisation are seen as largely bureaucratic exercises, with little room for mass participation. We have noted Lissak's remarks about the absence of seriously frustrated social groups in a country largely untouched by war or colonialism, and this reduced the need for soldiers to seek a mass base. Neither was there a strong nationalist vein to be exploited, as in Egypt and Burma with their long histories of foreign occupation. It was generally sufficient to confine civil–military alliances to an elite level, and the objectives of the military suggested in the literature are essentially conservative ones, including the protection of corporate interests, the maintenance of Buddhism, national security, stability, order, the prevention of communism and the ideal of an apolitical society (Thomas in Danopoulos, 1988, p. 112; Rathamarit, 1984, p. 1; Chaloemtiarana, 1979, pp. xxxiii–v; Lissak in Schriffrin, 1976, pp. 155–7; Hoadley, 1975, p. 27). While the military rulers of the 1930s were conservative in the sense that they did not want modernisation to be accompanied by major changes in the social structure or political participation, military rulers by the 1950s were men with much less foreign educational experience whose outlook was shaped more by internal politics and who rejected Western politics even as an ideal (Chaloemtiarana, 1979, pp. xxiii–v). As the war in Indochina gathered momentum, and social and economic changes stimulated new demands for political participation, left-wing politics was seen as both an internal and external threat, and the military were firmly on the side of the status quo.

Military Strengths and Weaknesses

The Thai army has not had to prove its strength in revolutions, on foreign battlefields or in civil wars, and only to a limited extent in combating terrorism, but the absence of such challenges has left it free to become more skilled in political manipulation. The army, like Thai society as a whole, is characterised by conflict between competing cliques, and there are divisions between politically oriented officers who want to manipulate the political system for the benefit of themselves and their clientele, and professionally oriented officers who want to develop a professional, disciplined and relatively non-corrupt military organisation (Hoadley, 1975, pp. 27–9; Marks, 1980, pp. 604–5, 612). But these divisions are transcended by a generally accepted belief that the army has a significant political role to play, and by the effects of historical continuity. The latter may not have produced 'professionalism' in the Western sense of an army concentrating on an accepted non-political role, but there is, as Thomas argues, professionalism in the sense of accepting military intervention as a means of protecting corporate interests (Thomas in Danopoulos, 1988, pp. 127–8), even if the extent of such intervention is in dispute.

To put it another way, military intervention in politics does not require the same elaborate justification that occurs with most new coups in most parts of the world. Having broken the royal stranglehold in 1932 and extended political participation, however modestly, in subsequent years, the existence of the army as a legitimate political actor has never seriously been disputed. This may change in the future as social change strengthens the bases of civilian groups, but so far the strength of the army has owed much to the weakness of potential civilian challengers.

The Military, Civil Society and Withdrawal

The existence of governments comprising both soldiers and civilians, each with their own power base, has been an almost constant feature of Thai politics since 1932, but there have been many variations within that broad framework. In 1957 the military government legitimised its rule with a dubious 'election'; after the 1971 coup the army created its own party (Hoadley, 1975, pp. 15, 31); in 1979 an election was held without parties, and between 1980 and 1983 General Prem adopted a 'divide and rule' policy towards rival parties (Rathamarit, 1984, pp. ii–iii). The retention of the monarchy emphasises an historical continuity that regular military coups have done little to diminish, and this precludes the direct election of the executive of the Latin American model. An effective miltary presence in the government therefore depended on manipulating, or sometimes bypassing, the party system to obtain a working majority in the legislature, and then ensuring an adequate military presence in the cabinet. Most recent prime ministers have been military men, and they have in turn appointed large numbers of soldiers to the Senate and top positions in the bureaucracy. Senior military officers have also played a significant role in coalition negotiations (Hoadley, 1975, p. 15; Thomas in Danopoulos, 1988, pp. 114–15).

Until recently the political system was described as one in which the mass of the population played little role. Lissak referred to a system in which military cliques handled moderate demands from the margins of the centre or the periphery, with most channels of communication operating from the top down (Lissak in Schriffrin, 1976, p. 160), and Rathamarit describes the parties as 'cadre parties' revolving around personalities in parliament, but he acknowledges that by the 1983 election there was a conflict between the army and parties over who should rule (Rathamarit, 1984, pp. 10–11, 277). He traces a legitimacy crisis as far back as the late 1960s, when economic development was giving rise to new demands, a greater interest in foreign ideologies and an increasingly vociferous student population (ibid., p. 2).

Thailand, like the Latin American republics, had the problem of a guerrilla war, but it was closer to the Uruguayan than the Central American model in that success, rather than failure, in combating terrorism contributed to military disengagement. The experience of nearby South Vietnam had shown that an authoritarian military regime could claim little legitimacy as an alternative to communism, and this realisation led to a growing civilianisation of government in the early 1980s. As the government won the ideological war and foreign support for the guerrillas waned, their numbers were reduced to barely 600 by 1986 (Thomas in Danopoulos, 1988, pp. 117–20).

With terrorism virtually defeated, and with new political demands largely contained within the existing party system, there was no obvious reason for the continuation of military government in the narrow sense. It did not come to a sudden end, and large numbers of retired soldiers continue to occupy prominent positions in political parties, the legislature, the executive and the bureaucracy, but governments since 1983 have emerged through competitive elections. Limited democracy has become less limited and more democratic. The answer to the question 'what had military intervention achieved?' is again an elusive one. If the army had not intervened, or not intervened as early as it did to end royal domination, the alternative might have been a more violent revolution later on. Instead, Thailand experienced five decades of government in which soldiers paid ample attention to their own needs and those of their clients, and attempted to pursue economic development as a bureaucratic rather than a political exercise. In contrast to Latin American, where much military behaviour has been explained in terms of increased military contacts with the outside world, Thai military rulers were initially influenced by Western ideals which they were unable to apply at home, but by the 1950s they were more obviously the product of the indigenous elite and bureaucracy, and were unlikely to depart very far from the values of that elite and bureaucracy. They might claim the credit for stimulating social and economic development to a greater extent than would have occurred under conservative politicans and bureaucrats alone, but they neither pressed for radical changes in political participation nor suppressed such changes consistently. Such a position blunted the distinctiveness of military government, but it also facilitated a relatively smooth transition to pluralist civilian politics. While Latin American civilians in the 1980s were agonising over questions about whether to put former military rulers on trial, and soldiers were agonising over what veto powers to impose on civilian successors, such questions were absent from Thai politics. Soldiers with a long experience of co-operation with civilians had less difficulty than most in moving from bayonet to ballot box, and many remained active in a nominally civilian political system. The poblem posed in Chapter 3 about 'controlling the pace and direction of democratisation' was probably not seen as a 'problem' by Thai soldiers, given the blurred distinction between military government and various forms of pluralist politics with military involvement.

Military rulers who had originally wrested power from an absolute monarchy had transferred it, almost imperceptibly, to a pluralist political system. For supporters of liberal democracy this is a positive achievement. The unanswered question is whether, in a country with a long experience of military involvement in government and where military men continue to occupy many prominent positions, the process might be reversed more easily than in countries where the return to barracks has been more complete and more clearly perceptible.

Indonesia: The Politicised Right

Pre-Military Government Politics

The Indonesian army, like the Thai, has been involved in politics continuously since 1945, but here the similarity ends. Whereas Thailand avoided both war and colonisation, Indonesia's history bears the scars of both. Some nationalists like Sergeant (later General and President) Suharto supported the invading Japanese as liberators from Dutch rule, but when the Japanese surrendered in 1945, a war of independence had to be fought without any foreign aid (McDonald, 1980, pp. 13–17). The army thus became a prominent political actor, but when independence was won, power passed not to the military but to long-standing nationalist politicians. President Sukarno led a nominally left-wing government which was supported by a substantial Communist Party, but the government lacked any firm party base and became increasingly dependent on the military for maintaining its authority.

The intertwining of civil and military institutions is indicated by the fact that General Suharto came to power at the invitation of the incumbent government rather than by force. Even under nominally civilian government in the late 1950s, 25 per cent of the cabinet, 16 per cent of the MPs, 20 per cent of senior civil servants and 43 per cent of the senior officials of state enterprises were military men (Hoadley, 1975, pp. 117–19). The country was under a state of emergency by then. As violence and disorder continued into the 1960s, the gradual transformation from civil to military government continued. After student riots and growing military pressure in 1966, President Sukarno signed all powers away to General Suharto, and Suharto was elected acting President by parliament in 1967 (Hoadley, 1975, pp. 109–10; McDonald, 1980, p. 66).

Military Ideology, Interests and Objectives

Indonesia belongs to the band of 'least developed' countries in which one would expect military intervention to come from the left rather than the right. Sundhaussen and Green argue that the right-wing nature of the military government is debatable, and that inequality is no greater in Indonesia than in Sweden or Yugoslavia (Sundhaussen and Green in Clapham and Philip, 1985, p. 106), and McDonald mentions the extent of state economic intervention and attempts to achieve greater equality under the 1979 five-year plan (1980, pp. 251–2), but much of the literature takes a different view. Many industries were privatised, army officers acquired extensive business interests, extensive violence was used against Communist Party members, and foreign policy was increasingly pro-Western (Crouch, 1978, p. 331; 1988, p. 166; Hoadley, 1975, p. 110), and even McDonald suggests that the army came to power as an old elite furthering old objectives (1980, p. 94).

National poverty alone does not guarantee that a military government will be left-wing. Like Bangladesh and Pakistan, Indonesia is an exception to the general trend. One explanation of this might be that once averting national disintegration becomes the major political issue, the priority accorded to law and order overshadows any concern with economic transformation or social equality, though one would still have to explain the presence of left-wing governments in Burma and Ethiopia. In the case of Indonesia there was also the distinctive position of the army as part of a broader nationalist movement, not integrated into any nationalist party, yet having to deal with the consequences of a failed socialist experiment which had produced inflation, economic and bureaucratic stagnation, and widespread corruption (McDonald, 1980, p. 68). In an ambiguous position of sustaining yet not supporting the Sukarno regime, Crouch suggests, by 1967 the army was already part of the political elite, and therefore in no position to launch a Nasserite coup (1978, p. 23), as in the underdeveloped countries where there was a clearer division between a traditional monarchy and a 'modernising' army.

Observers of Indonesian political institutions, like observers of military government in most of the world, admit that they can detect no clear military ideology. There were no new perceptions (McDonald, 1980, p. 94), only a vague nationalism (Crouch, 1978, p. 36) and a desire for consensus through consultation in preference to the divisiveness of liberal democratic competition (Hoadley, 1975, pp. 112–15). McVey gives us slightly more insight when she refers to the conflict between the revolutionary nationalist tradition and the reaction against Sukarno's flirtation with the communists, with the reaction becoming the more dominant tendency (McVey, 1972, pp. 148, 171). There are also hints at an Indonesian political culture which pervades the army as well as the rest of society, and which places the emphasis on a search for consensus in preference to the 'winner takes all' process which is seen as common to both liberal democracy and authoritarianism. Hoadley speaks of a search for consensus through consulting all (*sic*) groups in society (1975, p. 115) and McDonald mentions a culture which favours a 'corporate' political system with autonomous social groups combined with strong leadership (1980, p. 95). We can question, as we did with Central America, whether the concept of corporatism should be so stretched and made to travel to so many lands, but a clearer picture of what the military were for and against may be emerging. Bearing in mind that they did not suddenly stage a coup and release a list of indictments of the previous rulers, or a ringing declaration of objectives, but gradually edged Surkarno out of office on account of his inability to rule effectively, the immediate concern was to use whatever means were available to impose social, political and economic order. Communists were seen as divisive, alien and too implicated in the previous regime, and a less extreme brand of socialism seemed to have proved ineffective. This left little alternative but to turn towards a more market-oriented economy, and to American and Japanese aid.

Military Strengths and Weaknesses

If the army is characterised as 'non-ideological', it cannot be characterised as 'apolitical' or inexperienced in the art of political conflict. In Luckham's terminology, civil–military boundaries are 'permeable', and Indonesian soldiers did not think in terms of removing a distinctive group of civilian politicians or transferring power to another group. The army has always been in politics, initially in a violent struggle for independence, then in trying to shore up the Sukarno government in the face of growing disorder, and ultimately as the senior partner in government.

The army's strengths and weaknesses stem largely from the same roots. It was heterogeneous from the start, with some soldiers coming from the Dutch colonial army, some serving under the Japanese and some entering as nationalists in pursuit of liberation (Crouch, 1978, p. 27). In the early post-war years authority within the army depended heavily on the charismatic leadership of officers in individual units (McVey, 1971, pp. 142–5). The weakness of civil institutions already described enabled officers to penetrate many of these institutions extensively. Such a diffusion of roles might be thought incompatible with military professionalism, and both Crouch and Kahane mention the rivalries and jealousies created as some officers acquired large fortunes, some acquired smaller ones and others were left to subsist on their army salaries alone (Crouch, 1978, p. 27; Kahane in Schriffrin, 1976, pp. 252–4). Yet the wealth acquired by many officers, both from legitimate earnings and from such supplements as favourable treatment over licences, credits, contracts and avoidance of taxation (Crouch, 1978, p. 23), gave many officers a strong interest in maintaining military government, and Suharto's ability to distribute patronage on such a large scale helped to secure his own position. There were ample positions to which potential challengers could be posted in the fields of administration, diplomacy and business (Crouch, 1978, pp. 221–2).

The level of military professionalism could hardly be described as high, compared with Chile or Pakistan, or even Thailand, but it is probably higher now than when a more heterogeneous army took power in 1966. For a military government to survive under one leader for over twenty years is a remarkable achievement which would be envied by Latin American generals leading more professional armies, but one has to ask how far this is attributable to civilian weakness as well as military strength and also, paradoxically, to the extent to which civilian participation in the political process has provided a safety valve for any dissatisfaction with military leadership.

The Military, Civilian Elites and Society

The strength or weakness of civil institutions in Indonesian society is difficult to gauge if one uses Western measures. The country has never experienced liberal democracy in the sense of governments succeeding one another through free elections, yet society in pluralist in the sense that it has had strong party groupings ranged across the political spectrum, including socialialists, nationalists and Muslim fundamentalists. As in Thailand, the response of the military to party competition fluctuated between repression, when the opposition was seen as a serious threat, to toleration when the military-created party seemed more secure. Election-rigging was most blatant in 1969, when government violence against communists was at its height and most autonomous centres of power were being crushed (Crouch, 1978, pp. 347–8), but the military came to realise by the 1970s that attempts to ban all parties would only provoke retaliation. Their solution was to set up a military-backed party, Golkar (Crouch, 1978, pp. 245–6), which was able to win competitive elections regularly from 1971 onwards if only because there was little to be gained from supporting opposition parties in the legislature when the military were firmly entrenched in the executive. McDonald describes Golkar as a 'functional group organisation' rather than a party — a coalition of professional and community associations who stressed shared interests and national harmony (McDonald, 1980, pp. 89–90). The party included a total of 260 occupational, professional, functional and territorial groups (Hoadley, 1975, p. 117). Yet the diversity of interests which could not be accommodated in any monolithic structure was reflected in a steady vote of 35–38 per cent for opposition parties. The permeability of civil and military institutions again emerges as a sign of strength, when in other countries it is a symptom of instability. The army had penetrated many key civil institutions even before it took power formally, but it also allowed much autonomy to the civilian political infrastructure rather than attempting the repression found in Central America. Such toleration was made easier, as noted at the beginning of this chapter, by the fact that societies in countries with limited democracy are less polarised between elites and masses on account of the existence of a greater diversity of ethnic, regional and religious groups.

If we move from the legislature to the executive we find a similar inter-penetration of civil and military institutions. The army had taken many top posts in the cabinet and the bureaucracy under nominal civilian rule. When it took power it returned the compliment by appointing civilian technocrats to many top posts (McDonald, 1980, pp. 251–3; Crouch, 1978, pp. 328–9, 241–4; McDougall, 1982, p. 101), while the ruling party itself became increasingly civilianised (Crouch, 1988, p. 171). Many of the technocrats were part of what we might call a 'civil–military elite' which shared common values and interests, including American-trained economists who had been lecturers at the army's training school (McDonald, 1980, pp. 251–3). Like the military, they were generally pragmatists who sought order and stability in place of the inefficient state bureaucracy inherited from Sukarno. To the extent that they favoured greater scope for market forces and looked to the West for aid and investment, they were 'right-wing', but not in the rigid mould of the Chicago Boys in South America.

The Politics of Non-Withdrawal

With the aid of rising oil prices, these pragmatic policies helped to achieve an annual rate of economic growth of over 7 per cent for much of the 1970s, only to suffer a downturn as oil prices fell in the 1980s (Crouch, 1988, pp. 167–8). Whether the stability of military government is threatened more by economic success or economic failure is an open question. Success may lead to the emergence of new social groups demanding more political participation, and Kahane detected such a development as early as 1976 (Kahane in Schriffrin, 1976, p. 247), but relative failure can lead people to question the credentials of any government, especially one with little claim to legitimacy via the ballot box. Crouch argues that the downturn of the 1980s led to greater dependence on civilians (1988, pp. 167–8). Latin American experience certainly suggests that if military governments stake their claim to rule on administrative competence rather than democratic legitimacy, then a perceived failure to produce any better results than civilians will leave them vulnerable — hence a general retreat to barracks in the 1980s. This, however, assumes the availability of some known alternative model of government, whether a return to pre-coup party politics, as in Uruguay and Pakistan, or to elected civilian government subject to a powerful military veto, as in Guatemala and El Salvador. But the alternatives previously available in Indonesia cannot be brought back to life. The Dutch and the Japanese will not reoccupy the country, and the shaky autocracy of Sukarno could not be resurrected, even if anyone wanted such outcomes. Sundhaussen and Green consider a range of possibilities which acknowledge the incongruous state of the Indonesian social and political systems. There are extremes of social and political cleavage which have facilitated the survival of autonomous party organisations and prevented centralised dictatorship, yet no democratic political culture; substantial interpenetration of civil and military elites, yet limited civilian ability to maintain order; attempts by rulers to develop catch-all parties to sustain them, yet no dominant, mass-based party comparable with those in Singapore and Malaysia (Sundhaussen and Green in Clapham and Philip, 1985, pp. 112–20). They see 'authoritarian clientelism' as the most likely outcome, with the military retaining power but expanding participation to absorb more of the middle-class, rural 'kulaks' and independent labour into a corporate system. The likelihood of a straightforward handover to civilians is also rejected by McDougall and Crouch. McDougall emphasises the web of clients built up by the military who have an interest in continued military rule, and sees anomic change as more likely than a smooth transition (1982, pp. 91, 99, 108), while Crouch, emphasising the extent of military penetration and the civilian technocrats' lack of any power base, foresees changes only 'within the context of military domination' (1988, p. 175).

At the time of writing Indonesia stands out as an exception to the general retreat from power to right-wing military governments, and those experts willing to speculate see no reason why such government should not continue. It is difficult to bring any general theory to bear by way of explanation. The previous civilian government was incompetent, but that did not prevent a return of many former political masters in Pakistan and much of Latin America. The army came to power gradually and had the opportunity to build a firmer base than many, but the same could be said of Uruguay and of Pakistan in the 1950s. A more empirical approach might be to look at the longevity of other regimes in Asia in contrast to the rest of the Third World, for example India, Japan, Malaysia, Singapore and Taiwan. In all these countries, taking power at the right moment may be the key to longevity, irrespective of the means by which power was taken. In Japan and Singapore, economic success enabled governments to reward their supporters and ward off opposition. In India and, to a lesser extent Malaysia, cultural diversity made it difficult for any one opposition group to mount a serious challenge once the ruling party controlled the flow of patronage. The military government in Indonesia enjoyed both a period of economic success in its early years, and the absence of a single effective opposition group in a culturally heterogeneous society and, as in the other five countries, there was no pre-existing model of government to which its opponents could advocate a return.

The achievements of the military government may have been modest, but for a country which had suffered colonial exploitation, enemy occupation and ineffective nationalist rule, economic growth and political order were probably as much as realists could demand. From a right-wing perspective these achievements strengthened the existing elites. (The extent to which the benefits trickled down to the non-elite remains a matter of debate.) The achievements would seem even greater if one could envisage a process by which the changes wrought by the government could ensure political continuity. In the other Asian countries there is always the possibility of change through the mechanics of inter-party or intra-party competition. In Indonesia it is still difficult to envisage either a peaceful transfer of power to civilians or the entry of soldiers into the world of pluralist democracy.

Turkey: The Statist Right

Pre-Coup Politics

The claims of the Turkish governments of 1960–1, 1971 and 1980–3 to be right-wing or military might be disputed even more hotly than the claims of their Thai or Indonesian counterparts. The left–right divide in Turkey is complicated by the country's long history of centralised state control, initially to maintain an empire and from the 1920s to achieve Western-style modernisation under the aegis of a military leader, Kemal Atatürk. By the

1950s supporters of the centralised, secular bureaucratic state which the military had done much to fashion might be regarded as 'conservative', while emerging groups of urban merchants, industrialists and market-oriented farmers, who were by-products of modernisation but largely excluded from the older military–intellectual–bureaucratic elite and the patronage dispensed by it, might be regarded as 'radicals'. The Democratic Party won a landslide victory in 1950 with an appeal to the interests of these counter-elites, which disliked centralised government and the large military budget, and with a populist appeal to the provincial and rural population which had remained hostile to secular-statist values (See especially Dikerdem in Birand, 1987, pp. 9–10; Karpat in Heper and Evin, 1988, pp. 137–9).

The 1960 coup by junior officers might thus be regarded as an attempt to replace a *petit bourgeouis* government committed to a market economy with one committed to the left-wing virtues of centralised planning, but the story is more complicated than that. The self-interest of officers who had lost power and status since the defeat of 'their' party was important (Dikerdem in Birand, 1987, pp. 10–11), but there is also the conceptual question of whether supporters of state economic intervention with only minimal popular participation should be described as 'left-wing'. Atatürk's Republican People's Party (RPP) had not attempted popular mobilisation to the same extent as the more 'conservative' Democratic Party, and the army subsequently had to pay for its isolation from society. It had the strength and professionalism to take over the government again in 1971 and 1980 and to spell out the terms of civilian restoration, but it could not persuade the population to vote for its preferred successor. The RPP became more explicitly 'socialist' in the conventional sense of trying to build a working-class base, but in the process it drifted further from the army that had nurtured it, as the latter became more preoccupied with the role of the state as a vehicle for order and national unity rather than economic development and social welfare (Karpat in Heper and Evin, 1988, pp. 137–9).

Military Ideology, Interests and Objectives

One can disentangle a variety of strands in the ideologies of Turkish soldiers. The middle-ranking and junior officers who carried out the 1960 coup included, according to Dikerdem, left-wing nationalists wanting industrial self-sufficiency and '*étatist* reformers', while a 'Nasserite' coup was only averted in 1971 by a pre-emptive strike by senior officers (Dikerdem in Birand, 1987, pp. 13–14). Yet divisions of opinion on the role of the state in economic planning and redistribution have been overshadowed by a more deeply rooted consensus on the proper role of the army and its relationship with civil society, which can be traced back to the Ottoman Empire. There were three important aspects of this consensus. Firstly, there is a clear notion of the professionalism of the army, in the sense that hierarchical leadership has seldom been disputed. The coup makers of 1960 quickly handed power over to their superiors, and over 4,000 officers were purged, just as senior officers subsequently maintained their authority over radical plotters in 1971 when hundreds of officers were again retired or arrested (Dikerdem in Birand, 1987, p. 12; Dekmejian in Kolkowicz and Korbonski, 1982, p. 45). Although the senior ranks included some radicals (though many of these were purged), the maintenance of a professional hierarchy was generally a factor making for conservatism.

Secondly, the Ottoman inheritance legitimised a significant role for the army in politics, but with integral boundaries between civil and military institutions left much more intact than in Thailand or Indonesia. As in any empire built on force, soldiers performed significant political roles, as they continued to do under Atatürk, but they did so mainly through the medium of the army rather than by infiltrating civilian institutions. This meant that 'military government' in the sense of serving officers wielding executive or legislative power directly, was something alien to them. If they intervened in politics, the main objectives was to control what politicians did rather than to usurp their functions for more than brief periods. The legitimacy of civil political institutions was therefore accepted by soldiers much more willingly than it was by their counterparts in the civil–military authoritarian countries, but the soldiers had their own notions as to how such institutions should function. This brings us to the third aspect of the military consensus.

There was a reluctance to accept the legitimacy of intermediate groups between government and governed (Sunar and Sayari in O'Donnell *et al.*, 1986, p. 170). Under Atatürk this helped the modernising thrust of the government by bypassing aristocratic and religious leaders but, once greater industrialisation and urbanisation had been achieved, such an attitude implied limiting the role of political parties, trade unions and newly emerging pressure groups, and could easily lead to an aloof form of right-wing authoritarianism. When the army returned to power in 1980 the coup had widespread public support on account of the growing disorder and economic stagnation of recent years, but it had little *organised* support from any party or pressure group, even from its erstwhile allies in the RPP and the intelligentsia (Karpat in Heper and Evin, 1988, pp. 148–9, 153; Harris, ibid., p. 211; Karakartal in Clapham and Philip, 1985, pp. 54–7). The constitution which restored civilian rule in 1983 again reflected a distaste for the free play of pluralist politics. Only three political parties were ultimately permitted, and these were seen principally as vehicles for achieving consensus and acquiescence rather than means of aggregating diverse interests, hence restrictions of their links with pressure groups (Harris in Heper an Evin, 1988, pp. 193–4; Karpat, ibid., pp. 154–5).

Military Strengths and Weaknesses

As a disciplined instrument for taking power and repressing opposition, including opposition in its own ranks, no one could doubt the strength of the army. Three times in twenty years it toppled governments which it deemed to be the cause of disorder and national disunity, it ruled without compromising its own professionalism and then returned power to civilians largely on its own terms. It rewarded its own constituency generously with the provision of amenities and business opportunities for officers (Dekmejian in Kolkowicz and Korbonski, 1982, p. 41), and defence spending which maintained the Turkish army's position as the second largest in Nato (Dikerdem in Birand, 1987, p. 17). The 1961 constitution gave the armed forces greater autonomy from future civilian governments to avoid a repetition of the inroads made by the Democratic Party in the 1950s, while at the same time giving the military substantial influence in civilian politics through the creation of the National Security Council (NSC), a body consisting of senior officers which considered all security matters in consultation with senior ministers (Harris in Heper and Evin, 1988, p. 182). The army also ensured that the President of the Republic was a military man throughout the decade of civilian government between 1961 and 1971.

The army returned to power with relative ease in 1971 and 1980 after periods of disorder which they saw as the product of divisive party politics in which extremes of both left and right contributed to growing violence, but which others might have attributed to the problems of failing to institutionalise political conflict in a period of rapid social change in a society which was more used to long periods of single-party domination. The rapid growth of the urban population from 20 per cent to 47 per cent of the total population between 1950 and 1980 (Birand, 1987, p. 45) was an indication of social change that would have put a strain on any political system. By treating violent party competition and weak coalition governments as a cause rather than a symptom of disorder, the military limited their scope for positive political influence. They had ample powers of veto and ability to look after their own interests but, as we have seen, the culture of the army and society precluded long-term military government on the Indonesian model to shape the nation's destiny, quite apart from the embarrassment that such government would create in dealing with Nato allies or in seeking EEC membership. Soldiers could not become kings, but neither were they successful as kingmakers. For all their success in constitutional engineering, the first two military governments were succeeded by a series of weak coalitions rather than the strong 'national' government for which they had hoped, and when the third military government did produce a constitution more conducive to strong majority rule, the majority went to the party it least wanted.

This may suggest that we are moving towards the frontier beyond which 'pure' military government cannot easily survive. Although Turkey is no more 'developed' than most of Central America in terms of most socio-economic indicators, its army has for historical and strategic reasons acquired a 'professionalism', in the narrow sense of giving a high priority to preserving its own integrity, hierarchy and differentiation from civil society, which severely limits its room for manoeuvre in civilian politics. While soldiers in Central America and South-east Asia are willing to compromise military unity and hierarchy in pursuit of political goals and alliances with civilian factions, and see nothing improper in such a role when much political conflict is concerned with governments using violence against their opponents, the Turkish army has seen itself as 'above' political conflict and as the guardian of a higher national interest. As a referee in such a conflict it can sometimes stop the game or change the rules, but it is reluctant to become one of the players.

The Military, Civilian Elites and Society

The changing relationship between the military and civilian elites in Turkey was the reverse of that found in most other countries experiencing military intervention, in that each successive intervention left the military more isolated from civilians. The 1960 coup was largely a partisan attempt to restore the RPP and the relationship the army had enjoyed with it. The military made their party preferences clear by hanging the erstwhile prime minister, arresting many of his MPs and bringing into government members of what Karpat calls the 'state secularist wing of the RPP' (Karpat in Heper and Evin, 1988, p. 141). But after the return to barracks the electorate's preferences proved different from the army's, and a multiplicity of parties emerged. When the army re-intervened in 1971 to deal with the accompanying disorder, it had fewer political allies. It had, as we have seen, moved in the opposite ideological direction to the RPP, which had anyway become a smaller fish in a growing multi-party pond. The solution of an exclusive military junta was still rejected, presumably on account of the long tradition of soldiers not usurping civilian roles, and parliamentary institutions were allowed to continue under a new prime minister and a cabinet of technocrats, but with the National Security Council still playing an important role. As there was no longer any political party on which the military could rely, soldiers put their faith in a more authoritarian constitution to curb the excesses of pluralism (Dikerdem in Birand, 1987, pp. 13–14).

The 1971 constitution was no more successful than that of 1961 in containing or suppressing political conflict, and the government which terminated it in 1980 has the greatest claim to be both right-wing and military. The policies pursued, admittedly under International Monetary Fund pressure, increased unemployment by 1.5 million, reduced the annual growth rate from the 7 per cent of the previous fifteen years to 2 per cent, increased the power of the private sector and reduced that of trade unions (Birand, 1987, pp. 211–12). It is true that all political parties were banned, not merely those on the left, and there was a degree of even-handedness in the punishment of politicians, which included over 65,000 detentions and 27 executions (Birand, 1987, p. 212). Muslim fundamentalism was regarded as a threat just as much as left-wing terrorism, but the general policies of suppressing political activity, purging the bureaucracy, suspending professional associations and imposing greater state control over the universities (Sunar and Sayari in O'Donnell *et al.*, 1986, p. 183) might be compared with the demobilisation policies of right-wing military governments elsewhere, especially when combined with the economic measures. This is not to say that the policies were congruent with those of any right-wing civilian party. Hale claims that few politicians were willing to co-operate with the regime for fear of loss of support (Hale in Heper and Evin, 1988, pp. 167–8). This might be explained partly in terms of the traditional hostility between the successors to the Democratic Party and the army (which centred largely on questions of how great a role the military should have in politics and how much control politicians should have over the military), but there also appeared to be a conflict between the military desire for a strong state in both the political and economic spheres, and the desire of right-wing parties for freer competition in both spheres. In the absence of co-operation from civilian politicians, power was kept in the hands of five senior members of the armed forces, aided by specialist commissions of experts. This narrow apex ensured the exclusion of radical soldiers as well as radical civilians (Hale in Heper and Evin, 1988, p. 164), but the absence of a broader base meant that military government could not easily be sustained for long. Karakartal suggests that in the absence of natural allies, the military built up clientelistic networks at many levels, notably in trade unions and the universities (Karakartal in Clapham and Philip, 1985, p. 54), but the army did not appear to have the will or the ability to outstay its welcome. This was in keeping with the tradition of the military as the referee who made and interpreted the rules (the 'moderator role') rather than the player who compromised his integrity by participating in political conflict. The problem now was to withdraw from politics without allowing the system to degenerate into the disorder of the 1960s and 1970s.

Military Withdrawal

It was suggested in Table 3.1 that one of the problems for 'limited democracies' was the possible lack of consensus between soldiers and civilians on the direction in which democracy should go, with soldiers fearing a loss of control over events and civilians fearing military retaliation if they strayed too far out of bounds. In Turkey both these problems arose clearly after the 1961 and 1971 military withdrawals. In 1961 the military's main fear was of a return to the abuse of majority rule by the Democratic Party, and they therefore devised a constitution with checks and balances which included a constitutional court, a strong second chamber, a constitutional guarantee of civil rights and the retention of the National Security Council to provide general military oversight, if not veto power (Sunar and Sayari in O'Donnell *et al.*, 1986, pp. 174–5). This was a case of soldiers expecting the next war to be like the last one. The problem over the next decade was not of arbitrary one-party rule but unstable multi-party competition spilling into violence and disorder. Military leaders now felt a threat not merely to the army but to the unity of the nation. The military imposed a more authoritarian constitution in 1971, but the threat of a military veto to enforce it was weakened by the army's internal divisions at a time when senior officers had struggled to impose their authority on their more radical subordinates (Dekmejian in Kolkowicz and Korbonski, 1982, p. 45; Karpat in Heper and Evin, 1988, pp. 186–90). By the 1980s the army had eliminated most of its dissidents and there appeared to be a greater willingness to accept a 'doctor's mandate' from the military to deal with the growing disorder. The prescription was not prolonged military government but a constitution, approved by 91 per cent of the electorate in 1982, which would have met with more approval from Rousseau than John Stuart Mill. It referred to 'the absolute supreme will of the nation', prohibited publications which contravened the 'indivisible integrity of the state', and banned political parties with class, religious or racialist ideologies or which violated constitutional laws. Parties could not receive financial support from outside organisations, and could not obtain parliamentry representation if they received less than 10 per cent of the vote. Most of the prominent pre-1980 politicians were disqualified from standing for office, as were over a 1,000 prospective parliamentry candidates who were eventually selected (Tachau, 1984, p. 44; Turan in Heper and Evin, 1988, pp. 65–71, 75). The constitutional proposals asked for and received the endorsement of General Evren, the existing head of state, as the sole candidate for the presidency for the next seven years, and endowed that office with much greater power than any other post-Ottoman constitution, including control over the use of the armed forces and the right to proclaim martial law (Harris in Heper and Evin, 1988, pp. 194–6). There was thus ample insurance against any civilian attempt to punish former military rulers for their misdeeds, and there appeared to be little desire by the new civilian rulers for such punishments. The military had, after all, smoothed the new politicians' paths by disqualifying so many of their predecessors.

Only three political parties were able to meet the rigorous requirements of the constitution and compete for office, but the election was won by the party least favoured by the military and least subservient to them, and Motherland Party. Karpat suggests that the vote for a military-sponsored constitution but against military sponsored parties indicated a desire for a strong executive, but without an authoritarian regime dictating the day-to-day activities of citizens (Karpat in Heper and Evin, 1988, pp. 154–5). The fear of the military was not so much that of a left-wing takeover, as was feared in much of Latin America, but of a right-of-centre government building on the power bases of newer business interests rather than the old civil–military bureaucracy, which would end the army's traditional role as the ultimate guardian of the national interest — a subordinate Western-style army rather than a freer-ranging Third World army (See especially Rustow in Heper and Evin, 1988, pp. 243–6). Liberal democrats might welcome such a development, but the question for Turkey's future is whether it will be willing to perform such a subordinate role, and whether civilian opinion will be strong enough to resist if the army attempts to return to its former role. Much will depend on whether political conflict can be contained within the tight constraints of the 1982 constitution.

An army which has attempted to influence the political process as a referee rather than a player (or perhaps as a back-seat driver) would expect to be judged less by such criteria as economic innovation or social welfare provision, and more by its influence on the broad political environment. The Turkish army could claim that it helped to eliminate, or at least accelerate the removal of, two major obstacles to the development of liberal democracy: the authoritarian one-party government of the 1950s which had shown few signs of allowing itself to be challenged in a free election, and the political disorder of the 1960s and 1970s which left little scope for the consensus which democracy requires. Critics might argue that both authoritarianism and disorder are unavoidable growing pains in 'political development', but the army hastened the demise of both. It might have performed each task more effectively if it had looked beyond constitutional mechanics and military oversight to questions of how to harness political participation and conflict in a rapidly urbanising society, but that would have required a military penetration of civilian institutions which conflicted with the Ottoman tradition of integral civil–military boundaries, and would have made military extrication from politics more difficult and more easily reversible, as in the case of Thailand. The political structure handed over to civilians may be crude in design, but it is a structure in which civilians can consolidate a pluralist system, and which leaves the army with the relatively modest role that befits such a system.

7 Variations on Right-Wing Themes: Some Conclusions

Introduction

Our attempt to impose some conceptual order on three groups of diverse countries is illustrated in Table 7.1, where we look at six variations in the underlying socioeconomic, political and military conditions, and four variables in political outcomes. Critics may question whether the most significant conditions or outcomes have been chosen, but those chosen suggest a substantial degree of conformity within each of our categories of right-wing military government: personalist, military authoritarian, civil–military authoritarian and limited democracy. In the first group, Chile diverges from its conceptual neighbours on only one of the nine variables, Uruguay on none and Pakistan on four. In the second, Guatemala, El Salvador and Bolivia all conform to the same broad outlines and differ only in matters of detail. The third group exhibits the greatest diversity, with Thailand diverging from other limited democracies on two of eight variables, Indonesia on four and Turkey on two, while on the ninth variable of 'opportunities for military re-intervention' all three countries differ from each other. How far do the political outcomes depend on the unique circumstances of each country, and how far can they be explained by our general framework of underlying conditions? There is obviously much in the rich history and culture of each country that cannot be reduced to broad categorisations: the multiplicity of diverse political parties in pre-coup Chile, the resilient professionalism of the Pakistan army, Thailand's avoidance of the disruption of colonialism and Turkey's inheritance of the Ottoman culture, yet we can still argue that certain common variables are likely to produce common results. The study of nine countries is not, of course, sufficient for the construction of any watertight theories. It is merely intended to illustrate some common themes. One could, however, argue that the inclusion of the remainder of the Southern Cone in the first category, more of Central America is the second, and South Korea in the third, would strengthen many of the propositions.

Table 7.1: Underlying conditions and political outcomes in nine countries

	Chile	Uruguay	Pakistan	Guatemala	El Salvador	Bolivia	Thailand	Indonesia	Turkey
Underlying conditions									
Military professionalism.	High	High	High	Low	Low	Low	Medium/high	Medium/high	**High.**
Socioeconomic development.	High	High	**Low**	Medium	Medium	Medium	Medium	**Low**	Medium.
Pre-coup civilian political experience.	Pluralist, extreme competition.	Pluralist moderate competition.	**Limited competition**	Limited competition, fraudulent elections.	Very limited competition, fraudulent elections.	Limited competition, fraudulent elections.	Limited, moderate competition.	**Accommodation between groups, largely outside the electoral framework.**	Limited competition.
Civil-military boundaries.	Integral	Integral	Integral	Fragmented	Fragmented	Fragmented	Fragmented.	Fragmented.	**Integral.**
Military dependence on civilians.	Low	Low	Low	High	High	High	High	High.	High.
Degree of common interests between the army and allies in civilian elites.	High.	High.	High.	Low.	Low.	Low.	**High.**	Medium.	Medium.
Outcomes									
Nature of right-wing policies.	Extensive socio-economic restructuring	Limited socio-economic restructuring	**Restoration of order.**	Preservation of elites.	Preservation of elites.	Preservation of elites.	**Preservation of elites**	Restoration of order.	Restoration of order.
Extent and effectiveness of terror.	Extensive, effective.	Extensive, effective	Extensive effective over short periods.	Extensive, ineffective.	Extensive, ineffective.	Extensive, ineffective.	Very limited.	**Extensive, effective over short periods.**	Limited.
Restoration of civilian rule.	**Resisted by military.**	Accepted.	Accepted with extensive military veto.	Accepted with extensive military veto.	Accepted with extensive military veto.	Accepted with extensive military veto.	Accepted. Military veto depends largely on military-penetrated institutions.	Resisted by military.	Accepted with limited military veto.
Scope for re-intervention.	Low.	Low.	**High**	High.	High.	High.	**High.**	**Not applicable.**	Low.

Note: Entries in bold type indicate divergence from rest of group.

Right-Wing Policies

If we begin with the nature of right-wing policies, two of the three personalist/military authoritarian categories sought socioeconomic restructuring with a shift to free market economic policies, greater inequality and the repression of popular movements, the three civil–military authoritarian categories were more concerned with the preservation of existing civil and military elites than with any radical new departures, and two of the three limited democracies were concerned mainly with the restoration of order (although 'order' may, of course, imply a freezing or strengthening of existing privileges and inequalities). In the first category there is a clear link between the search for restructuring and the underlying conditions of high socioeconomic development and pluralist pre-coup politics. The threat from non-elites was particularly great in these circumstances, and the ability of the military to counter it was helped by the common features of integral civil–military boundaries, a low level of military dependence on civilians, and the shared interests of the military and their allies in civilian elites. These conditions enabled military governments to recruit civilian technocrats and businessmen whose belief in the discipline of the market fitted well with the discipline of the parade ground, but with the civilians lacking any independent power base, hired and fired rather than co-opted, and with soldiers free to impose the necessary repression to enforce the policies. In the deviant case of Pakistan, the restoration of order after periods of ineffective civilian government was given a higher priority than free market economic policies, though the latter were not absent. Here the background has been one of limited political competition over a short period in an economically under-developed country, rather than the extensive, deep-rooted party competition of South America. Military intervention in countries with Pakistan's social and political background often degenerates into a 'praetorianism' in which effective authority is lost, but the survival of a highly professional army, with only limited dependence on civilian politicians, kept Pakistan in the military authoritarian category. This should warn us against assuming that armies are merely a product of indigenous society. We have already questioned Huntington's assertion that 'the most important causes of military intervention in politics are not military but political' (1968, p. 194), and we must certainly guard against purely 'political' explanations of the behaviour of military governments. The army can be a powerful independent variable: in Pakistan and Turkey because of its inheritance of an imperial tradition, and in Indonesia because of its role in the struggle for independence.

Two of our three military governments in limited democracies, Indonesia and Turkey, also gave high priority to the restoration of order. The opportunity for extensive disorder to flourish might be attributed to the lower level of development in these countries compared with Chile and Uruguay, but the success of restoration, as in Pakistan, owed much to the degree of military professionalism, although this professionalism manifested itself in different ways in each country. The Turkish army maintained its integral boundaries with civil society, and laid down the framework within which civilian politicians could operate, whereas the Indonesian army exercised control by penetrating civil institutions extensively. In both cases dependence on civilians was higher than in the personalist/military authoritarian model largely because of the interdependent way in which civil and military institutions had evolved, with the army underwriting the initial modernising and nationalist governments. While Chile and Uruguay swung abruptly from pluralism to military dictatorship, Indonesia and Turkey moved less perceptibly from civilian governments dependent on military support to military governments, which felt less threatened by the rise of mass movements and which allowed limited democracy in the form of competitive parliamentary (but not presidential) elections.

Thailand deviates from the other limited democracies in that greater historical continuity reduced the likelihood of disorder, and military governments after 1945 were more concerned with preserving existing elites. The motives for the different coups varied, and they were often little more than the product of intra-elite squabbles. The historical continuity not only minimised disorder but made for fragmented civil–military boundaries in the absence of any thoroughgoing attempt to 'Westernise' the army and differentiate it more sharply from civil society, as in Pakistan. The army might have remained mainly an instrument for intra-elite squabbles but for the socioeconomic changes from the 1960s onwards which gave rise to new popular demands. These pushed the army into a more explicitly conservative position as a defender of the elite, but it was a more deeply rooted elite with wider public legitimacy than its counterparts in Latin America, just as the Thai popular movements were less strident. The elite could thus survive in a climate of limited democracy in which relatively free elections were allowed, but with extensive military penetration of civilian political institutions and with the ever-present threat of more explicit military intervention, should the need arise.

All our civil–military authoritarian governments, like Thailand, were more preservers of elites than radical innovators which dismantled popular participatory structures. There were fewer such structures to start with, compared with more developed countries such as Chile and Uruguay, although both Guatemala and Bolivia had experienced periods of reforming left-wing government, but the capacity of the military governments to impose their own wishes was more limited than in either the personalist/military authoritarian or the limited democratic types. There had been long periods of military involvement in politics but, unlike Thailand and Turkey, this was not based on any broad consensus on what the proper role of the army should be. Armies had evolved as bodyguards of the landed elites, rather than soldiers of the king or sultan in a country with a long national history, and the enemies were often non-elites rather than foreign foes. Military professionalism remained low, if only because the 'client' served by the profession was more an employer with limited political legitimacy, offering material rewards, than a nation offering a role for heroes. This does not mean that the soldiers were mere mercenaries, since a continuous military history was likely to imbue some corporate spirit, but civil–military boundaries remained fragmented as rival contenders for power sought the enlistment of the military, or military factions.

A long background of governments emerging through fraudulent elections or military coups meant that no civilian government could enjoy widely accepted legitimacy through the ballot box, and survival depended on keeping on good terms with the military. The military for their part lacked the professionalism to govern effectively without support from civilian elites. We have thus characterised the regimes as civil–military authoritarian. The whole venture depends on conceding areas of power and influence to civilians with strong, largely economic power bases, unlike the militarian authoritarian regimes where civilians are hired and fired at the government's convenience. Yet, paradoxically, the congruence of interests between civil and military elites is less than in countries where civilians are hired and fired. This may be partly because the military have less freedom in choosing civilian allies and partly because the armies are themselves more ideologically heterogeneous, if not incoherent. There is always a conflict over the allocation of scarcer resources as business interests seek lower taxes and interest rates, while soldiers demand more resources for self-enrichment and for waging largely ineffective anti-guerrilla wars. We have seen that in Guatemala civilian elites were able to win major concessions in such conflicts, and that in all our civil–military authoritarian cases it was the dissatisfaction of civilian elites with military corruption, economic failure and (in the cases of Guatemala and El Salvador) failure to restore peace, which hastened the return to barracks.

Styles of Right-Wing Government

Actual styles of right-wing military rule are difficult to characterise. We looked at the concept of bureaucratic authoritarianism and found that the 'bureaucratic' element was difficult to reconcile with reality. Technocrats such as the Chicago Boys in Chile and Argentina, and rather paler imitations in Uruguay, may be appointed to senior policy-making posts, with the advantage to the military that they have no independent power bases which might pose a threat. They can pursue free market politics which will weaken mass movements, but the employment of such people may have been no more than a passing phase which was abandoned speedily when the extent of damage to the economy was realised. We also rejected the concept of charismatic rule, which has not been attempted extensively by any right-wing military leader since Peron. Charisma normally implies some attempt to build up mass support, whereas most of the governments we have examined have wanted to curb, if not reverse, mass mobilisation, and have not generally followed the sort of policies which would attract such support.

Corporatism and clientelism are other concepts which appear fitfully in the literature. We are told that in Guatemala there was a 'corporate' relationship between the military and powerful private interests (Black *et al.*, 1984, pp. 48, 130) and that Indonesian culture favours a 'corporate' political system with autonomous social groups combined with strong leadership (McDonald, 1980, p. 95), but the term is not defined with any rigour. We can willingly acknowledge the interdependence of civil and military elites in both the civil–military authoritarian and limited democratic models, but if corporatism is taken to mean a clearly structured interdependent relationship, the evidence so far is inadequate. Clientelism is in a sense the reverse of corporatism, with rulers 'buying' the support of particular groups or individuals in the absence of a structure providing for a more institutionalised means of chanelling political demands and resources. Such a clientelistic system was said to exist in Pakistan after corrupt landlords and businessmen gained control to Ayub Khan's Basic Democracies (Maniruzzaman, 1971, pp. 225–8), only to wane as resources dried up after the outbreak of war with India. In Bolivia clientelism has enjoyed a longer life, and acted as both a barrier to and substitute for more formal relations between government and governed (Malloy and Gamarra in Malloy and Seligson, 1987, p. 98), and in Turkey the army was said to have compensated for its growing isolation from civilians after 1980 by building up clientelistic networks at many levels, notably in trade unions and the universities (Karakartal in Clapham and Philip, 1985, p. 54). These examples suggest that clientelism either emerges as a last resort in the terminal stages of a military government that is short of civilian allies (Pakistan and Turkey), or holds a rudimentary system together when governmental authority is weak (Bolivia), but it can hardly be a major long-term element in the dynamics of military government. Indonesia may be an exception in that benefits from clientelistic arrangements have limited any desire to hasten the demise of military rule, but the absence of a united opposition is probably a more important factor in preserving the regime.

Unless more conclusive evidence can be produced of the existence of bureaucratic authoritarianism or corporatism, we are left without any neat concepts for describing or distinguishing the styles of different right-wing military governments. Of the variables in Table 3.1, we are left with the extent of terror and the extent of co-option of civilians, both of which are obviously matters of degree rather than 'models' against which we can approximate real governments. They may lack conceptual elegance but they tell us much about the distinguishing features of our types of right-wing military government. The personalist/military authoritarian types rely extensively on terror and use civilian technocrats to suit their convenience without becoming dependent on them; limited democracies have a much more interdependent relationship with civilians — politicians as well as technocrats — and make much less use of terror, except for limited periods in Indonesia, while civil–military authoritarian regimes are dependent on both the co-operation of civilian elites and the use of terror, though the former has frequently been a source of instability and the latter has been largely ineffective in combating guerrilla movements. These differences can again be explained in terms of the underlying conditions in each type of system. Personalist/military authoritarian regimes require a high degree of coercion to combat relatively developed mass movements and have a high degree of success, especially in the short term, on account of the existence of highly professional armies, clearly differentiated from civil institutions and owing few debts to them. The extent of terror in Pakistan was probably less than in other countries in this category because of the interrelated features of fewer threatening mass movements and a less ambitious government policy of political demobilisation.

In the limited democracies we have noted the way in which civil–military interdependence evolved in a 'benign' way, with armies helping to sustain civilian governments in the early years of independence or modernisation, with the result that there was less need to resort to terror. The military could make incremental change to increase their role in government if they perceived a threat to order or elite power, without the need for sudden military intervention in the form of a 'big bang'. Indonesia deviates furthest from the rule of non-violence in that there were extensive purges of the erstwhile civilian government and its allies in the late 1960s, but this subsequently gave way to a more accommodative style.

In the civil–military authoritarian regimes, terror has continued even after the nominal restoration of civilian government. We have explained the uneasy interdependence between military and civil elites, based as much on a fear of non-elites as on common ideologies or interests, but the elites themselves did not enjoy the same deep-rooted legitimacy or support as their counterparts in Thailand or Turkey, or even Indonesia. While non-elites in military authoritarian systems might wait for the pendulum to swing back to the restoration of pluralist democracy and free elections, as it eventually did in Argentina, Uruguay and Greece, experience of pluralist politics in the civil–military authoritarian countries was mainly of fraudulent elections. If social discontent could not be resolved by the ballot box or by a left-wing coup, the alternative was for non-elites to pursue their demands through violence. This they did increasingly, especially in Guatemala and El Salvador, and although they did not win, neither did their political masters. Terror has so far achieved little more than stalemate, with armies more limited in their professionalism and the resources they can draw on, compared with the military authoritarian regimes, and unable to crush guerrilla forces in spite of both all-out warfare and the use of death squads to kill and torture selected opponents.

Military Withdrawal and Beyond

The willingness and ability of our different types of regime to restore civilian rule, and the subsequent ability of civilians to prevent further military intervention, presents a mixed picture. The greatest uniformity is again in the civil–military authoritarian group, where the military in Guatemala, El Salvador and Bolivia have all restored nominal civilian rule but have retained an extensive power of veto. This was spelt out formally in the case of Guatemala, where the civilian contenders for power were persuaded to renounce any left-of-centre policies and to promise not to prosecute soldiers for human rights violations. There was no such formal agreement in El Salvador, but the limited scope for the new Christian Democratic government to deviate from previous policies, in a country suffering economic decline and riven by civil war, was soon realised. In Bolivia the more disorganised state of the army and the economic chaos which had accompanied its rule made it more difficult for it to impose any conditions for returning power to civilians, but the successor left-wing president was left with little room for manoeuvre in the face of hyperinflation, and he survived for only three years before being succeeded by a more orthodox right-wing president. In all three cases similar pressures had left the military with little alternative to withdrawal. Their failure to cope with the worsening economic conditions of the 1980s meant that not even competence in government could compensate for authoritarianism, the violation of human rights, corruption and, in the case of Guatemala and El Salvador, their failure to win civil wars. Abandoned by their civilian allies and lacking the support of the wider population, they had little alternative but to retreat. Underlying conditions such as the low level of military professionalism, which reduced the armies' ability to cope with the strains of government or the waging of civil war, and the uneasy relationship with civil elites which, was based more on short-term expediency than long-standing shared culture or ideology, all helped to undermine the military rulers.

There is, none the less, a danger of searching for distinctive causes of military intervention or military withdrawal when we may be looking at little more than the general causes of political victories or defeats which at other times and places would be channelled through the ballot box. Concerns about inflation, strikes, law and order, dubious economic ventures in the public sector or redistributive taxation, either as the consequences of current policies or threatened future policies, may give rise to right-wing electoral victories in many parts of the world, and dissatisfaction with the subsequent handling of these problems may then lead to the pendulum swinging the other way. In countries with little tradition of free elections, military intervention and withdrawals may be seen partly as a reflection of changing currents of opinion, with soldiers most likely to intervene when public support for incumbent governments is low, and to depart when their own popularity is low. Such swings of the pendulum are clearly important, but we need to qualify this model by remembering that it is not necessarily 'public opinion' in the broad sense that is important (though it obviously helps if military rulers do not face a hostile populace), but the interests of the military constituency, and views of civilian elites and potential foreign backers whose support the military need.

The existence or otherwise of an articulate public opinion will clearly have some bearing on the prospects of the military recapturing power. In the (former) civil–military authoritarian countries there seems to be little reason, except perhaps possible United States disapproval, why right-wing military governments should not come to power again if soldiers are dissatisfied with the performance of civilian governments. Little has changed in the underlying political culture or in the socioeconomic structure to make intervention more difficult, though soldiers may calculate that they would cope no better with these countries' intractable social and economic problems, and prefer to maintain a role as a pressure groups with ample power of veto over policies they dislike.

The attempts to restore and retain civilian rule in the personalist/military authoritarian systems have produced more varied results. The Uruguayan military government faced apparently similar problems to those in the civil–military authoritarian countries, with only shallow legitimacy and few civilian allies or foreign backers to sustain it at a time when worsening economic conditions reduced its ability to deliver material benefits, but there were important features of the military authoritarian model which made Uruguay's position different. Firstly, in a country with a higher level of socioeconomic development, there was a long pluralist tradition which found military government repugnant, and long-standing parties were pressing for a return to electoral politics. Secondly, a more professional army was able more effectively to negotiate its way out of office through a formal agreement with the parties. The terms were not all that the army had wished for, but it was able to retire without any fear of prosecution for its misdeeds or any increased civilian control over the military. The nature of the Uruguayan polity and society, with a long acceptance of moderate pluralism, makes it difficult to conceive of circumstances in which the military would re-intervene. Civilians would presumably be fearful of such an outcome, in view of the last military government's unexpected repressiveness and limited competence, and would read the danger signals more carefully to rectify any faults in the polity which might provoke re-intervention. (But sceptics might argue that this assumes a greater 'rationality' in the behaviour of politicians than is justified in the light of experience.)

The Pakistan military also restored civilian government, and to a party which would not have been the military's choice, but in somewhat different circumstances. In a much less developed country with little history of pluralist politics, there seemed to be no reason why a strong professional army should not preside indefinitely over a limited democracy, similar perhaps to Indonesia, with an elected legislature but a strong military president. The untimely death of General Zia might be seen as the immediate reason for civilian restoration, but there were other forces at work. The wider population, although largely rural and illiterate, had already shown its strength in bringing down the first military regime and electing a more populist government under Bhutto, and was mobilised relatively easily behind demands for competitive party elections, in preference to the return of the weak non-party parliament which Zia had favoured. But the veto power retained by the army and its capacity to re-intervene suggest common ground with the civil–military authoritarian countries. Benazir Bhutto and her followers openly acknowledged the need to trim defence and foreign policies to avoid a further coup, and ensured that the Pakistan People's Party presented a more moderate image, in terms of policies and personnel, than it had had under Zhulfikar Bhutto. Having retired in good shape, with its professionalism intact, and with the (largely non-democratic) Islamic funamentalism that it had encouraged continuing to flourish, the army remains a powerful force. In a country where a government has never been voted out in a democratic election, it would be foolhardy to predict that the military will not intervene again.

Chile is much closer to Uruguay than Pakistan on most of our indicators but it took much longer to achieve a return to barracks. While economic failure, or at least failure to cope with worsening economic conditions to the satisfaction of key groups, drove most Latin American military governments back to barracks in the early 1980s, the Chilean military survived, and it was the right-wing technocrats and their monetarist policies that were jettisoned. The most obvious variables which might explain the tenacity of the Chilean military are the greater polarisation of pre-coup political competition and the personalist nature of the regime. Whereas in Uruguay the restoration of power to pre-coup (mainly moderate) politicians competing under the same pre-coup party system was something that the military accepted, albeit reluctantly, in the belief that their own position would be secure even if their mission to transform the system had failed, a similar restoration of (more polarised) pre-coup politics in Chile would have posed a major threat to the lives and liberty of right-wing soldiers, with left-wing politicians seeking to avenge the death of President Allende and his followers. If pre-coup politics could not be resumed, what were the alternatives? The military had for a long time excluded politicians of the right as well as the left from the political process, partly because they had taken power with little help from civilians and had few debts to repay in terms of patronage, and partly because they looked with disfavour on the moderate right, whose ineptitude when seen as a cause of the emergence of a Marxist government. The military thus left themselves out on a limb, with no right-wing civilian successor readily available. The personalist nature of the regime meant that its strategy depended heavily on the personal whims of General Pinochet. Pinochet's ideal appeared to be a form of limited democracy with a strong military president and a weak congress, but his defeat in the 1988 presidential plebiscite, in which he was the sole candidate, left him with the task of negotiating a military withdrawal on the least unfavourable terms available. There was little motivation for the military to seek to retain power, and little prospect of them doing so successfully, once the process of pluralist politics had been set in motion with Pinochet's unsuccessful plebscite and the unpopularity of the regime which it had revealed. Any attempt to do so would almost certainly have met with substantial resistance and would have required massive repression by an army that no longer seemed to have a distinctive cause to defend.

To consider the prospects for military re-intervention in Chile requires us to speculate two steps ahead, and might be considered a rash exercise. But assuming the initial withdrawal is completed effectively, it is difficult to envisage successor civilian politicians behaving incompetently or foolishly enough to create conditions which would provide a pretext for reintervention, in view of their experience of a regime which was much harsher and more prolonged than most politicians, and not merely those on the left, had wanted or expected. Pluralist competition had worked relatively smoothly in the four decades before Pinochet intervened. To paraphrase Oscar Wilde, to allow the excesses of such competition to usher in a repressive government once might be regarded as a misfortune. To allow it to happen twice would seem like carelessness. As for the army itself, it could hardly expect the support or acquiescence of politicians and their supporters on the right and centre of Chilean politics which it enjoyed in 1973. At that time anything might have seemed preferable to an embattled Marxist regime. In the 1990s politicians might offer resistance to any attempt at military intervention, in the belief that occasionally losing power to the 'wrong' party is preferable to not being able to complete for power at all.

In the limited democratic group, the Turkish military returned power to civilians after getting their own constitution approved by a referendum and disqualifying large numbers of unacceptable civilians from standing for office, but were unable to prevent their least favoured party from winning power. The precision with which the army conducted the constitutional exercise can be related to its professionalism and its traditional role as a political facilitator rather than a political actor, while its inability to achieve the desired election result might be related to the integral civil–military boundaries which precluded the military from penetrating, and thus influencing behaviour within, civilian political institutions. The insistence on the continuation in office of a powerful military president and the retention of the National Security Council gave the army a limited veto power, protecting its own interests, and over matters of law and order, but with less control over the wider political sphere compared with the civil–military authoritarian countries. This may not matter in the short term, since the successor regime is, if anything, further to the right than the retiring generals, but if policies creating higher unemployment and greater inequality, in a country already poorer than most of those in which monetarist experiments have been conducted, leads to further urban discontent to fuel extremist parties on the left, while doing little to appease Muslim fundamentalists on the right, Turkey might head towards the sort of violent polarisation that led to military intervention in 1971 and 1980. The preconditions for re-intervention still appear to exist, but the desire not to embarrass partners in Nato or prospective partners in the European Community might impose constraints on both soldiers contemplating intervention and civilians pursuing or contemplating policies which might provoke such intervention, though we are again left with the question of whether 'rationality' will triumph over instinct or immediate self-interest. A further constraint is the army's long-standing distaste for compromising its integrity through direct political involvement, in a country where civil–military boundaries are probably more integral than in any other we have studied. Turkey may have to suffer the instability that many countries have suffered in the early stages of urbanisation and industrialisation, but there is no guarantee that the man on horseback will ride in to rescue it.

The case of Thailand is, perhaps, more straightforward in that military arrivals and departures there have generally been accompanied by less disruption to the political system or society. The differences between the underlying conditions in Thailand and Turkey indicated in Table 7.1 — Thailand's more fragmented civil–military boundaries and its greater convergence of civil and military elites — have helped to smooth the departure of 'military government' (in the sense of rule by men who came to power by means of a military coup rather than an election) by replacing it with government through civil institutions extensively penetrated by the military. Questions of a military veto to protect soldiers from prosecution for misdeeds in power, or from civilian 'interference' in the functioning of the army, hardly arise, since the civilian elite was itself widely involved in previous 'military' governments and the army has an ample foothold in the successor regime without needing any special protection. It may be that this informal veto power will persuade the military that further coups are unnecessary, but the opportunities still seem to exist if the motivation is there. There is still little in the culture of the army or society that would regard a coup as repugnant, in the way that it would be in a more socially and economically developed country, should there be no other way of resolving an intra-elite conflict or a left-wing challenge.

Indonesia shares with Thailand a system of fragmented civil–military boundaries, and the interpenetration of civil and military institutions has ensured that soldiers retain control not only over the broad shape of the political system but over detailed areas of policy. In these circumstances one might have expected Indonesia to follow a similar gradual transition to civilian government to that in Thailand, but such a transition has not so far occurred. Indeed the survival not only of military government, but of one military head of government, for over two decades is remarkable for a relatively 'under-developed' country when compared with the transitory military regimes found in most of Africa. This survival and reluctance to withdraw can be explained in terms of constitutional, political and military factors.

Constitutionally, General Suharto had the advantage of taking over an executive presidency, rather than a prime ministership under a king, like his Thai counterpart. Such constitutional niceties may seem unimportant in a Third World where constitutions are frequently not worth the paper they are printed on, but the difference meant that while Thai military prime ministers could discreetly 'civilianise' themselves by seeking a mandate through a parliamentary election, with varying degrees of manipulation of the party and electoral processes, General Suharto could only civilianise himself through the more drastic and risky process of a presidential election. He preferred instead to allow relatively free elections to parliament but only uncontested presidential elections, while retaining the army as his main power base. Politically, Suharto enjoyed, in common with civilian leaders in several other Asian states, the advantage of having taken power at the right time, before the political system had settled into any clear mould, and while opposition groups were still sufficiently weak and divided (largely as a result of the heterogeneous social structure) to be crushed or bought off. While Thailand and Turkey could contemplate returning to largely familiar forms of pluralism after military rule, Indonesia's pre-military politics had consisted of a complex process of accommodation between diverse groups, but without competitive presidential elections. It had not been a 'one-party state' because the main party was too weak, neither had it been an autocracy or a pluralist democracy. Such a curious political system could not easily be reinvented, so Suharto's opponents had no obvious model to offer.

If there is insufficient civilian pressure for military withdrawal, there are many groups outside, and more especially inside, the army that have an interest in the patronage that flows from continued military rule, especially when we bear in mind the extensive military penetration of state structures. Indonesia is an exception to the general rule that armies become more divided the longer they remain in power. Soldiers had learnt many of the political skills as they tried to maintain order under the Sukarno regime, before they took power formally. Having taken power at the invitation of a weak civilian regime and enjoyed sufficient fruits of office from their leader to remain loyal to him, they have been in no hurry to restore power to civilians.

The hypothetical question of how easily Indonesian soldiers might re-intervene in the event of their returning power to civilians is not worth pursuing in detail. Unless one envisages the sort of civilian uprisings which drove the first Pakistan military government out of office — and this is difficult to imagine in a country with such fragmented civil–military boundaries — any civilian restoration would probably be much closer to the Thai than the Turkish model, with soldiers retaining many key 'civilian' posts. In those circumstances any civilian successors would have to work within narrow constraints if they were to prevent a reassertion of military power.

The Effects of Right-Wing Military Government on Politics

In Chapter 1 I raised questions not only about the immediate effects of right-wing military intervention, but about its long-term impact on the political process, especially in terms of the extent of political order, democracy or authoritarianism, the balance of power between different groups and political parties, and the subsequent role of the army itself. The relevance of some of these variables to individual countries is suggested in Table 7.2. Our study of individual countries suggests that in no case has military intervention from the right produced revolutionary changes comparable with intervention from the left. Egypt, Libya and Ethiopia clearly have different polities today from those which existed under previous civilian management. This is not to say that all left-wing coups produce such changes, but the fact that some do is in contrast to coups on the right. In none of the countries we have studied, with the possible exception of Turkey, has there been a significant transfer of power from one elite to another. Some political parties have benefited at the expense of others, but the rules of the political game have not changed fundamentally.

This is not an invitation to skip the remainder of this chapter. The search for explanations of continuity, or of failed attempts at radical change, can be as interesting as explanations of revolution, and some of the subtle changes which have occurred may yet have important long-term implications. The absence of radical changes, one might argue, is attributable to the nature of conservatism, and that what we should be looking at is the sorts of potential change which have been forestalled rather than at striking innovations, but not all our right-wing leaders were mere guardians of the status quo. Generals Pinochet, Ayub Khan and Zia, and the various Turkish leaders all had ideas about how society and the polity should be ordered which were different in significant ways from those of the politicians they displaced, while the Central American military envisaged an orderly society undisturbed by civilian mass movements or guerrillas, yet all had only limited success in extinguishing the political tendencies they disliked. A second explanation might be that the limitations were not imposed by conservatism as such but by the political naivety of some of the objectives. The Chilean economy could not stand the prescriptions of the monetarists, Pakistan could not be ruled without acknowledging the need for wheeling and dealing with politicians, and public resistance to authority in Central America was too great for order to be

Table 7.2: The impact of right-wing military intervention on the political systems of nine countries

	Chile	Uruguay	Pakistan	Guatemala	El Salvador	Bolivia	Thailand	Indonesia	Turkey
Degree of order, consensus and coercion.	Still largely coercion.	Apparent return to consensus within elite. Not clear if it extends to non-elites.	Military accepted unfavourable election but extensive veto power.	Continued dissensus and disorder. Conflict resolution through violence.	Continued dissensus and disorder. Conflict resolution through violence.	Continued dissensus, disorder.	Continued party competition, largely at elite level.	'Corporate' conflict resolution has survived. Military have achieved greater order.	More extensive conflict from late 1960s. Moderated by military, though over-rigid constitution may encourage extra-constitutional violence.
Relative power of elites and non-elites.	Non-elites weak after post-coup purges.	Little obvious change.	More elite penetration of PPP.	Demobilisation after end of 1954 left-wing government.	Little change.	Demobilisation after 1964 left-wing government.	Little effective challenge to post-1945 elite, despite social changes in 1960s and after.	Restoration of order reinforced economic elites.	Military failed to restore pre-1950 elite, failed to prevent rise of new capitalist elite.
Party balance.	Unclear. Extreme right discredited; Left hit by persecution.	Little change.	Right-wing parties lost despite military support.	Election won by party not threatening military.	Power passed from Christian Democrats to extreme right.	Parties still weak; continued instability.	Parties have gained some autonomy from army: still mainly cadre parties.	Previously dominant left-wing party crushed. Military party created and sustained.	Failure to restore pre-1950 dominant party. Election of free-market right-wing party.
Subsequent military role.	Military still in power.	Limited veto.	Strong military veto; limited civilian control.	Very strong military veto. Limited civilian control.	Very strong military veto. Limited civilian control.	Strong military veto.	Limited military veto via penetration of civil institutions.	Strong military veto.	Limited veto.

restored through anti-guerrilla warfare. This might lead us on to a third explanation which focuses more on the nature of societies in which right-wing military intervention is most common, which we saw tend to be located in the relatively 'developed' Third World countries where urbanisation, literacy and industrial employment are sufficient to provoke resistance to political demobilisation, yet insufficient to sustain the sort of inegalitarian conservatism in which the rich can get richer but without the poor suffering such extreme deprivation as to drive them to militant resistance. Right-wing policies in Chile and Guatemala may thus require more repression and enjoy less consent than in Britain or the United States, and this may reduce their prospects of success. We have noted that many left-wing military governments in poorer countries have created single political parties to strengthen their legitimacy and their links with the wider population, whereas no recent right-wing military government has done this (though some have supported individual parties within semi-competitive systems). While not all left-wing single parties have been effective, the willingness to create them suggests a willingness to attempt to mobilise public opinion which is seldom found on the right. In much of South America, Pakistan and Turkey the degree of military professionalism would be difficult to reconcile with such incursions into the civilian sphere, while in our civil–military authoritarian systems and Indonesia, pluralist competition has passed the point where an army would be strong enough to force party activity into a single channel. Let us now look at some of the individual cases.

We have characterised our personal/military authoritarian countries as having highly professional armies, integral civil–military boundaries and, except in the case of Pakistan, a relatively high level of socioeconomic development giving rise to what Finer called a (relatively) 'high political culture' in which the governed will not willingly accept arbitrary non-elected government. This does not, however, extend to a willingness to lie down in front of the tanks of the oppressor, and in the short term the Chilean military met with considerable success in restoring order and repressing all political parties. The Marxist left was severely damaged by terror, and this may weaken its prospects in any post-military system in a way comparable with Spain. In the 1970s the extreme right appeared to be the most obvious beneficiary of the coup, but the removal of the Chicago Boys after the perceived failure of their policies left this faction discredited in the eyes of the population as well as the government. Pinochet's defeat in the 1988 referendum owed much to the efforts of more moderate parties, and might augur well for those who envisage a post-military world of moderate pluralism, in contrast to the extreme polarisation before 1973, although this was hardly the outcome for which the military had striven.

The army had shown itself more effective as a destroyer than a builder. Its integral boundaries with civil institutions after a long period of abstinence from politics had left it with extensive freedom to destroy these institutions, but it also prevented it from building new structures which might have smoothed the transition to an approved post-military polity. Without military intervention Chile might have a prolonged continuation of unstable government. The army's achievement was to end such disorder, but it could not impose a new order of its own choosing.

The impact of military intervention on the wider society may prove to be less spectacular than had seemed likely in earlier years. The Chicago Boys have come and gone, leaving many import-substituting businesses destroyed by the foreign capital which monetarism encouraged, but the economy recovered well from the disasters of the early 1980s. While individual businesses have suffered and monetarism has been modified, the broad thrust of economic policy has remained one of capitalist growth in which no attempt has been made to share the fruits more equally. Gross domestic product grew at an annual rate of 5 per cent in the late 1980s, but average incomes by 1988 were 15 per cent lower than in 1970 (Coad, 1988, p. 14). A right-wing military government which began by displacing a Marxist regime, and ended by handing over to a civilian regime an economy in which capital has fared much better than labour, can hardly be judged a failure by its own standards.

Military intervention in Uruguay had a much less significant impact. In the political sphere the country returned to the same moderate pluralist competition between the same parties, and in the economic sphere soldiers had remained closer to the national consensus in favour of a welfare-oriented mixed economy. Although a substantial consensus arising from relative prosperity, ethnic homogeneity and a long history of pluralist politics could not prevent military intervention, the prevailing political culture placed severe limits on the ability of the military to make radical changes. There were, of course individual beneficiaries and sufferers as a result of military government, but society, the economy and the polity had all developed autonomously to such an extent that the military interregnum left them largely unscathed.

Pakistan presents a more interesting case for academic speculation. The military intervened to restore order, yet they provoked much disorder; to end the divisiveness of party competition, yet they left the country with a more vigorous party system, dominated by their opponents, than they had inherited; to restore national unity, yet their inflexibility contributed to the secession of Bangladesh. But in fairness to the military we should remember that the political system which they took over, in contrast those of to Chile and Uruguay, was an infant one in which few conventions of authority or competition had evolved. The army had less difficulty than in the former countries in crushing political institutions it disliked, and we noted Rizvi's assertion that it restored some power to economic elites at the expense of 'representative elites' (Rizvi in Clapham and Philip, 1985, pp. 201–4), or what sceptics might call elites based on party patronage. But the level of economic development was such that there were few powerful indigenous economic allies to be courted. While attempts were made at privatisation and greater reliance on the discipline of the market, the survival of any government in Pakistan has depended heavily on the distribution of economic rewards and patronage to groups whose support the government needs, especially in the absence of well-developed political institutions as power bases. This meant that any economic transformation was difficult, and political change was largely limited to the options of continued military government with some limited democracy or a return to party competition over which the army had limited control, given its lack of penetration of civil institutions. The outcome of a victory for the 'wrong' party, but subject to a substantial military veto, might seem to be a limited achievement until one considers the alternatives. The absence of any strong tradition of party competition in Pakistan, and the ability of dominant 'catch-all' parties in similar countries to retain power through patronage and ballot-rigging, might suggest that without the threat of military intervention, Pakistan would have developed a one-party system on the Indian model but in a society with fewer traditions of restraint and tolerance than India. There is, of course, no guarantee that military intervention will be used to promote democratic virtues, but the post-1988 balance of power between soldiers and party politicians may at least provide some check on the worst forms of authoritarianism.

The civil–military authoritarian countries again present a greater picture of uniformity than the military authoritarian when we look at the broader impact of military intervention. In all of them the violence and disorder of the military periods has continued into civilian rule, the dominant elites remain free to ply their trades without surrendering much of their power or wealth to non-elites, and the machinery of government, even where it has passed to more moderate parties, has not generally been used in such a way as to upset either the army or the economic elites. If it were, or if parties further to the left seemed likely to win an election, the military would be quick to exercise their power of veto. Yet if we compare the actual political outcomes with what might have happened if the military had not intervened or, more realistically, if they had had to surrender power on less favourable terms, we can see that the stakes were much higher in these countries than in many others. The military in both Guatemala and Bolivia overthrew left-wing governments which might, for all their weaknesses, have established some form of social democracy which would have blunted political and economic inequalities, as was the case in Costa Rica. If anti-guerrilla warfare in Guatemala and El Salvador had been less successful, which it might have been if the United States had developed qualms of conscience earlier, a Cuban or Nicaraguan-type outcome is conceivable. Despite the apparent divisions, ideological incoherence and lack of professionalism of soldiers in these countries, their impact on the course of political history may prove more significant than in the other types — a clear victory for the forces of the right which could hardly have been achieved without them.

The Turkish story has superficially similar features to that of Pakistan. A highly professional army was largely successful in restoring order and establishing limited democracy but, largely because integral civil–military boundaries limited its penetration of civil institutions, failed to ensure the election of its favoured party. A major difference was, however, that political institutions and elites were much more developed in Turkey and were thus more difficult to control. They had stronger bases in society and were less dependent on the manipulation of state patronage. The capture of power by the military thus failed to ensure the restoration of the pre-1950 military–bureaucratic–intellectual elite and the party which sustained it, and failed to prevent the rise of a new capitalist elite, which emerged with urbanisation and industrialisation. The military had some limited success in moderating the violence and political extremism which arose with the accompanying social changes, and showed sufficient skill in constitutional engineering to restore power to a three-party system under a strong military president in place of the polarised multi-party system of the 1970s. But the question remained as to whether constitutional engineering would be sufficient to achieve stability in the face of continued social change. The policies of the successor right-wing civilian government did little to prevent further violence and polarisation yet, unlike Pakistan and the civil–military authoritarian countries, the prospect of a military veto as a deterrent to political misbehaviour seemed barely plausible in a country anxious to show its maturity as a member of the democratic European community. Much had changed between the initial intervention of the military in 1960 and their departure in 1983, but the ability of the military to exert any further influence is now in doubt.

In Indonesia the immediate objective of restoring order (or perhaps establishing it for the first time) was achieved after an initial period of repression. The balance of political power has shifted with the eclipse of the former ruling party and the communists, but in social and economic terms what has been loosely described as a 'corporate' relationship between ruling elites, and a diversity of groups whose co-operation is required, has remained largely intact. The system remains pluralist, but non-democratic in the sense that there is little prospect of a change of government through the ballot box, just as before the military takeover. Such a reinforcement of elite power might be regarded as a substantial conservative achievement, facilitated partly by the heterogeneity of the opposition and partly by reaping the benefits of economic success, but largely through the strength and professionalism of the army and its judicious use of patronage and effective penetration of civil institutions. The major problem for the functioning of the political system is the mirror image of the Turkish problem. The Turkish army has apparently reached the stage where it has lost its power of veto to forestall either disorder or the emergence of a left-wing government, whereas the Indonesian army has reached the stage where it cannot easily extricate itself from government, partly because of the existence of a variety of groups with a vested interest in maintaining it, and partly because of the country's lack of experience of any form of democratic government which might offer a suitable model. Stability has been bought at the expense of dynamism, and it is a stability which may prove vulnerable if a means of succession to office cannot be evolved.

The achievements of right-wing military government in Thailand, for good or ill, seem modest compared with most of the countries we have examined, apart from Uruguay. In the 1930s the reforming military government did much to widen the political arena, but more conservative post-war governments have been more concerned with maintaining or restoring order, settling intra-elite conflicts and blunting relatively mild left-wing challenges. It would be tempting to see the function of military intervention as similar to the tropical African model of facilitating the circulation of elites in what might otherwise be a system of prolonged one-party rule by a catch-all party, which could use patronage and a limited amount of coercion to keep the opposition at bay. This still leaves us with the question of why one party failed to reach such a dominant position in the first place, as in India and Singapore, which takes us back to the fact that, as in Turkey and to a lesser extent Indonesia, it was the army that provided the early thrust for modernisation, and that this may have stunted the growth of parties. We suggested that, in these two countries, the problem for further conflict resolution was that either the army had been pushed off the political stage and was barely able to threaten errant politicians with re-intervention, or that it was almost irremovable from the centre of the stage and was blocking further development. The Thai army, like Goldilocks with her third bowl of porridge, may have found a solution that is 'just right'. It has left the centre of the stage, but through its penetration of civil institutions it may be able to pull sufficient strings to get the political system to perform in the way it wishes, or even to resume a more prominent role. This may not please liberal democrats, who feel that governments of whatever complexion or quality should be allowed to emerge through the free play of pluralist forces, but it may be comforting for conservatives, who want an additional check on disorder or perceived left-wing extremism. But if further social change did promote more such extremism, the Thai political system's limited experience of handling polarised conflict would put it under considerable strain.

Right-Wing Military Government and 'Political Development'

The concept of 'political development' is a contentious one, with its implications of movement from one recognisable set of variables to another, yet readers with tidy minds may still want to know whether one can generalise about the relationship between right-wing military intervention and the subsequent political process. Attempts at such generalisations pose at least two problems. Firstly, we cannot easily discover when a particular phase is over. Should we refer to right-wing military government in Pakistan or El Salvador in the past tense and assume that these countries are entering a new 'phase', or are we merely living through a brief interregnum between military governments? Secondly, is right-wing military government as much a symptom as a cause of political systems which are unable to achieve a consensus or means of resolving conflicts, and if there is a failure to achieve liberal democracy, socialism, political stability or any other desired end, can this be blamed on soldiers alone? And what is intervention symptomatic of? We have seen that the circumstances which brought right-wing soldiers to power in different countries varied considerably, and we would therefore expect their impact on subsequent events to vary. Any Barrington Moore-type of analysis to relate right-wing military government to particular patterns of political evolution seems doomed to failure. All we shall attempt to do here is to sketch out four main types of civilian political system which frequently follow right-wing military government.

1. Pluralism with limited military veto

This is frequently found in countries that have experienced military authoritarianism, which has sometimes been followed by a transitional phase of limited democracy, as in Brazil and South Korea. If we placed the countries in this category along a continuum, Spain would occupy one end, with the army apparently reduced to a Western liberal democratic role and unlikely to re-intervene successfully, while Argentina would occupy the other, with civilian politicians having to tread warily in the pursuit of defence policy and the allocation of resources to the army for fear of provoking another coup. But within this group day-to-day pluralist politics may continue vigorously, even where an election has been won by a party not favoured by the military (as has generally been the case, except in South Korea). Socioeconomic development and pre-coup experience of politics in these countries is such that pluralism can flourish unless a very determined effort is made by a strong, professional army to suppress it. Indeed the harshness of military government which was necessary to suppress pluralist politics may have the effect of putting subsequent civilian politicians on their guard to ensure that extremes of confrontation do not provide a pretext for the military to return.

2. *Pluralism with no apparent military veto*

There are few final victories or defeats in politics, but some countries at least appear to have moved completely outside the orbit of military intervention. Greece is an obvious case, Spain appears to be moving in the same direction and Uruguay may yet join them. These are countries near the borderline between the First and Third Worlds. In Greece and Uruguay military intervention was an aberration, following a phobia about left-wing extremism and threats to order which existed largely in the minds of the military, and the military interregna made little obvious difference to the course of civilian politics. In Spain the military presence was longer and stronger, but once the conflict they had originally intervened to resolve had subsided, and its partisans passed on, the pressures for popular participation that socio-economic development had generated made liberal democracy relatively easy to sustain.

3. *Limited pluralism sustained (and limited) by the military*

Pakistan belongs to this category, as do countries with longer periods of limited democracy under military tutelage such as Thailand, Turkey and Indonesia (where the tutelage still continues). Without military intervention these countries might resemble their socioeconomic peers in sustaining one-party dominance based on a blend of patronage and coercion, as in India, Malaysia and much of East Africa. Right-wing military intervention has interrupted or forestalled such development, and the relatively free 'restoration elections' have given opposition politicians an opportunity they might not otherwise have enjoyed, provided they are not deemed too extreme to participate. Military intervention in these countries has generally been more concerned with restoring order than meeting a left-wing challenge, so the number of competing parties regarded as beyond the pale is relatively small. Intervention may thus facilitate a circulation of (or within) elites not found in one-party states, but the underlying socioeconomic conditions will make pluralist democracy difficult to sustain. In Finer's terminology, the 'low political culture' will minimise public disapproval of further intervention, and opposition parties anticipating defeat in unequal electoral contests may positively encourage it. In these circumstances, the nature, extent and duration of pluralist politics may continue to depend on soldiers' perception of the political system and their role within it.

4. Nominal pluralism with a strong military veto

This is especially common in civil–military authoritarian regimes where shifts between military and civilian governments are barely perceptible. One could argue that it is in these countries that the impact of right-wing military government on subsequent civilian politics is most far-reaching. Countries which have overthrown right-wing military dictators through revolution, such as Cuba and Nicaragua, or which have avoided them by disbanding the army, as in the special case of Costa Rica, have had a very different subsequent history from Guatemala or El Salvador, despite the apparent socioeconomic similarities between these countries. Where civilian government has been restored without a revolution, the army's veto power has been so great that election results have been of only marginal significance. Either the election or the count has been arranged to ensure the defeat of left-of-centre parties, or the combined effects of national economic fragility and military veto power have rendered them impotent when they have won. There was no inevitability about this. Groups on the left in Guatemala and El Salvador had shown a willingness to search for compromise, but soldiers saw the suppression of guerrillas and the social forces they represented as an essential part of their mission. Having made such a choice, they have sustained right-wing parties and entrenched elites more effectively than has been the case in our other three categories.

The legacy of right-wing military government is, then, a largely negative one. Whereas left-wing military governments have facilitated the evolution of relatively durable, stable (though not generally democratic) political systems in countries such as Algeria, Egypt and Libya, right-wing soldiers outside Central America have, more often than not, been succeeded by parties they did not favour, and have had to content themselves with the consolation of relative autonomy for the armed forces and the implicit threat, with varying degrees of credibility, of re-taking power as a last resort. For those who had hoped that right-wing military intervention would create conditions for stable political development in countries where both democracy and order had previously failed to take root, this may be a disappointment. For liberal democrats who believe that stable democracy can only evolve through a process of trial and error, even if elections are not perfectly free, if politicians are not perfectly honest and neither government not governed are perfectly law-abiding, the outcomes may appear more promising.

PART III
Beyond Military Government

We now move from rule by the military to their attempts to hand power back to civilians, and the nature of the successor regimes. I have already hinted at the mortality of military governments in the previous section. If the government's authority is based on force, there is no reason to expect people to obey that authority indefinitely, especially if it fails to deliver adequate material benefits. At the same time, only a tiny proportion of soldiers will be in the government, and some of the majority who are left outside, and are thus denied the status and privileges of their superiors, may be tempted to seek power by the same violent means as their superiors had done. The mere threat or fear of both civilian non-cooperation and counter-coups, together with a realisation that there are many problems which soldiers can solve no better than civilians, leads to thoughts of disengagement, but the process is never a simple one. Soldiers will want to ensure that a successor government does not reverse too many of the policies they have followed, for reasons of ideology, pride and self-interest, or even self-preservation. It would be foolhardy to risk allowing the election of a civilian government that would punish the erstwhile military rulers by depriving them of their wealth, their liberty or even their lives. The nature and extent of disengagement depends not just on a desire that it should happen, but on a series of subtle relationships between the military and society, which may either ensure a smooth transition or leave soldiers attempting to restore the coherence of the army and wanting to divest themselves of the responsibilities of office, yet wary of civilian politics gaining a momentum which could work to their disadvantage.

If some form of civilian succession is negotiated, this will not close the book on the story of military government. Our interest in military government extends beyond the taking and using of power by soldiers, to the impact of this on subsequent political development. Will the subsequent civilian regimes be the creatures of their military predecessors, subject to substantial military veto power and haunted by the fear of military re-intervention, or will experience of military oppression lead to a civilian determination to establish democratic institutions and keep the army out of politics? The answers will clearly vary between different times and places, and we again need to look at the different combinations of variables which help to explain a continuing military influence, or a reaction against the previous military domination, or even a subsequent political history which owes little to the arrival and departure of the military.

PART III
Beyond Military Government

8 The Politics of Military Disengagement

Introduction

Right-wing military governments seldom seek to hold power indefinitely. While their left-wing counterparts often build single-party bases to sustain their authority, as in Algeria and Egypt, or build governments around dominant military personalities, as in Iraq and Libya, in order to continue the work of the 'revolution', the more modest objectives of conservative military leaders set limits to their tenure of office. Generals Franco and Pinochet were more reluctant to depart than most, but they were exceptional in their determination to eliminate their opponents and the alternatives they represented. General Stroessner's success in taking over the dominant party as a long-term power base in Paraguay is another exception, as is General Suharto's more tenuous grip on the party he created in Indonesia. Otherwise a variety of pressures have driven right-wing military governments to disengagement, even though we cannot be sure that their departure is permanent or that their influence behind the scenes does not continue. In this chapter we shall consider the different explanations of right-wing military withdrawal, the sorts of civilian political system the military attempt to establish, and the processes by which they attempt to make the transition. The processes, and the forces that influence them, need to be seen in the context of governments which seek limited rather than revolutionary changes, but which may be fearful of the changes that might take place if they no longer control or manipulate the political system.

Much has been written about individual cases of military disengagement, but there have been relatively few attempts to build a broader framework. Table 8.1 indicates some of the authors who have attempted to do this, and the variables they have emphasised. Such an attempted classification is bound to oversimplify, since no one is likely to believe that one single variable explains everything, but different authors have claimed different vantage points as the most suitable for observing the process of disengagement. Much depends on whether one is seeking to explain immediate events or long-term trends. Our first variable, civilian attitudes, is liable to change in the short term, with public support, acquiescence or opposition to any government liable to change as the government tackles, or fails to tackle, new problems. The second and third variables — political structures and institutions, and the nature and

Table 8.1: Main variables in the literature on military disengagement

Variables emphasised	Authors
1. Civilian attitudes.	Finer (1985), Levine (1988).
2. Political structures, institutions.	Baloyra (1987), Schmitter in O'Donnell *et al.* (1986), Welch (1987).
3. Nature and objectives of the military government and its military constituency.	Baloyra (1983), Finer (1985).
4. Socioeconomic development.	O'Donnell (1986), Sundhaussen (1984).
5. Political culture.	Schmitter in O'Donnell *et al.*, (1986), Welch (1987).

objectives of the military government and its military constituency — can be regarded as medium-term variables. They may not alter from day to day, but particular individuals or groups do have the power to create, destroy or restrict the operations of legislatures, political parties and pressure groups; and the beliefs, powers and behaviour that emanate from them can have an impact on the government's tenure of office. Finally, socioeconomic development and political culture can be seen as long-term variables, produced by a variety of complex forces over a long period, and not subject to the direct control of even the most powerful ruler.

We may also note the variables which are not given so much prominence in the general literature, even though they play a part in case studies of individual countries. Relatively little is said about the actual performance of military governments, whether in terms of the distribution of material benefits, in fighting wars at home and abroad or in the extent to which they kill, torture or restrict the freedom of their subjects, though some of this will be reflected in the study of civilian attitudes. Neither are external influences, such as the greater unwillingness of the United States to sustain authoritarian regimes, generally emphasised as the most significant factor, though it may be argued that such influence is generally indirect (Welch, 1987, p. 24). While there have been many cases of external pressures precipitating right-wing coups, there have been few cases, if any, of a foreign power toppling a right-wing military government, though the threat of reduced aid might hasten its departure if it is already divided or unpopular.

Civilian Attitudes

Finer examines disengagement largely in terms of the interaction of civil and military attitudes at different levels, while also allowing for the influence of failed military ventures abroad and the withdrawal of external support (Finer, 1985, pp. 16–30). It is not merely a case of acceptable civil institutions being available to take over the reins of power, but of civilian challenges actually forcing military withdrawal, as in Cuba, Nicaragua and the more dubious example of El Salvador. Levine also places much emphasis on the impact of mass public opinion, in response to the more deterministic literature. He argues that civilian democracy has emerged in Latin America and southern Europe not just as a compromise between civilian elites weary of authoritarianism and economic failure, and soldiers wanting to repair the army's shattered morale after the strains of office, but because elite demands for democracy are strengthened by the positive support of the masses, frequently transmitted through political parties (Levine, 1988, pp. 377–94). He also argues that disengagement is helped by the 'moderate' demands of the civilian population, which ensure the election of right-of-centre parties acceptable to the military without any need to rig the ballot (ibid., pp. 381–2). Little concrete evidence is produced to support such a view, but one might speculate that people who have suffered material deprivation, the loss of liberty, and sometimes the loss of friends and relatives to the mercies of the security forces, may feel that a competitive party system is more likely to respond to their interests. Citizens in virtually all the countries with right-wing military governments have had previous experience of such a system and, for all its faults, it may arouse greater enthusiasm in retrospect in view of the authoritarianism that has followed it.

The 'moderation' and acceptability to the military of civilian demands is more difficult to concede, as is the concomitant assertion that elections are not rigged it favour of the right. Several key politicians were disqualified from contesting elections in Turkey and Uruguay, the military's manipulation of the electoral system in South Korea ensured a narrow victory for their candidate on a minority vote, and the Pakistan military helped to prevent Benazir Bhutto from winning an overall majority by preventing people without identity cards (generally the poorest citizens) from voting. In Central America, even when elections are not rigged blatantly, the main contenders have been expected to declare their opposition to nationalisation, reconciliation with the guerrillas or punishment of soldiers for violating human rights. Voters have come to understand that, if they elect a left-wing party, it will not be allowed to take office, and that it is therefore more prudent to restrict their choice to parties acceptable to the military. The pattern may be less one of soldiers and voters (and the parties representing them) subscribing to the same right-of-centre consensus, than of each calculating how far they can go without antagonising the other to such an extent that the whole disengagement venture is shelved. The Pakistan military thus allowed an election to be held in 1988 on the tacit understanding that the Pakistan People's Party would tone down the policies it had favoured in the 1970s, and Argentinian parties were careful not to jeopardise the prospects of a free election by promising over-rigorous prosecutions of soldiers who had served under General Galtieri.

The fact that most right-wing military governments outside Central

America, South Korea and possibly Thailand have been succeeded by parties which were not their first preference says much for the vigour of civilian opinion. But does the fact that the electoral choice was still within the limitations acceptable to the military indicate the existence of a viable right-of-centre consensus, or does it indicate the realism of voters in not pushing their luck too far? In Greece and Spain voters chose 'acceptable' right-wing parties in the first post-authoritarian elections, only to move further left on the second occasion when prospects of a military veto had receded. These varied forms of electoral behaviour suggest a major problem with the emphasis on 'civilian attitudes'. Voters do not begin by deciding which of an infinite variety of choices they will make, but choose from a limited menu vetted by a narrower (largely military) elite, and in the knowledge that some of the more exotic dishes are likely to be 'off'. (They tend to steer clear of the 'chef's specials' cooked up by the military, which are rejected as a rehash of unpalatable ingredients.) They may help to secure the return of civilian rule by keeping their choice within prudent limits, but this is largely a reactive role. In a few rare cases a civilian revolution may drive out the military, but where this does not happen it may be more fruitful to move away from the masses in our search for explanations of disengagement.

Political Structures and Institutions

Disengagement comes about not merely because there is a desire for it, but because institutions and structures are available to sustain a civilian regime. Finer contrasts the availability of viable institutions to take over from the military in Pakistan and Turkey with the absence of any viable alternative to the military in Northern Ireland (1985, pp. 28–9) and Baloyra notes that in southern Europe and much of Latin America 'political parties were able to intermediate and channel the energies unleashed by breakdown [of military regimes] into peaceful processes of implementation'. In contrast to Levine's emphasis on the masses, he suggests that 'factors related to elite conflict appear to be more relevant than any configuration conjuring up a vision of masses rushing to the barricades' (Baloyra, 1987, p. 38). The availability of suitable political structures emerges again in Schmitter's anticipation of the prospects for democracy in southern Europe, where the history of these countries and their neighbours offers more varied forms of democratic system than Latin America, where variations on the United States presidential model are the rule (and executive power-sharing is presumably inhibited) (Schmitter in O'Donnell *et al.*, 1986, Part I, pp. 3–10). The 'Gaullist'-type solution in Turkey, where extremist parties are kept at bay by a relatively strong president, constitutional monarchy in Spain, with its blend of parliamentary democracy and historical continuity, and parliamentary republicanism in Greece, where an unpopular monarchy has given way to largely decorative presidency, might all be cited as supporting examples of the varied forms of pluralist democracy. 'Structures', in the sense of formal bodies such as parties, legislatures and presidencies, can be created or destroyed at will, but 'institutions' in Huntington's sense of stable, recurring patterns of behaviour

(1968, pp. 244–5), can only evolve in the fullness of time, though Huntington has definite views on how such evolution might be aided. Welch suggests that institutional development is helped by either a revolution, which presumably confers legitimacy on political structures because they have been forged by the popular will, or by a long period of independence, which leads him to be more optimistic about the prospects for disengagement in Latin America than in Africa (Welch, 1987, p. 17). Within limits, differences in structures and institutions can make a difference to the prospects for disengagement. Mainwaring (1988) has shown how South American countries which appear similar in terms of socioeconomic development have vastly different party systems which have made for different patterns of transition (or non-transition) to civilian rule. In Brazil's 'top-down' political system, parties have always been heavily dependent on the state, and the state allowed them to continue to function even after the military had taken over, albeit with attempts by the military to tilt the party system in their favour. Such continuity also implied the continued existence of an elected congress and state governors. The transition to civilian rule was less abrupt than elsewhere, with the military gradually retreating in the face of a succession of electoral setbacks. The Chilean system, in contrast, was one of strong, autonomous parties, in a powerful legislature, less willing to moderate their behaviour for the benefit of the head of state. This autonomous, polarised system was deemed incompatible with military government, and parties suffered a long period of suspension. It is still not clear whether a party system compatible with the wishes of the military can emerge. Uruguay is different again, with the main parties largely frozen in the narrow elitist mould of an earlier generation. Their restoration posed no immediate threat to the military, but their inability to incorporate new social groups contributed to the growth of extra-constitutional activity before the military intervened, and may yet prove to be a weakness under the restored civilian regime (Mainwaring, 1988, pp. 91–120).

The perennial question is the extent to which political structures can be treated as independent variables, separate from the socioeconomic structure on the one hand, and the power of those who control the machinery of state on the other. Most of the authors I have mentioned would acknowledge that it is a matter of degree. Civilian government was restored in Greece and Spain not only because the right constitutional models were available but because the underlying social conditions sustained moderate political competition; the difficulty of finding acceptable political parties to succeed General Pinochet could be explained not only in terms of the historical impact of Chilean parties on the polity, but in terms of the high-handed way in which the military spurned politicians of the moderate right and preferred to rely on technocrats with no independent power base. We must therefore move on to look at the impact of military behaviour on the socioeconomic structure.

The Nature and Objectives of the Military Government and its Military Constituency

Both Finer and Baloyra give much prominence to the motivations of military men themselves, while acknowledging that their decisions on disengagement will depend partly on how far military objectives are congruent with the demands of civilian groups (Baloyra, 1987, pp. 9–10, 38–43; Finer, 1985, pp. 24–5). Most military governments face tensions after a few years in power between 'soldiers in government' and 'soldiers in barracks' which can threaten the integrity of the army unless a long-standing tradition of professionalism helps to maintain the hierarchy, as in much of South America and Pakistan, or sufficient patronage can be dispensed to keep subordinates contented, as in Indonesia and possibly Thailand. The actual or threatened breakdown of the military hierarchy may itself be a major reason for disengagement, as in much of Central America, and justifications in terms of the virtues of civilian democracy may be little more than excuses for a hasty departure, but in other cases the decision to depart will depend more on the underlying values of soldiers and the policy choices to which they give rise. Finer cites the case of the Turkish army's strongly held belief in civilian supremacy, with military intervention undertaken only reluctantly when there seemed to be no other means of restoring order (Finer, 1985, p. 25), whereas soldiers in Central America might have felt less troubled by the suspension of pluralist politics and might have had few qualms about enjoying the fruits of office until guerrilla threats, the withdrawal of United States support and civilian resistance made their position untenable.

Between the extremes of the speedy restoration of order and the plundering of public coffers, soldiers may have a variety of motives for taking power and then retaining it for varying lengths of time. The vagueness of the Greek and Uruguayan soldiers' desire to combat left-wing threats left them with little positive to do once they faced real political choices, and disengagement became a matter of seeking the best terms available for the military rather than facilitating the implementation of highly valued policies. The Chilean military, in contrast, had a much clearer vision of the sort of society they wanted, and the redistribution of political and economic resources necessary to bring it about. This has meant that any effective disengagement will require many more safeguards to protect the political and economic edifice the military have built, and the personnel who have built it, unless civilians are able to remove the regime on their own terms. In still other cases, noably Indonesia, the military constituency may pose as great an obstacle as the military government to disengagement, with subordinate soldiers not wanting to lose the patronage they enjoy, and offering the implicit threat of a counter-coup if the process of civilianisation goes too far.

Are we to explain these variations in motivations largely in terms of the preference of individual soldiers or armies, or are these shaped by more discernible forces such as the degree of professionalism in the army, the structure of the military government or the society within which it functions? A relatively low level of professionalism, as in Central America, will make it difficult to speak of 'objectives', since the army will contain soldiers with a heterogeneous range of values, and any unity of purpose may be limited to a lowest common denominator in an attempt to preserve some sort of power structure that will resist the challenges of mass movements and guerrillas. A more professional army, even in a poorer country such as Pakistan, will have a clearer unity of purpose and sufficient autonomy to spell out its terms for disengagement, which in the Pakistan case has meant the retention of an ample military veto in defence and foreign policy. The importance of the structure of the military government is emphasised by Baloyra, who contrasts the breakdown of 'bureaucratic authoritarian regimes' (a concept which we have approached with caution) in Argentina, Brazil and Uruguay with the greater longevity of personal dictatorships in Chile and Paraguay (Baloyra, 1987, p. 297). Personal dictators may appeal over the heads of soldiers to the wider population, thus giving the government a certain popular legitimacy, but this still does not explain why, beyond explanations of personality and sheer chance, a relatively wealthy country like Chile and a poor one like Paraguay should have a type of military government different from the more collective ones of their neighbours. As to why dictators should have returned to barracks despite the advantages of powerful professional armies to sustain them, we are left with the question of whether this was the result of individual choices made by military rulers, some of which were designed to facilitate disengagement and some of which inadvertently had that effect, such as the Falklands invasion or violations of human rights, or whether there were also underlying socioeconomic conditions which made their tenure insecure.

Socioeconomic Development

Much has been written about the socioeconomic conditions which facilitate military intervention, but the relevance of these conditions to military disengagement has not been explored so thoroughly. Those who are pessimistic about the prospects for disengagement might appear to have powerful arguments at both ends of the development spectrum. If a country is 'underdeveloped' in terms of the indicators we have used, such as per capita income, literacy, industrialisation and urbanisation, it may be difficult to find acceptable civilian elites able to generate sufficient legitimacy from a largely apolitical population. Sundhaussen cites the examples of Indonesia and Paraguay, and argues that:

> Certain kinds of reasons and preconditions for military withdrawal are unlikely to surface if a society has a low level of development. In many parts of the world freedom from hunger will enjoy a higher priority than civil rights. Since strong government, including military regimes, is often — rightly or wrongly — regarded as the possible solution to economic misery, sufficient pressures for less authoritarian forms hardly eventuate. (Sundhaussen, 1984, p. 552)

Yet in the more developed Third World countries such as Brazil, Chile and South Korea, it was fashionable to argue, at least until recently, that capitalist elites and their foreign supporters had too much to lose from pluralist democracy, which would threaten to divert resources from capital accumulation to mass consumption and social welfare. In the absence of traditional aristocracies, which enjoyed sufficient legitimacy to maintain authority when nineteenth-century Europe went through a comparable stage of development, civilian elites must rely on military governments to maintain order. The extensive inequality created or sustained by military governments may itself make it difficult to achieve the sort of consensus that democracy requires (O'Donnell, 1986, Part II, p. 9), and may stunt the growth of political parties which are important both in negotiating military withdrawal and in maintaining communications with the wider population.

Military governments are, none the less, departing from most of the more developed Third World countries, even if their permanent abstention from government remains in doubt and the nature of their civilian successors is not clear. Has disengagement occurred in spite of, or because of, socioeconomic development? The arguments about capitalist accumulation requiring authoritarianism, and a damping down of popular demands and participation, are powerful ones, but there is no guarantee that the sort of authoritarianism provided by the military will achieve the desired economic growth, as the disastrous experiences of Argentina and Chile bear witness, though the experiences of Brazil and South Korea suggest that a military road to capitalism does exist. Clapham argues that economic success makes civilian succession easier, contrasting the examples of South Korea and Brazil with Argentina and Chile (1988, p. 287), whereas Blakemore argues that the biggest element in military withdrawal in Latin America has been the failure to deliver what was expected of the military (1986, p. 1078). Seligson suggest that the economic records of military government in Latin America have been no worse than those of civilians during the same periods, but that the military were vulnerable because their claim to superiority could not be sustained (Seligson in Malloy and Seligson, 1987, pp. 5–6).

There are, then, only tenuous links between high socioeconomic development and military disengagement. The fact that it would suit the convenience of capitalist elites to have right-wing military governments to sustain them at particular stages of development is no guarantee that the military will be able or willing to oblige. Other pressures will be at work, such as the democratic demands in South Korea from a growing body of workers and students, many of whom owed their social positions to the development fostered by the military; or in Brazil from voters expressing anti-military preferences through political parties which the military had kept alive, and in Argentina from less articulated mass protests against economic mismanagement, failure in the Falklands and state-authorised terror. We return to the observation made earlier that military intervention and disengagement are merely two of several processes for changing a government, alongside revolutions, competitive elections, foreign invasions and takeovers of party politburos. If a government is seen to be incompetent or unjust, those who are able will seek its removal by whichever of these processes is appropriate in the circumstances. In that context the reasons for the departure of different right-wing military governments may be as diverse as the reasons for the downfall of American presidents, Italian coalitions or

Soviet party leaders, though dissatisfaction with the extent of material well-being, and personal liberty and status are often key factors.

A military government, like any other, may be punished for economic failure, but Welch makes a useful distinction between disengagement related to short-term negative trends, which may make for only a transitory civilian regime if its policies fare no better, and long-term disengagement related to positive economic trends (1987, p. 23). On this argument, civilian successions would prove more durable in Brazil and South Korea than in Argentina and Central America. We might even speculate that there is a developmental threshold beyond which military re-intervention will not occur because wealth, education, and the evolution of democratic institutions would create too much resistance both within and without the army. None of the thirty most developed countries of the world has experienced successful military intervention (in the sense of establishing a military government) since 1945 (See Table 1.1) and we have speculated that Spain, Greece and Uruguay may have crossed the threshold, but it would be dangerous to assume that if and when the countries of Latin America and Asia acquire the same levels of wealth, education and industrialisation as those of present-day Western Europe, they will also acquire the same attachment to liberal democracy. This is partly a question of political culture, to which we shall return presently, but also of a tradition of using the machinery of state, whether bureaucratic or coercive, to further the interests of the current holders of power and their supporters, to a much greater extent than in Western Europe where the state has traditionally provided a framework for political competition rather than unlimited scope for winners to enjoy all the spoils. Even the experience of a country like Japan, with its prolonged period of one-party rule based on extensive patronage, suggests that a high level of socioeconomic development will not necessarily produce Western-style pluralism. The dismemberment of the Japanese army after 1945 ruled out the possibility of military intervention in that country, but can we predict with confidence, if other countries enjoy comparable development but fail to provide adequate mechanisms for democratic political succession, that opposition groups will not look to the army for salvation?

At the other end of the scale, 'underdevelopment' is clearly no barrier to the dissolution of military governments, as the experience of Pakistan and the Central American republics indicates. Where potential economic rewards are fewer, and coercive resources more limited, most governments, whether civil or military, lead a precarious existence especially if they lack the legitimacy conferred by either traditional authority or democratic election. Disengagement thus tends to be partial, with the military retaining substantial veto powers and able to re-intervene relatively easily. Of the eleven least developed countries which have experienced right-wing military government since 1960 (all those below Turkey and Nicaragua in Table 1.1) it is difficult to think of any, apart from South Vietnam and Laos which have been absorbed into the Communist Bloc, which are not either still under military rule or subject to extensive military veto powers which could easily percipitate re-intervention. Socioeconomic development does not guarantee military disengagement, but lack of development ensures that any military withdrawal will be only partial or temporary.

Political Culture

The concept of political culture, like that of political development, has been used much more frequently in explaining military intervention than military disengagement. If we take political culture to mean the different attitudes to the political process and to political authority which are found in a country, there is clearly enormous diversity within the group of countries which have experienced right-wing military government. Turkey, Bolivia, Thailand and Guatemala occupy 80th, 84th, 85th and 86th positions respectively on Sivard's ranking on development, yet this proximity of development is not matched by cultural similarity. Turkey and Thailand both have long histories as independent nations, and populations which are relatively homogeneous in terms of race, language and religion, the presence of Armenian and Chinese minorities notwithstanding. A powerful monarch was for centuries accepted as the legitimate centre of power in each country, and much of this legitimacy was transferred intact to elected governments, or military governments which were expected to civilianise themselves and submit themselves or their successors to relatively free elections at an early opportunity. In both countries powerful civil bureaucracies provided an additional symbol of nationhood and ensured, together with equally long-standing military bureaucracies, that the government's writ ran throughout the nation. Bolivia and Guatemala, in contrast, acquired independence at a time when there was little consensus on who should rule or how, and contained heterogeneous populations of Europeans and indigenous 'Indians'. Authority depended more on the economic and coercive resources that different groups and individuals could wield than on the legitimacy of national symbols such as a monarch or a state bureaucracy. None of this is to suggest that the machinery of state in Turkey and Thailand was not frequently used in the interests of elites against non-elites, but there were at least some accepted conventions as to how authority should be wielded, which were based on broadly accepted values.

These cultural differences, which obviously penetrated armies as well as civilian populations, have influenced not only the circumstances and nature of military intervention but processes of disengagement. The Turkish military had a long tradition of integral boundaries with civil society, and its role was seen, by both soldiers and civilians, as a 'policing' one of intervening in politics to restore order but not usurping the functions of civilians. Transferring power in 1983 to an elected party not favoured by the military was culturally more acceptable than retaining power and the benefits that went with it. The Thai military's relations with civil institutions were more fragmented, with much interpenetration, but there were again underlying values which required at least partial disengagement in the sense of soldiers contesting relatively free elections or sharing power with civilians. In Bolivia and Guatemala, disengagement has come less as a result of widely accepted notions of correct military behaviour than as a result of threats to the integrity of the army as a result of frustration with economic mismanagement, the failure to win a guerrilla war and the fear of losing United States support. The survival of civilian successor regimes remains precarious while there are few values to challenge the desirability or scope of further military intervention.

Can we relate these examples to any more general propositions about the relationship between political culture and military disengagement? Our example of ethnic homogeneity in Turkey and Thailand does not appear to be an essential prerequisite for successful disengagement. Schmitter mentions the importance of a diversity of ethnic, linguistic, religious and social groups in southern Europe, capable of acting autonomously in defence of their own interests and ideals, but able to work together when occasion demands it, and existing independently of the state (Schmitter in O'Donnell *et al.,* 1986, Part I, p. 6). These features seem at first to be the opposite of those in Thailand and Turkey, but it may be that no one group is strong enough to dominate the others, so that mutual tolerance develops, though the experience of civil wars in Greece and Spain may do something to spoil such an idyllic picture. The emphasis on autonomy from the state rather than the effectiveness of a strong state again points to a contrast. The requirement for a successful transition to democracy may depend not so much on the extremes of state strength or group autonomy but on a more subtle balance. An exceptionally strong state, as noted in the previous section, may promote a form of 'winner takes all' politics which will make constitutional opposition challenges to governments so difficult as to encourage extra-constitutional plotting as an alternative. The prospects for democratic government in Argentina or Brazil might be examined in such a context. Yet a state which enjoys little legitimacy and which has to rely heavily on force, as in Central America, is equally unlikely to facilitate democratic development. What may be more important than the existence of group autonomy or state effectiveness is the extent of consensus on how far autonomy or state control should go, without the need for violence to be used in pursuit of different claims. Even between the Western democracies there are substantial variations in the extent of executive discretionary power, centralisation, limitations to civil liberties and the use of electoral systems to weaken opponents, but these variations may not matter if they are broadly congruent with the prevailing culture — hence the greater toleration of official secrecy in Britain than in Sweden, and the greater acceptance of centralised authority in France compared with the United States. Similarly, in building a viable successor to a military regime, it is not a question of offering a single blueprint but of developing something compatible with generally held values.

If the prevailing political culture is not conducive to any sort of consensus, attempts at successful long-term disengagement will obviously face serious difficulties. We noted the problems of Bolivia and Guatemala, but Welch suggests that even the Latin American republics have better prospects than most African states, on account of the social differentiation based mainly on economic position in the former rather than on language and kinship, as in the latter (Welch, 1987, p. 196). It can be argued that economic conflicts can sometimes be resolved by 'splitting the differences' in conflicts over the distribution of resources, and can be blunted by the fact that different social groups blur into one another, whereas conflicts between tribal groups take on a more 'absolute' form. Yet it is difficult to be optimistic about the prospects for disengagement in Central America, or even much of South America, when class conflict is as polarised as it is at present.

I have implied so far that the object of disengagement is to replace military government with pluralist democracy. There is no conceptual reason why this should be so. One could conceive of a military government or civilian groups preferring one-party rule, totalitarianism or absolute monarchy, but there are obvious practical reasons why pluralist democracy is generally preferred, or is at least claimed to be preferred. We have noted that, unlike some of their left-wing counterparts, right-wing military rulers do not generally attempt to pro-long their rule through creating a single party, since they are not attempting to consolidate a 'revolution'. A civilian dictatorship would leave little scope for military veto, so the option of pluralist democracy emerges if only by default. There are also positive influences at work. Pluralist democracy will give a variety of civilian groups the hope of winning power and influence, and thus ensure substantial public support for the transfer of power, and the government which eventually emerges will enjoy greater legitimacy at home and abroad. But if pluralist democracy is intended to be the outcome of disengagement, not only in southern Europe where it appears to be viable but in much of Latin America and Asia, the cultural barriers in its way are considerable. Perhaps, as in Rustow's thesis, culturally diverse rival groups will eventually come to realise that they can neither defeat one another nor exist independently of one another, and must therefore come to an agreement on peaceful ways of regulating conflict in order to pursue their mutual interests (Rustow in Lewis and Potter, 1973, pp. 117–30), but looking at present-day politics in Guatemala and Bolivia, or even Chile or Indonesia, it is still difficult to detect the emergence of such a 'rational' pattern of behaviour.

The Process of Disengagement

The actual forms of military disengagement may vary from formal agreements, made at specially convened meetings of civil and military leaders, through informal understandings, and terms spelt out by the military with which civilians have little choice but to comply, to civilian revolutions and handovers following counter-coups precipitated by alliances of disaffected soldiers and opposition politicians. Some of the variables are spelt out in Table 8.2, where it is suggested that the outcomes will depend on such variables as military strength and professionalism, and the strength of civilian political structures. 'Military strength' in this context is concerned with the ability of soldiers to disengage on the terms they demand, rather than the firepower and skill they enjoy in fighting wars. The Argentine army thus had greater strength in the former context than the latter, while the Bangladesh army was successful in a war of independence but has had difficulty in achieving a smooth transition to civilian rule. 'Civilian political structures' refers not only to those engaged in the formal political process, but to any groups able to wield power or influence, including pressure groups and revolutionary movements.

Table 8.2 suggests the possible outcomes of different combinations of military strength and professionalism, and civilian strength. When all are high

Table 8.2: Military disengagement in relation to civil and military structures

Military strength	Military profes- sionalism	Strength of civil political structures	Nature of disengage- ment	Prospects for civilian government
1. High	High	High	Formal pacts	Durable, e.g. Uruguay, Turkey, South Korea, Argentina, Greece
2. High	High	Low	Military- imposed terms	Government subject to strong, relatively predictable veto, e.g. Pakistan
3. Medium	Low	Medium	Military- imposed terms	Government subject to strong, unpredict- able military veto, e.g. Central America
4. Medium to Low	Low	Low	Informal under- standings, often following counter- coups	Unstable civilian government subject to unpredictable military veto, e.g. Laos, South Vietnam, Iran in the 1950s
5. Medium	Medium	Medium	Informal under- standings, possibly aided by civil– military interpene- tration	Unstable civilian governments, with the military exercising veto power largely from within govern- ment, e.g. Thailand
6. Low	Low	High	Civilian 'revolution'	Populist civilian government, often penetrating the army, e.g. Cuba, Nicaragua, Bolivia 1952

(Category 1), civil and military leaders will both have a disciplined following and generally be able to come to terms through formal pacts, whether in the form of an actual meeting to settle the terms of disengagement, as in Uruguay, or through an agreed constitutional settlement which may be approved by a wider electorate, as in South Korea and Turkey. Such pacts generally make for a durable successor regime which knows clearly the sorts of activity that would be vetoed by the military, and acts accordingly. Where military strength and professionalism remain high but civilian structures are weaker, as in Pakistan (Category 2), the military can more easily impose their own terms for disengagement and can, in the last resort, cling to power if civilians seem unwilling to accept these. The style of the civilian successor regime will be more cramped on account of the wider area of military veto (covering most of defence and foreign policy in Pakistan), but the strength and unity of the army will ensure that it will not intervene in an unpredictable way because of the whims of one or two officers, as often happens in Africa. The civilian government may therefore be relatively stable and durable, even if its scope for action is limited.

In much of Central America and Bolivia (our civil–military authoritarian countries) military professionalism is lower but the army's coercive control of the civilian population is still relatively high (Category 3). Civil political structures enjoy a strength somewhere between the extremes of the well-developed Uruguayan party system and the fragile, immature pluralism of Pakistan. Civilian political parties and elites have a long history, but have been heavily dependent on the military for retaining their positions in the face of challenges from mass movements and guerrillas. The military are therefore again able to impose the terms of disengagement, as they did when they persuaded the main contenders for power in Guatemala and Honduras to renounce any left-of-centre policies or prosecutions for human rights violations, but the lower level of military professionalism makes for a more unpredictable military veto on subsequent civilian governments. General Noriega's return to power in Panama in 1988 might be attributed more to personal whim than to a professional army protecting its integrity and values.

Where low military professionalism is matched by weak political structures (Category 4), disengagement is more likely to involve informal understandings between civil and military elites, often following a counter-coup by officers anxious to find civilian support, rather than a formal agreement or distinctive terms imposed by the military. Iran in the 1950s, or Laos and South Vietnam in the 1960s and 1970s, might fit such a pattern, as might many of the non-right-wing military governments in Africa, but the underlying conditions of low civil and military development are not normally met in countries with right-wing military governments. Where such outcomes do occur, the subsequent civilian regime is likely to be even more unstable, and subject to an unpredictable military veto — praetorianism in all its glory.

Where soldiers and civilians confront one another at intermediate rather than low levels of professionalism and development (Category 5), disengagement may again be based on informal understanding, but the under-standing will have more deep-rooted support on each side and will be aided by interpenetration of civil and military institutions. This will ensure that although the successor regime may again be unstable, with the possibility of military re-intervention at any time on quite flimsy pretexts, any change of government is likely to be an 'incremental' one involving changing degrees of civil and military participation and moderate shifts of policy, in contrast to the more sweeping changes which have marked the ending of civilian interregna in Argentina, Pakistan and Turkey. Thailand is a prime example of such a succession, and any eventual disengagement in Indonesia might follow a similar pattern.

Finally there have been cases where military professionalism has been reduced to a low level by prolonged, unpopular military government and where civil political structures with substantial popular bases are strong enough to challenge them, sometimes with the help of disaffected soldiers, as in Bolivia in 1952, Cuba and Nicaragua (Category 6). Purists may argue about whether such a challenge constitutes a coup or a revolution, but disengagement will clearly be on terms dictated by civilians, and the subsequent government is generally a populist one which will try to repoliticise the army in its own image to prevent any counter-coup. The Cuban and Nicaraguan governments have so far been successful in that respect; the Bolivians, as suggested in Chapter 5, failed because socio-economic development was not congruent with the political changes they were attempting. Right-wing military governments overthrown by popular pressures have not figured extensively in this study because the governments caught up in this sort of pressure tend to be old-fashioned autocracies led by long-retired military men, and resting largely on civilian bases supplemented by personally controlled terror, rather than military juntas relying heavily on military bases. These autocracies are more difficult to sustain in the modern world, where pressures for greater popular participation have to be met with either the legitimacy of the ballot box or the coercion of the bayonet, rather than reliance on blind obedience to a long-standing dictator. A variation on this theme occurs where dictators develop an effective party base, and they or their successors gradually transform military into civilian government, as in Spain and Paraguay. Such a course is unusual for right-wing military governments because it requires either a docile population which can be relied upon to vote the right way (Paraguay) or a semi-totalitarian apparatus to ensure compliance (Spain). In Brazil, where neither was available, the demise of military government was brought about because the electorate rejected the military-created party.

What help does this categorisation offer us in assessing the prospects for successor civilian regimes? Two of our six categories appear to be anachronisms, and another two appear to be the product of unique circumstances found in only a few countries. Category 4, where civil political structures are very weak, implies a low level of development not normally associated with right-wing military intervention. Where such intervention has occurred in the past in the Middle East and South-east Asia, it has been aided by the sort of United States subversion that has become less prevalent after defeat in Vietnam. Category 6, produced by strong civilians confronting a weak army, may also be a dying breed, requiring old-fashioned dictators who prefer to use the army as a personal bodyguard rather than develop it as a professional force which shares in government. They thus run the risk of dividing or alienating the army, many of whose members will make common cause with equally repressed civilians. Few modern military leaders are likely to take such a risk.

Category 2, the professional army in an underdeveloped society, is likely to arise only where the army has a long historical tradition and where the country's strategic position enables the army to live (with foreign aid) in a manner to which the rest of society is not accustomed. Pakistan appears to be unique in this respect. Turkey, the next most likely candidate for Category 2, has gone further in developing a pluralist political system. Category 5 requires a subtle interpenetration of civil and military structures which Thailand has achieved largely through avoiding 'Westernising' influences which prescribe more integral boundaries, and which Indonesia has achieved in a more incoherent way on account of the interdependence of civil and military groups in the years after independence. It is difficult to think of any other countries where such developments have taken place, or are likely to take place.

This leaves us with Categories 1 and 3 as the most common types, and they point us in divergent directions. Category 1, with high military professionalism and strong political structures, implies relatively durable, stable civilian government, able to act autonomously as long as it keeps out of clearly labelled 'out of bounds' areas demarcated by the military. This is not to say that the governments will necessarily be competent, honest or scrupulous in upholding democratic rights, but they will at least have some control over their own destiny. Most of our military authoritarian regimes, together with Turkey but excluding Pakistan, appear to have been succeeded by governments of this sort. Category 3, in contrast, where civil political structures are weaker and military professionalism is much lower, leaves the door open to weak civilian regimes subject to a military veto which is both extensive and unclearly defined. The interrelated problems of raising the level of military professionalism, so that even if soldiers do not abstain from politics they at least participate within more clearly structured conventions, and institutionalising civil political conflict so that political actors are willing to accept defeat without enlisting the support of soldiers to avert it, are still a long way from resolution. In the next chapter we shall look more closely at the successor civilian regimes which do, or might, emerge.

9 The Politics of Civilian Succession

Introduction

What is the long-term effect of right-wing military intervention? Can it be defended as a necessary evil which can rescue a country from disorder, and then establish the necessary stability for pluralist democracy to flourish? Does it inhibit democratic development by encouraging the use of violence as a means of resolving political conflict? Or is military intervention irrelevant to subsequent political development, either because such intervention is merely a symptom of wider political disorder, or because one intervention is merely an aberration in an otherwise stable civilian political system? In this chapter we look at both the possible relationships between military governments and civilian successor regimes, and at the actual performance of these successors in promoting such developments as democratic competition, individual liberty, social equality and economic advancement. Again I risk criticism for using the extent of achievement of pluralist democracy as a major criterion for measuring success, but again I must blame right-wing military governments and their successors for setting this as their stated objective, unlike non-right-wing military rulers such as Bokassa, Gadafi, Nasser, Ne Win and Rawlings. The alternatives of indefinite personal rule, one-party rule with totalitarian undertones or continued terror, have been regarded as unacceptable on ideological or practical grounds, even if the pluralist democracy envisaged is less than pure.

In Table 9.1 I suggest five models of civilian succession. The focus is different from that used in the previous chapter in that I attempt to assess the nature of the civilian outcome in dynamic terms rather than merely looking at the relative strength of civil and military institutions. In each case we are concerned with the relationship between the nature of the civilian successor regime and the army, and military government which preceded it.

I suggest five models:
1. A strong professional army is able to disengage on its own terms, leaving any successor civilian regime in the shadow of a potential military veto (the military domination model in Table 9.1). Argentina is an obvious example, and Paraguay may develop along similar lines. Brazil and South Korea hover uneasily between this model and the next.

Table 9.1: Types of civilian succession

Military domination model	Pluralist democracy model	Civilian populist model
Military intervened originally to reinforce power of military (and civil) elites.	Military intervened originally to protect civil–military elite from imminent electoral defeat or to reverse actual defeat.	Original military take-over of economically backward country develops into personal dictatorship, remote from much of the army.
↓	↓	↓
Suppression of participation and mobilisation.	Coercion proves inefficient in long run, with strong resistance.	Social and political inequality preserved or increased.
↓	↓	↓
Democratic development stunted.	Military government disengages because of inability to deliver material benefits, protect elites or establish legitimacy, or to satisfy its military constituency.	Ruler refuses to disengage or democratise.
↓	↓	↓
Civilian succession is largely controlled by the military.	Succession involves civil–military bargaining.	Civilians stage revolt, possibly supported by disaffected soldiers.
↓	↓	↓
Substantial military veto under civilian government. Right-wing parties and elites strengthened; left-wing parties contained. Pluralist democracy stunted by privileges of right-wing parties and elites, and military threats of re-intervention.	Extreme right-wing parties weakened on account of association with previous military government. Support for extreme left-wing parties hampered by voter's fears of military re-intervention. Good prospects for pluralist competition between moderate parties.	Succession passes to populist civilian government. Pluralist democracy inhibited by underlying economic and cultural conditions and by fears of counter-revolution.

Table 9.1 Contd.

Unstable model		Societal model

Right-wing military intervention is a symptom of political instability.

Military intervention in a relatively developed country reflects personal preferences of military leaders rather than social or political breakdown.

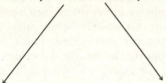

Military intervene because pluralist system cannot cope with consequences of early industrial- isation, and civil elites have limited legitimacy (much of Latin America).

Military intervene to meet threats to order in newly independent country (Indonesia, Pakistan) or country facing demands for wider participation in early stages of urbanisation (Thailand, Turkey).

Military government enjoys little elite or mass support, and has diffi- culty in imposing its will.

The military's capacity to resolve these problems is little greater than that of civilians. Succession involves civil– military bargaining.

Isolated military government disengages on terms favourable to pre-coup politicians.

Disengagement is only partial. Economic and cultural conditions cannot sustain pluralist democracy (unless it is underwritten from outside). Successor regime lacks secure political base, and is subject to extensive military veto.

Character of successor civilian government owes more to indigenous society than to short- lived military govern- ment.

2. Civil institutions are strong, and the initial military intervention was to remove or forestall a left-wing challenge. Civilian pressure is strong enough to persuade the military to disengage on terms relatively favourable to the dominant civilian parties. This strength, together with a determination not to provide a pretext for renewed military intervention and repression, may provide a foundation for pluralist democracy (the pluralist democracy model). Spain is a current example, with Chile as a possible future case.

3. A military leader has transformed military government into a personal dictatorship and has become remote from his military constituency, yet refuses to make concessions to demands for democratic participation. Civilians stage a violent revolt, possibly supported by disaffected soldiers, and a populist civilian government is installed, for example Cuba and Nicaragua (the civilian populist model).

4. Right-wing military intervention is merely a symptom of political instability. Soldiers are no more able than civilians to establish legitimate authority, restore order or resolve economic problems. Any disengagement is partial, leaving behind a weak civilian government which can be removed by the military at any time (the unstable model). Much of Central America and Bolivia belong to this category, together with Pakistan and, in a rather different way, Thailand.

5. Military intervention occurs in a relatively developed country more on account of the personal preferences of military leaders than social or political breakdown. Civilian resistance is even greater than in the pluralist democracy model, forcing an isolated military government to disengage on terms favourable to pre-coup civilian politicians. Pluralist democracy returns after the brief hiatus, and its character owes more to underlying social conditions than to the superficial military interregnum, for example Greece and Uruguay (the societal model).

Let us now look at the components of these models in more detail.

The Military Domination Model

Military intervention may have occurred partly to forestall a left-wing threat, but it was also part of a regular political process in which soldiers asserted their authority to protect themselves and their allies in civilian elites. This meant that even if mass movements and participatory structures were not actually dismantled, as they were in Chile, their development was stunted. Even if military government becomes unpopular, there are few civil institutions strong enough to press for disengagement on their own terms, and the military thus control the process of succession and retain substantial powers of veto under the successor regime. Left-wing parties will be banned or severely restricted, even if the army does not give implicit support to any party on the right for fear of such support losing more votes than it would win. In both Argentina and Brazil, the stength of the army as an institution has continued, even though individual military leaders have had to depart. The civilian government removed most of the top military leadership in Argentina in 1983, only to find that their replacements subscribed to the same values and continued to interfere in government decisions (Vacs in Malloy and Seligson, 1987, pp. 31–9). In Brazil, Fleischer asserts that the military 'maintain real power after withdrawal', with control over crucial areas of policy such as the arms industry, much foreign policy and internal security (Fleischer in Drake and Silva, 1986, p. 299). Eight to ten thousand army offers were retained in state posts after the army's formal withdrawal from politics, and in 1985 the government agreed to increase the authorised size of the army from 183,000 to 296,000 and to provide more modern equipment (Skidmore, 1988, pp. 306, 273).

The economic performance of the civilian successors seems little better than that of the military, with continued stagnation in Argentina and inflation reaching 1,000 per cent in Brazil in 1988 (Rocha, 1989, p. 8). Existing inequalities were preserved or increased. The proposed land redistribution in Brazil was modified after opposition from landowners and the military, and after the 1986 election the government reverted to economic orthodoxy (Skidmore, 1988, pp. 300, 308–9). The terms of civilian restoration have so far left little scope for any challenge to entrenched civil or military elites, but one could argue that the new regimes should be judged less by their ability to transform the social or economic order, which they clearly lack the resources to do, and more by their ability to sustain democracy itself.

> Conservative transitions are more durable . . . it is wise to avoid polarisation wherever possible, . . . the left rarely has massive electoral support, and . . . popular groups often value civil liberties and political democracy as much as they prize issues of equity of redistribution. (Levine, 1988, p. 392)

This argument may underestimate the extent to which the rejection of left-wing alternatives is influenced by manipulation of the electoral process, and by actual or implicit military vetoes, but the fact that pluralist democracy has survived, that the torture and arbitrary arrest of citizens has ceased, and that Argentinians in 1989 even enjoyed the rare experience of removing a government by the ballot box, all suggest that durable democratic foundations may have been laid. The long-standing tradition of military intervention, coupled with the parlous economic state of the countries emerging from military rule, may not augur well for democratic development, yet both the harshness and, especially in the Argentina case, incompetence of recent military governments, in comparison with the less oppressive Caudillo regimes of earlier times, may strengthen public determination to cling to the new democratic structures, however inadequate these may be.

The Pluralist Democracy Model

This differs from the military domination model in the extent to which the initial military intervention was designed to protect the military elite and its civilian allies from the imminent threat of electoral defeat by the left, or to reverse an actual defeat by the left, as opposed to merely reinforcing elite domination in the time-honoured manner. If Brazil and South Korea are borderline cases, Chile and Spain are clearer examples of the right restoring power through the might of the army. Such a regime may survive and function effectively for longer than any of our other models, as civilian elites close ranks behind a strong professional army to ward off the threat of their supremacy, but ultimately the regime faces a dilemma. If it presides over a period of economic development, as in Spain and South Korea, new social groups may arise demanding more political participation. Yet if it fails to deliver economic benefits to elites or masses, or to satisfy its military constituents, it has only a limited reservoir of legitimacy on which to draw, having already alienated the substantial proportion of the population which favoured a left-of-centre government. The military government in thus in a much weaker position than in the military domination model when it comes to negotiating the terms of disengagement, and the commitment of much of the population to democratic civilian government will reduce the scope for any subsequent military veto. Parties on the extreme right will be weakened because of their association with the previous military government and its policies, while those on the extreme left will be weakened by voters' fears (whether unfounded or not) or provoking a military backlash. Such a situation may set the scene for democratic competition between moderate parties. But the foundations for democracy, or potential democracy, are based on something more than the impact of soldiers on voting behaviour.

> Countries that have had relatively stable authoritarian rule (such as Spain and Portugal) are more likely to evolve into relatively stable democracies than countries that have regularly oscillated between despotism and democracy (such as Peru, Ecuador, Bolivia, Argentina, Ghana and Nigeria). In the latter, neither democracy nor authoritarian norms have deep roots among the political elites, while in the former a broad consensus accepting authoritarian norms is displaced by broad consensus on or acceptance of democratic ones. (Huntington, 1984, p. 210)

This is to describe rather than to explain. If the prospects for democratic development are greater in Spain, or eventually Chile, than in Argentina, might this have something to do with the strength of the state, not merely as an instrument for coercion but as a focus of legitimacy and loyalty, and as a relatively effective distributor of resources which can be used to reward friends and punish foes? This might seem to conflict with the emphasis in much American literature, including Huntington's, on the requirement for democracy of strong, autonomous groups to limit the power of the state (Huntington, 1984, pp. 204–5). This may have been the pattern of democratic development in the United States, but one could argue that in countries such as France, Germany and Austria, democracy was helped by the existence of a strong state which could disarm groups that threatened democracy: one could contrast the strength of the state in the Federal German Republic with its weakness in the Weimar Republic. In post-military countries, the weakness of the state in El Salvador and Guatemala, where it cannot effectively contain violence, control the army or check the excessive power and wealth of civilian elites, has done little to foster democracy, compared with the relatively strong states in Spain or even Brazil. This is not to advocate an all-powerful state subject to no checks and balances, but to suggest that we need to consider not just the dimension of strength and weakness in the state, but the extent to which there are rules and conventions about the ways in which its powers should be used. A state which can effectively suppress opposition and protect the wealthy today, without losing control to a megalomaniac dictator such as Hitler or Amin, may be equally effective in conducting free elections or distributing welfare benefits tomorrow, whereas a ramshackle arbitrary dictatorship may give way to a ramshackle civilian regime in which power derived from wealth and guns cannot be checked by power derived from votes.

This still leaves us with the question of why some countries evolve rules and conventions about using the power of the state for democratic ends. We shall return to this point in more detail later, but we may speculate here that it has something to do with the fact that countries approximating to this model either have a richer previous history of pluralist competition (Spain, Brazil) than countries in the military domination, civilian populist and unstable models, or that they have achieved the sort of economic development which helps (but does not guarantee) such competition (South Korea).

The small number of countries graduating unambigiously from military government to liberal democratic competition, and their brief life in it so far, makes any generalisation about their performance difficult. Spain made considerable progress towards greater social equality in its early post-Franco years. Parties on the extreme right wanting to continue the Franco tradition were shown to have little electoral support. Barnes *et al.* suggest that conservative organisations had traditionally operated through personalised systems using local notables and brokers. In the Spain of the 1970s and 1980s they lacked skill in using the media, and had no focus for unity, especially as the church had moved to a more liberal position (1986, pp. 64–5). The moderate right-wing government of Suarez taxed wealth more heavily, ended much of the tax evasion of the middle and upper classes, and used the revenue for public works and social security to alleviate unemployment. It made a 'social pact' with the trade unions in return for wage restraint (Meisler, 1977, p. 206). A less formal pact was also made with the military. The army was modernised and promotion procedures were revised, and it was given a more positive role within Nato. This, acccording to Heywood, contributed to the effective elimination of 'the army's obsessive interest and interference in domestic politics' (1987, pp. 397–8).

Much of this might, however, be seen as a process of catching up with the rest of Western Europe rather than a reaction against the previous authoritarianism. The subsequent ability of the electorate to replace the moderate conservative government with a socialist one without any serious attempt by the military establishment to stand in their way (despite one abortive coup attempt which appeared to have little support from the top), suggested that Spain was evolving a political system not so very different from other Western European democracies, most of which had themselves shown their resilience after periods of fascist rule or enemy occupation. The socialist government pursued policies which were not always to the liking of socialist purists with regard to monetarism, privatisation and unemployment, but these might be seen as responses to the economic problems of contemporary Europe rather than any shadow of Francoism.

Of the other countries approximating to the pluralist demcoracy model, South Korea's experience has been too brief for adequate analysis, although a non-democratic tradition seems to have survived both in the violent ways in which protests are articulated and in the ways in which the government responds to them. Yet Han notes that experience of oppression helped to unite opposition to the military government (Han in Diamond *et al.*, 1989, p. 292) and this negative factor may strengthen the determination to preserve the democratic alternative. In Brazil any progress towards instigating liberal democracy owes more to public attitudes than economic preconditions. We have noted that little progress has been made towards greater equality, and the 'top-down' tradition of institutional development leaves the country with an unstable party system in which the ruling party is said to be more of a broad electoral front than a united party (Cammack in Randall, 1988, pp. 131–3), yet optimistic observers see a determination, as in South Korea, to maintain pluralist democracy, if only because of the experience of harsh authoritarianism. Cammack suggests that a long battle against dictatorship had made democracy a popular demand (Randall, 1988, pp. 131–3), and Skidmore sees a broad consensus stretching from the military to the left which is willing to accept bourgeois democracy (1988, p. 310). These limited examples, and the so far untested case of Chile, might suggest that right-wing military government functions as a form of purgatory through which some countries have to pass before reaching the relatively stable condition of pluralist democracy. In the European context, and including Spain and Greece, Huntington suggests a 'dialectical model'.

> The development of a middle class leads to increased pressures on the existing authoritarian regimes for expanded participation and constestation. At some point, there is a sharp break, perhaps in the form of what I have elsewhere called the 'urban breakthrough', the overthrow of the existing authoritarian regime, and the installation of a democratic one. The regime, however, finds it difficult or impossible to govern effectively. A sharp reaction occurs with the overthrow of the democratic system and the installation of a (usually right-wing) authoritarian regime. In due course, however, this regime collapses and a transition is made to a more stable, more balanced, and longer-lasting democratic system. (Huntington, 1984, pp. 210–1)

This does not explain why the democratic outcome should ensue, or why the first attempt at democracy should fail, but one might infer an element of trial and error, in which the initial democratic experiment is undervalued and discarded in favour of an authoritarianism which promises to give greater stability (through military government in Spain and Brazil, and civilian fascism in Germany, Austria and Italy). The oft-expressed belief that a mild dictatorship would resolve many problems ('At least Hitler made the trains run on time') becomes discredited with a realisation that one cannot control the mildness or otherwise of dictatorships, and that the harshness deemed necessary by rulers to suppress or control mass movements creates a form of government which people are determined not to endure again. This determination, as much as socioeconomic developments or pacts between elites, may be the key element in explaining why the strongest right-wing military governments are followed by long-lived democracy. How such democracy will compare with that in northern Europe and Anglo-Saxon countries which have not followed the 'military route', but have evolved through elites coming to terms with one another and then broadening political participation, it is too early to say. However, a major question must be the extent to which memories of the previous authoritarianism and the consequent determination to avoid its return remain significant, especially if the underlying economic conditions (as in Brazil) or the underlying political culture (as in South Korea) offer little reinforcement to democracy.

The Civilian Populist Model

This model is largely outside the scope of the present study because the right-wing military government at the centre of it is of a type not commonly found today. A coup takes place in an economically backward country, if only because that is the easiest way of removing a government, and a military leader subsequently emerges as an autocrat, increasingly remote from the army and relying largely on a personal military bodyguard. Few rulers today would rely on such a precarious power base, with the support of neither the army as a whole nor a tailor-made political party, and with the risk of both a military revolt and a popular uprising. Where they have relied on such a structure in the past, as in Cuba and Nicaragua, their rule has been characterised by corruption, social inequality, brutality and lack of economic development. This ultimately gives rise to a civilian revolt, a radical coup or a combination of the two, and the installation of a populist left-wing civilian government. The desire for pluralist democracy may be as great as in Brazil or Spain, but the economic base is weaker and the presence of counter-revolutionaries may require, or be used to justify, restrictions on political competition and civil liberties.

The Unstable Model

Here military intervention is a symptom of political instability rather than merely an attempt by one elite to displace another. Within this category military intervention may be a response to two different sets of circumstances. Firstly, the military may intervene because an embryonic pluralist system cannot cope adequately with the consequences of early industrialisation and urbanisation, and civilian elites have not built up reserves of legitimacy, in the absence of any long-standing aristocratic tradition (Bolivia and much of Central America). Secondly, the military may be less concerned with rescuing a civilian elite as its main objective, and more with meeting threats to public order, or even national unity and survival, in a newly independent country (Indonesia, Pakistan), or a country with a long history of national independence and unity facing demands for wider political participation as it undergoes the early stages of urbanisation (Thailand, Turkey). In all these cases, the capacity of the military to resolve these political problems is little greater than that of civilians. Their failure leads to demands for civilian restoration, both from civilians who have been deprived of the fruits of office and from soldiers who fear for the unity of the army. Civilian succession thus involves bargaining between soldiers and civilians who are both in weak positions, and any military disengagement is likely to be only partial, with the retention of an extensive military veto, as in Central America and Pakistan, or extensive military penetration of civil institutions, including the legislature and the executive, as in Thailand. The prevailing political culture, and the low level of socioeconomic development, make it difficult to sustain pluralist democracy (unless external pressures intervene to underwrite it, as in Turkey), quite apart from the ability of soldiers to ensure that elections are fixed to prevent the emergence of a government which deviates too far from the status quo.

In these countries the impact of right-wing military government on subsequent political development stands out particularly sharply. Why is the political environment different in Pakistan than in India, in Thailand than in Burma, in El Salvador and Guatemala than in Cost Rica and Nicaragua? We have argued that military intervention was a symptom of instability, but there is nothing inevitable about its timing, its form or even its occurrence, which may depend on such unpredictable factors as the preferences, behaviour and competence of soldiers, and the attitudes of foreign powers. Soldiers who become personal rulers divorced from the army may, as we have just seen, be succeeded by populist civilian governments, whereas military men who rely more on the army as a power base will have more control over the process of succession and over the subsequent government. The ability of the army to retain some semblance of unity and professionalism in a society where there are few widely accepted norms for the regulation of political conflict, and where elites are desperate to retain the support of the military to preserve their wealth and privileges, ensures that the civilian successor will display clearly the marks of its parentage.

It is difficult to find much literature in praise of civilian governments in our unstable countries, whether in terms of economic achievement, social justice or democratic development. Some have reduced three-digit inflation to two digits, but few have achieved any significant economic growth, and most have increased social inequality. In Pakistan the army has continued to secure a large share of the budget, while a quarter of the population remain unemployed, and businessmen and landowners resist any modestly redistributive taxation (Brown, 1989, p. 23). In Bolivia real wages in 1989 were a third lower than in 1985, and large numbers of public sector workers became unemployed as a result of monetarist policies (Reid, 1989, p. 6); and in El Salvador the moderate reforms attempted by the Christian Democrats came to little in the face of military pressure and a hostile economic climate. Real wages fell, unemployment soared and land reforms were resisted by civilian elites (Karl, 1985, pp. 317–26; Karl in Drake and Silva, 1986, pp. 29–36). Civil wars in Central America, and the insistence of the Pakistan military on involvement in the Afghan civil war, drained these countries' resources still further.

Until recently it was also fashionable to argue that civilian government had done little to enhance democratic choice. Thailand is a special case, in that a less polarised society than in Central America facilitated relatively free elections with minimal risks to civil or military elites, but armies in Guatemala and Honduras have ensured that left-of-centre parties will have no chance of success. Civilian rule in Bolivia and El Salvador has endured long enough for incumbent governments to be removed by competitive elections — a test frequently applied to establish the strength of democracy — though in each case the new government has been further to the right than its predecessor, and has thus posed no threat to the military. Did these elections represent a consolidation of democracy, however much liberals might deplore the choice the voters made, or was it a matter of merely allowing people to make a selection from the limited menu permitted by the military? In El Salvador the unwillingness of the Christian Democratic government, under pressure from the military, to negotiate with the guerrillas, had the effect of excluding a substantial proportion of the population (mainly the poorest) from electoral participation in 1989, and this deprived the left of even an opportunity to use the balance of power to support the Christian Democrats against the far right. But this is part of the rough justice of Central American politics, and it seems that it was the Arena Party's promise of order, rather than any massive electoral fraud, that enabled it to win the vote. In Bolivia, too, right-wing policies which increased unemployment and social inequality, but achieved a degree of economic stability, received electoral endorsement in 1989 (Gott, 1989, p. 13). One can again speculate on the extent to which fears of military re-intervention or manipulation by civilian elites deterred potential left-wing voters, as they may do in many parts of the world, but it may also be true that there is only a limited belief in the practicability and desirability of left-wing policies. In Latin America, as in much of Western Europe and Australasia, belief in the virtues of centralised planning and state ownership has waned in the light of experience: 'It seems likely that the ideologists of neo-liberalism will fill the vacuum . . . The overwhelming state power once available to be seized by the military now looks to be a thing of the past' (Gott, 1989, p. 13).

It would require a separate study to explain this decline of socialism, or even Peronism in its original form. Here we merely note that although the pressures which constrain left-wing parties are greater in Central America, Bolivia, Pakistan and Thailand than in most of the world, we should not dismiss the significance of relatively free competitive elections, some of which have produced peaceful changes of government. Whether such political competition eventually contributes to equality, social justice or the relief of poverty depends on a variety of economic, social, political, military and external imponderables, but it may be regarded as vastly perferable to the military repression which preceded it. Of more immediate concern is whether even the present fragile civilian structures can survive. Apart from the possibly greater reluctance of the United States to support a coup, little has changed in these countries to make further military intervention more difficult. Civilian regimes still lack secure legitimate bases, and it may be fear of the heavy governmental burden which soldiers would have to shoulder, if they returned to power, rather than fear of civilian power or respect for the democratic process, which has so far kept them back in barracks.

The Societal Model

In contrast to the unstable model, civilian governments emerging through the societal model owe little to their military antecedents. Greece and Uruguay are the most obvious examples, where there was a long history of pluralist politics in relatively developed countries, and where the military intervened to forestall a perceived left-wing threat, even though such a 'threat' seemed capable of resolution by the normal democratic process. These were not highly polarised societies like Chile, Argentina, or even Brazil, where military intervention might be justified on the grounds that major political groupings were not operating, or might not operate, within the democratic arena, even though the Tupamaros in Uruguay posed a more serious threat than the smaller terrorist groups found in Western Europe.

The military were not greeted by civilian elites as saviours, but treated as usurpers. They were not able to build any effective bases of support, and had difficulty in imposing their will. Isolated from most of civil society and ineffective as rulers lacking legitimacy, they were eventually forced to disengage on terms favourable to the pre-coup politicians, who were still seen as the rightful heirs. In Uruguay politics soon returned to the pre-coup pattern, with the scene dominated by the same parties. In Greece the contrast between pre- and post-military politics was greater, but this owed more to long-term social changes than to anything the military had done. By the late 1970s the domination of parliament by elites from the older professions had been replaced by groups such as engineers, teachers and white-collar salaried workers, and party networks controlled by clientelistic figures have been superseded by a centralised, populist ruling socialist party (Mowzelis in Featherstone and Katsoudas, 1987, pp. 271–87). The military rulers had been unpopular and generally incompetent, and their abortive invasion of Cyprus finally destroyed them as even the military constituency turned against them. Once civilian rule returned, the military were in no position to exercise a veto power or to threaten re-intervention (Veremis, ibid., p. 225), though, like the Uruguayan military rulers, they did manage to escape punishment for most of their misdeeds.

At the most, military intervention in countries of this sort might serve as a warning to civilian politicians that undue neglect of problems perceived as important by the military, such as terrorist or communist threats, or economic decline, might lead to the suspension of democracy, but it is difficult to envisage re-intervention except in the event of a crisis so deep that politicians would be in no position to respond to such warnings. From a long-term perspective, the impact of military intervention on political development may be no greater than that of a brief period of enemy occupation.

The Search for Democracy

Implicit in much of this chapter is a search for theoretical explanations about why pluralist democracy has taken root in some countries, and about the prospects for democracy in others. There is no shortage of general explanations of the preconditions for democracy. These include adequate socioeconomic development (Lipset, 1959, pp. 69–105); compromises between elites, subsequently extended to the masses, about the conditions under which they compete for power (Huntington, 1984, pp. 212–13; Rustow in Lewis and Potter, 1973, p. 122), and the refusal of powerful foreign backers to tolerate undemocratic behaviour (Levine, 1988, p. 392). What is lacking in much of the literature is a distinction between historical cases in which democracy evolved as an unknown quantity, and current ones in which it is a known model that political actors may or may not attempt to emulate. Political actors in Britain in 1832 had no way of knowing that their behaviour might ultimately produce a system in which a cabinet was answerable to a mass electorate via an elaborate system of parties, pressure groups and bureaucracies, whereas political actors in present-day El Salvador or Pakistan have some awareness that some actions may contribute to institutionalised political competition while others may lead to greater authoritarianism or disorder, even if they cannot always be sure of precisely which actions will produce which results.

We can acknowledge that there are certain minimal conditions without which democracy is unlikely to flourish. These include adequate levels of per capita income, literacy and urbanisation (lacking in tropical Africa), some tradition of toleration of the cultures and ideologies of groups other than one's own (lacking in much of the Middle East) and freedom from external powers strong enough to impose authoritarian rule directly or by proxy (much of Central America and Eastern Europe, at least until recently), but beyond these minima much depends on the will of political actors at both elite and mass levels. A relatively developed country such as Chile was plunged into a long period of authoritarian rule largely because the most significant political actors were willing to allow democracy to be jettisoned as a means of ending a political crisis and toppling a Marxist government, whereas people in less developed countries such as Turkey have shown a greater determination to preserve or restore some form of democratic competition. One can argue that variables such as relative cultural homogeneity or the absence of forces making for extreme political pluralism may help, but they are not essential preconditions — democracy has survived in Italy, despite considerable electoral support for 'extremists'. Much of the literature we have reviewed suggests that the will to make pluralist democracy work can be explained in terms of the unattractiveness of the limited range of alternatives. Unlike our ancestors, who might have contemplated various forms of aristocratic or oligarchic rule, and who had no comprehension of the feasibility or likely outcome of government based on universal suffrage and competing mass parties, political actors in countries emerging from military government today know that pluralist democracy has worked in other parts of the world, and sometimes in their own countries, with varying degrees of success. They also know that in the absence of any monarchy or aristocracy with its own power base, the main alternatives are either the sort of populist authoritariansm practised in Cuba or a reversion to authoritarianism under the military, and it is especially the unattractiveness of the latter alternative that may strengthen the resolve to 'make democracy work'. It is generally acknowledged that recent right-wing military governments have been much harsher, in terms both of the sort of brutality they have employed and of the extent to which they have penetrated a wider society, than the Caudillo-type regimes of the nineteenth and earlier twentieth centuries, partly on account of the greater public resistance, actual and potential, of a more urbanised, educated and articulate population, and partly on account of the facilities offered by modern technology and weaponry. An ineffective man on horseback might have been an acceptable alternative to the risky venture of pluralist democracy, whereas a government terrorising millions on citizens was not, especially when such a government could not even deliver benefits such as stability and economic development as substitutes for democratic partici- pation and individual liberty. In Latin America, Malloy claims, all sections of society have learnt that the best way to further their interests is 'through regular and predictable participation in central decision-making' (Malloy and Seligson, 1987, p. 248), and we noted Levine's argument that democracy is the product of mass demands, and not merely the outcome of elite compromises (1988, p. 385). In countries as far apart as Brazil and South Korea, we have noted, there is a widespread preference for democracy in the light of recent experience of authoritarianism, and Rustow praises the maturity of the Turkish electorate, the resourcefulness of its economic and political leadership, and the generals' readiness to bow to the voters' verdict, all of which are said to make further military intervention unlikely (Rustow in Heper and Evin, 1988, p. 243).

All this suggests that we need to emphasise behavioural, as well as social, economic, cultural and external explanations of democracy. Social, economic and cultural conditions have not changed appreciably over the past decade in the countries we have studied, yet most of them have discarded right-wing military government and many have changed their governments, or chosen rulers not favoured by the military, through the medium of competitive elections. The fact that the military have not so far arrested this process, and that relatively few civilian elites have urged them to do so, points to a shared belief that pluralist democracy offers a better form of government than any conceivable alternative. Such a preference does not ensure that triumph of democracy, as we have seen in Central America, but in many cases it has so far tipped the balance in its favour.

10 Conclusion

Our search for right-wing military governments, and for explanations of their emergence, nature and, in some cases, disappearance, has taken us to a variety of lands. There are many who would have doubts about the utility of such a search. Can we make any useful distinction between governments consisting largely of soldiers and dependent on the army as their main power base, and governments, whether headed by military men or not, which rely heavily on force rather than power? And even if we can, is it useful to pick out and compare a variety of military governments which are classified as 'right-wing' according to certain specified criteria, when they rule over countries so diverse in history, culture and economic development? If one put all the heads of communist states in the same room, or all the heads of governments in countries with free competitive elections, or even all the heads of left-wing military government, one might find that, for all their differences, the occupants of each room would have certain common conceptions as to how society should be ordered. If one put all the heads of right-wing military governments in the same room, such a consensus might be much more difficult, if not impossible to arrive at. They would be frightened of socialism and communism, and of mass movements demanding greater social equality or popular participation, and would dislike foreign powers which sought to promote such development in their own countries. They would generally be suspicious of interventionist economic policies which were seen to channel resources away from the army to provide increased employment for the feckless, and would be doubtful, especially in the short term, of the ability of the civilian political process to arrest the policies they disliked. But this is essentially a negative consensus. When it comes to positive policies to be pursued, the alliances to be forged with different civilian groups or the political structures to be created or dismantled, there is no discernible underlying philosophy, nor even a clear set of useful precedents, since the nature and magnitude of different perceived threats, or policies requiring reversal, will vary between different times and places, as will the quality and quantity of resources and potential allies required to achieve new goals. In searching for tenuous links between Greece and Guatemala, South Korea and El Salvador, or Thailand and Uruguay, are we merely using 'right-wing military government' as a residual category, outside the spheres of liberal democracy, communism, revolutionary populism and autocracy, or is it a conceptually useful category because it tells us something useful about an experience common to countries which encounter particular social, economic, cultural or political conditions, and which then attempt to resolve their problems in a limited number of discernible ways?

I discussed the value of the concept of military government at the outset of this study and will not labour the point much further. While conceding that many governments rely on force rather than consent without necessarily being presided over by military men, and that many governments which are led by soldiers will enlist the support and participation of civil personnel and institutions, it still seems useful to treat governments which use the army as their primary power base as different from those relying mainly on elections, single-party hegemony, charisma or divine right. The military power base is significant because it provides a sharp short-term instrument for capturing power and enforcing authority, but frequently becomes a long-term liability as soldiers outside the government see no legitimate objection to using the same unconstitutional methods as their superiors to take (or threaten to take) power. The questions of what sort of alternative power bases should be developed in civil society, without driving the military leaders into an undue surrender of power, and of what sort of polity is acceptable in the long run if military rule eventually becomes unsustainable (as it generally does), become paramount. These are questions which do not exercise the minds of rulers of liberal democracies, communist states, absolute monarchies, or even civilian autocracies, in the same way. The question of whether 'right-wing' military governments require a special study is more difficult to answer. We can concede that they are recognisable more by their negative features than their positive, and that they are diverse in both the settings in which they flourish and the policies they pursue, yet they can be seen as a response to certain conditions which are common across many apparently different societies.

We have seen that military government in general, as opposed to rule by retired army officers who had initially taken power through *coups d'état,* is essentially a phenomenon of the second half of the twentieth century, facilitated by the ending of colonial rule and influence, which would previously have put down any army uprising, or by conflicts in society which cannot be resolved by all-out revolution or the co-option of new groups into a pluralist political process. Where the colonial retreat exposes a semi-feudal society, as in much of the Middle East, any military intervention is likely to be by left-wing armies which represent the 'modern' sectors of society against the old aristocracy. Where there is no powerful entrenched aristocracy but only embryonic business, professional and bureaucratic elites nurtured by the colonial power and enjoying little legitimacy after its departure, as in much of tropical Africa, and where economic development has been insufficient to produce a large articulate working class, military intervention generally takes the form of conflicts within and between elites, without attempting to make radical changes to the left or the right. I suggested in Table 1.1 that right-wing military intervention is more likely to occur when the level of economic development is higher, and mass movements in the growing urban and industrial sectors begin to make demands for a greater share of political power and economic wealth than ruling elites are able or willing to concede. Such a situation does not make military intervention either inevitable or necessarily right-wing, but there are plausible reasons why army officers, as members of a relatively wealthy elite group and with notions of responsibility for maintaining order, might install right-wing governments, quite apart from any external pressures which might push them in that direction. Such a scenario would fit much of Latin America and South Korea, and possibly Thailand, and might suggest that we can locate right-wing military government neatly somewhere along a developmental continuum. But this would omit Greece, which was much more developed when the military took power, and Pakistan and Indonesia which were much more backward. By placing the emphasis on variables in socioeconomic development, it ignores significant differences in political development. Turkey and Thailand both had long histories as independent kingdoms in which elites enjoyed a legitimacy that did not require constant military protection, in contrast to Latin America where authority depended heavily on military support, whereas Indonesia and Pakistan had not had any experience of handling the problems of political succession when the military first intervened, and there was therefore little consensus on who had the right to rule or on the way in which they should obtain it. Military intervention in these Asian countries has to be explained less in terms of some 'crisis of participation' or 'crisis of distribution' in which the rising masses were confronting capitalist elites, and more in terms of attempts to restore or impose order, which was being undermined either because no consensus on the regulation of political conflict had yet evolved (Indonesia and Pakistan) or because the existing consensus was too inflexible to adapt to changing conditions (Turkey). While the Asian military governments are (or were) less unambiguously right-wing than those in much of Latin America, I argue that the emphasis on 'order', which is likely to freeze existing inequalities without any notion of removing the causes of discontent by removing existing elites, places them in the right-wing camp.

Yet we appear to end up with two different types of right-wing military government which have come to power for different reasons in completely different circumstances, and we have still to justify bringing such groups together in one study. The main justification is that even though the countries have diverse backgrounds, their experience of right-wing military government gives them certain common features and problems. Even when the problems diverge, the divergence is not necessarily along the lines of 'Latin America versus the rest'. Thus the organisation of military government in Pakistan has, in many ways, more in common with Chile and Uruguay than Indonesia, and the dilemma of finding an acceptable civilian successor makes Indonesia closer to Chile than Thailand or Turkey.

Having established that certain socioeconomic or political conditions are particularly favourable to right-wing military intervention, we try to avoid getting caught in any determinist trap which implies that particular combinations of circumstances make intervention inevitable. Singapore, Malaysia and Taiwan have survived under the rule of a dominant civilian party. Italy has avoided the fate of Greece and Spain, and many of those Latin American countries which have experienced military intervention have been ruled by soldiers of less conservative persuasions than those of El Salvador,

Brazil and the Southern Cone. Yet the combination of early industrialisation, with the concomitant growth of literacy and urbanisation, and the existence of political structures such as mass parties, pressure groups and elections by universal suffrage, which were non-existent or much less significant when Western Europe and North America underwent comparable economic development, is an explosive combination. We questioned the adequacy of the bureaucratic authoritarian model, with its primarily economic emphasis on the coalition of indigenous and foreign capital and the military suppressing mass demands in order to promote advanced industrialisation, on the grounds that it is too rigid in both its description of economic circumstances and in the ways in which the various actors responded. Neither do explanations related to levels of political culture tell the whole story, since military intervention has extended to countries with 'high' political cultures such as Chile and Uruguay, while leaving many poorer countries unscathed. But if one brings together the social changes wrought by economic development and opportunities which political structures, largely copied from First World countries, furnish for articulating mass demands for more political power and material wealth, then existing elites can be seen to be facing a powerful challenge, especially when these elites have never enjoyed the deep-rooted legitimacy that European aristocracies enjoyed when they faced the first stirrings of industrialisation. To speak of a legitimacy crisis would be inaccurate, since Latin American governments from independence onwards have enjoyed only limited legitimacy, and political succession has frequently been resolved through violence, but the earlier conflicts were intra-elite conflicts rather than responses to actual or perceived challenges by the masses. Over the past thirty years fear of left-wing electoral victories, or the desire to reverse actual victories, has left elites with little hope unless they could enlist the support of the military. But even if we accept that the gulf between the elite and the masses is so wide, and the consensus on how political conflict should be resolved and how resources should be distributed so limited, that peaceful resolution is difficult, why should the military want to become involved, and why on the side of the right wing?

The balance of evidence suggests that soldiers are seldom merely the uniformed arm of a civilian elite. Indeed their quest for resources may make them competitive with such elites, and they may sometimes feel that national unity, generally one of their highest priorities, is best served by attempting to remove the causes of discontent among the poor, as in Peru. But it is more likely that as well-paid members of a disciplined profession, officers will have a greater affinity to civilian elites and will see the rise of mass movements as a threat to order, especially if the officers have been socialised by training under United States auspices. This would explain why the conflicts brought about in South America by the economic and political changes described in this book frequently end in right-wing military government. In Central America, the level of economic development and the degree of military professionalism are generally lower, and there is less guarantee that all soldiers will rally behind right-wing forces. In so far as they do, the explanation has to be sought less in terms of economic change and more in terms of the traditional historical role of soldiers as protectors of plantation owners against the peasants in societies where, again, governments and ruling elites enjoyed little popular legitimacy. As the challenges to authority became more structured than earlier peasant uprisings, and armies became more professional, right-wing military intervention emerged as a more formal continuation of what had gone before.

In Asia, our explanations of right-wing military intervention place more emphasis on the political than the social or economic. Levels of development were lower than in South America at the time of intervention, and there was not the same sharp polarisation between an insecure elite and rising mass movements. It was the inability of civilian governments to resolve political crises, thus threatening order or even the survival of the nation, which provoked military intervention. Preferences for order and national unity are not the exclusive property of conservatives, and the subsequent military governments were less stridently right-wing than those in Latin America, but I argue that they were nonetheless right-wing in that they saw left-wing politicians, sometimes apparently working in alliance with governments in neighbouring communist states as the main threat to order.

From the day a military government comes to power there is a time bomb ticking underneath it called 'illegitimacy'. No matter how economically backward the country nor how apparently indifferent the population to the usurpation of power, there is no reason to expect people to obey rulers who have come to power by force, unless the rulers can either demonstrate that they can serve people's interests better than civilians, or use sufficient force to maintain their position, neither of which is likely in the long run. The crucial question is, then, what sort of power structure can be developed in order to make force or civilian co-operation as effective as possible? I suggested a fourfold typology of right-wing military governments based on the power structure and its relationship with civil society: personal rule, military authoritarianism, civil–military authoritarianism and limited democracy. I suggested that the type of military government adopted would depend on such variables as the nature and extent of pre-coup civil–military relations, the strengths and professionalism of the army, and the strength and power bases of civil institutions. Economic factors are clearly important in that the most economically developed countries will normally have the greatest degree of structural differentiation — hence well-organised political parties, pressure groups and legislatures on one side, and a highly professional army on the other, with the latter needing to develop a highly authoritarian structure to crush its well-organised adversaries, but social, political and military factors may still vary independently of the economic. Turkey and Thailand had developed political institutions which generated widespread public support before the first right-wing military interventions, in a way in which the Central American republics had not; the Turkish and Pakistan armies had developed integral boundaries with civil society in a way that the Thai and Indonesian armies had not, and elite–mass polarisation in Central America was in contrast to the network of cross-cutting social cleavages in Asia.

In looking at countries approximating to each of our four types, we looked at concepts such as 'charismatic authority', 'bureaucratic authoritarianism' and 'corporatism' as possible means of characterising their styles of government, but generally found them unhelpful and too far removed from reality. The basic questions of how effectively and extensively governments rely on terror, and how far they co-opt, delegate power to, or share it with civilians seem more important in attempting to explain the dynamics of military government. Each country has its own individual tale to tell, but the general point emerges that no country experiencing right-wing military government has been transformed in a way comparable with Nasser's Egypt or Gadafi's Libya. Chile achieved substantial socioeconomic restructuring, the Central American governments preserved elites which might otherwise have been swept away, and governments in Pakistan, Indonesia and, to a lesser extent, Turkey restored order in countries where civilian politicians were unable or unwilling to do so. Most of them preserved or extended the degree of social inequality in already unequal societies. In a minority of countries, notably Chile and Argentina, there was a recognisably explicit ideology which encompassed respect for order, discipline and a particular interpretation of Christianity and market forces, but in the majority of countries right-wing policies were more a pragmatic reaction to the circumstances in which the military found themselves, and the sort of civil–military alliances most readily available. There were negative achievements, as befitted governments whose aims could be defined in largely negative terms, such as the prevention of socialism, the arrest of rising mass movements and the restoration of a degree of order in countries facing national disintegration, but in few countries, if any, can we say that right-wing military government has transformed the social, political or economic order. This may be explained partly in terms of the nature of conservatism, but there were generals in Chile, Central America and Pakistan who did have a vision of a more orderly, disciplined, God-fearing society, yet found that political reality stood in their way. The development of a dominant single political party, as in the countries under left-wing military government, might have helped, but this would have implied the mobilisation of groups which the right-wing military preferred to exclude from politics. This brings us to one of the central dilemmas: the desire to pursue changes which are likely to be unpopular with large sections of society, yet the reluctance to use a civilian political process to facilitate the implementation of the changes for fear of the process gathering a momentum of its own, as indeed it did in Brazil, until the military eventually found themselves run over by the juggernaut they had created.

There was also the problem that if, as I have argued, right-wing military intervention is a symptom of certain conflicts in certain types of society which cannot be resolved peacefully or on the basis of consensus, then any incoming military government is also likely to be a prisoner of these circumstances. Thatcher and Reagan achieved remarkable right-wing changes partly because the existing political cultures acknowledged the right of elected governments to carry out controversial policies without the people most adversely affected asserting extra-constitutional resistance, and partly because inequality and unemployment could be increased in the knowledge that there was some sort of safety net to prevent a return of nineteenth-century conditions of poverty. In countries prone to right-wing military intervention, traditions of voluntary obedience to authority are less developed and per capita income is much lower, so that attempts at radical right-wing policies that are likely to cause greater hardship meet with greater resistance, and this requires greater reliance on force, which has only a limited capacity to succeed in the absence of consent.

We may, however, be setting unfairly high targets of achievement. Chile, Guatemala, Pakistan and Indonesia would almost certainly be different countries today in terms of political structure and the distribution of power and wealth, if right-wing soldiers had not intervened, even if their capacity to make positive changes is limited. But have they left any longer-term legacies? If military intervention is precipitated by an unstable political system, does the order imposed by the military provide a foundation for stable democracy? The answer is generally 'no', but it needs to be qualified by examining the balance of power between different forces in society before and after military government.

Right-wing military rulers have fewer objections in principle to withdrawing from politics eventually, compared with those on the left. Apart from a few zealots like General Pinochet, their aims are more modest, and they acknowledge the ultimate goal of pluralist democracy, even if they define the rules of the game to exclude certain adversaries or to avoid certain outcomes. Only rarely will right-wing soldiers seek to perpetuate themselves in power as leaders of single parties, or as heads of revolutionary movements of indefinite duration. Yet the manner in which they have departed from government has varied from transitions in which soldiers have dictated most of the terms, and ensured the retention of a substantial veto power over the successor regime (Turkey), to a hasty surrender in the face of growing unpopularity (Greece). In the former case the assumption among the soldiers is that they have achieved as many of their objectives as they are likely to, in restoring order, curbing left-wing threats, reducing the social functions of the state or rewarding their military constituency. In the latter there is an eventual realisation that their policies are not wanted, and that the degree of repression necessary to impose them is either impracticable or too costly in terms of resources and risks to life and liberty.

We can examine these different circumstances of military withdrawal, and the types of civilian successor they may produce, by looking at such variables as the strength and professionalism of the army and the strength of civil political structures (See Table 8.2). These, in turn, can be related to the circumstances of the initial military intervention and the subsequent development of civil–military relations (See Table 9.1). Our analysis suggested five models of civilian succession. One of these implies a successor regime largely fashioned by the military, two imply succession fashioned largely by civilian initiative, one stalemate and one the irrelevance of military government. The differences are matters of degree, but it is useful to distinguish between cases where soldiers capture power to resolve a political or economic crisis, even though there is little immediate threat from left-wing forces with substantial support (the military domination model), and those where the existence of such forces is a major reason for the initial coup (the pluralist democracy model). The latter type ends in pluralist democracy because civilian resistance is stronger, and the military will be less able to dictate the terms of disengagement, especially if civilian voters show a willingness to shift their allegiance away from parties on the extreme left in return for the restoration of (at least limited) political competition. In the military domination model, in contrast, civilians are not strong enough to exert so much leverage over the terms of succession, and soldiers retain a greater veto power. Fitting countries into these categories is difficult as there is considerable overlap in practice, but one can recognise a more precarious successor regime, subject to greater military veto, in Paraguay, or even Argentina, than in Brazil or South Korea. In some cases, notably Spain and to a lesser extent South Korea, civilian pressure on the military government may grow as a result of major socioeconomic developments during the government's lifetime, with a more literate, urbanised and better organised population refusing to accept autocracy.

We looked briefly at cases where (now largely extinct) personal dictatorships by soldiers who have become detached from the army are overthrown and replaced by populist civilian governments (Cuba and Nicaragua), and then at the 'unstable model' where right-wing military intervention is a symptom of, and is unable to cure, widespread political instability (Central America, Indonesia, Pakistan). The failure of the military to find a cure, and civilian dissatisfaction with such failure, leads to an ending of direct military government, but the civilian successor remains precarious, unable to build a secure base or to resolve the country's intractable problems, and therefore vulnerable to military veto or further military intervention. Finally, we noted the case of relatively developed countries such as Greece and Uruguay where a single military interregnum was an aberration, and had little discernible impact on the political process for good or ill.

What, then, are the long-term legacies of right-wing military government, if any? They are difficult to separate from the legacies of the conditions which precipitated military intervention, including the impact of late industrialisation, poorly supported political structures and the inexperience of newly independent countries in handling political conflict, yet not all countries experiencing such conditions have had right-wing military governments. Our Asian countries offer an obvious contrast, with countries not experiencing military intervention generally developing one-party dominant regimes which are able to fend off opposition with a mixture of patronage and coercion, whereas countries with right-wing military governments have, paradoxically, kept party competition alive. They have realised that the vast majority of the electorate will not vote for a party explicitly supported by the army (if only because this would be seen as too much like a continuation of military government), and have therefore permitted competition between a range of other parties towards which they are largely indifferent. A limited form of party competition may thus ensue, with the power of the ruling party checked by the possibility of re-intervention, but it is a precarious form of pluralism in countries where social, economic and cultural conditions are of limited help in attempting to establish or sustain liberal democracy. There may also be a trade-off between pluralism and a circulation of elites on the one hand, and the violent resolution of conflict on the other. The rulers of Singapore, Malaysia and Taiwan have been difficult to displace through a democratic vote, but their subjects have escaped the widespread violence which has accompanied changes of government in Pakistan, Bangladesh and Indonesia.

In the poorer Latin American countries military government has generally given way to a limited form of pluralism, subject to extensive military veto. The most obvious impact of the military has been to reinforce political polarisation as they have removed, or prevented the election of, social democratic governments and rejected attempts at conciliation with left-wing guerrillas. Violence is not new to these countries but its continuation, and the continued suppression of political movements which seek increased political participation and reduced social inequality, can be explained at least as much in terms of the behaviour of the military as in terms of some inevitable collision of social forces wrought by economic changes. It may be that citizens of these countries will eventually be able to expand the limited choices between parties and policies and to incorporate rebel groups into the democratic process, and that armies that will be kept in check by a United States refusal to support their activities, but such developments would be more of a reflection of the will of civilian political actors than any legacy of military government.

This leaves the more economically developed countries of Latin America, Spain and South Korea. In South Korea the military's favourite won the first post-military presidential election on a minority vote, but in Chile the electorate rejected General Pinochet's offer to serve as a quasi-civilian president, and in most of the other countries voters have elected parties not favoured by the military. Whatever other impact military government had, it did not succeed in socialising people into accepting the political beliefs of soldiers or in strengthening right-wing parties, though it may have frightened some voters away from voting too far to the left for fear of the army overturning the whole pluralist process. Perhaps more important has been the unintended impact of military government in making citizens determined that it will not happen again. Military government in these relatively developed countries has had to be much more brutal, and has had to extend repression over a wider population, in order to crush rising popular movements, than was the case with earlier Caudillo regimes. Faced with a choice between such repression and an imperfect pluralist system which may produce incompetent or corrupt governments, or allow the 'wrong' side to win, citizens have indicated that they would rather take a chance with the latter. This raises questions about the preconditions for democracy and the future prospects for right-wing military government. Much of the literature on the emergence of democracy in the West places the emphasis on adequate socioeconomic development, a willingness of elites to compromise rather than engage in violent conflict, and the emergence of autonomous social groups to impose limits on the power of the state, but the democracy ultimately achieved was not positively sought by the participants, and indeed most were unaware of the existence, or potential future existence, of such a political phenomenon. The countries emerging from right-wing military government today, in contrast, lack many of the social and economic preconditions prescribed in the literature (and have not generally undergone any significant socio-economic changes since the military took over), yet they are aware of the existence of pluralist democracy at other times and places and, for the most part, have a positive desire to achieve it, if only because of th unattractiveness of the alternatives. There may not be the autonomous centres of power to counter the power of the state in South America and South Korea that there were in Western Europe, yet a powerful state can be used to facilitate the distribution of resources chosen by the electorate and to combat anti-democratic forces, just as it was previously used to support military repression.

The right-wing military legacy is thus an unclear one. It has done nothing to strengthen right-wing parties once they are exposed to the winds of competition, but it has not generally led to a reaction causing the overthrow of civilian elites which the military had sustained, still less to any attacks on the resources and privileges of the military. Successor elections have generally produced governments of the moderate right and centre, but it is not clear whether this is due to an implicit military threat to subvert any left-wing government or to the doubts of the voters about the efficacy of socialist policies. Where left-wing governments have been elected it has been in elections subsequent to the successor election, as in Greece and Spain, where the threat of military re-intervention is seen as minimal, or where the reality of a military veto makes the actual implementation of the more radical proclaimed policies unlikely, as in Pakistan. Yet the achievement of pluralist democracy itself is remarkable, even it it does not allow a choice right across the political spectrum, when military governments had previously seemed impregnable in view of their coercive resources, and their support from domestic and international capital, and sometimes foreign powers.

Most of the countries we have studied had experienced some form of pluralism before right-wing military intervention, but often in a form that did not produce competent, stable government, let alone equality or social justice, (though one could, of course, question how far these virtues are present in many Western liberal democracies). There were few civilians in key positions who made much effort to avert military intervention, and many who believed that such intervention would produce material benefits. When military governments proved no more competent and much more repressive than anything people had known before, civilian opinion began to value pluralist democracy much more. Supporters of the democratic ideal might feel that right-wing military governments are now a dying breed because their very success in coercing the population has created a determination to preserve democracy, even if it still produces less than competent governments and does little to alleviate the sufferings of the poor. Here we come back to Huntington's 'dialectical model', with its implication that, as in the former fascist countries of Europe, democracy succeeds at the second attempt after being undervalued the first time. But we are still building on shaky foundations. The social polarisation, the extremes of wealth and poverty and the absence of any elites around which much legitimate support may be generated, remain features of Latin American politics. The lack of experience in operating democratic institutions remains a problem in Pakistan, Indonesia and South Korea. Right-wing military government may have hampered democratic development by maintaining the tradition of using violence rather than elections to dispose of unwanted governments, or it may have helped by giving people a warning of the suffering that may ensue if they fail to resolve their conflicts within the democratic arena, but it has not imposed a new social order or a new way of thinking. Neither have reactions against it been sufficiently united to guarantee that a new social order will emerge in its place. But its fragility, especially in comparison with many of the one-party states of the Third World, has left an opportunity for citizens to seize which might, given the right combination of luck and judgement, allow pluralist democracy to flourish. The legacy is neither a defective political systems unable to function without violence, nor a brand new democratic structure which is bound to flourish because society has got authoritarianism out of its system, but a rough site on which the potential for building a democratic structure exists.

Bibliography

Ahmed, A., 1983. Democracy and dictatorship, in Gardezi and Rashid. pp. 94–147.

Ali, T., 1988. Benazir's legacy, *The Guardian*, 18 November, p. 23.

Ayub Khan, A. 1967 *Friends, Not Masters*, Oxford, Oxford University Press.

Baloyra, E.A. (ed.) 1987. *Comparing New Democracies: Transitions and Consolidation in Mediterranean Europe and the Southern Cone*, Westview Press, Boulder.

Barnes, S.H. McDonough, P. and Pina, A.L., 1986. Volatile parties and stable votes in Spain, *Government and Opposition*, Winter: 56–75.

Bienen, H. and Morrell (eds) 1976. *Political Participation Under Military Regimes*, Sage, London.

Binder, L. *et al.* 1971. *Crises and Sequences in Political Development*, Princeton University Press, Princeton, New Jersey.

Birand, M.A. 1987. *The Generals' Coup in Turkey: an Inside Story of September 12, 1980*, Brassey, London.

Black, G. *et al.* 1984. *Garrison Guatemala*, Monthly Review Press, New York.

Blakemore, H., 1985. Return to barracks: the Chilean case, *Third World Quarterly*, Vol. 7, No. 1 (January): 44–62.

Blakemore, H., 1986. Old soldiers never die: the military in Latin America, *Third World Quarterly*, Vol. 8, No. 3 (July): 1076–82.

Bouzutsky, S.T., 1987. The Pinochet regime: crisis and consolidation, in Malloy and Seligson pp. 67–89.

Brown, D., 1988. Benazir Bhutto advances rule of the dynasties, *The Guardian*, 18 November, p. 9.

Brown, D., 1989. When the sun sets, *The Guardian*, 2 May, p. 23.

Calvert, P., 1985. Demilitarisation in Latin America, *Third World Quarterly*, Vol. 7, No. 1 (January): 31–43.

Cammack, P. 1985. The political economy of contemporary regimes in Latin America: from bureaucratic authoritarianism to restructuring, in O'Brien and Cammack pp. 1–36.

Cammack, P., 1988. Brazilian party politics, 1945–87: continuities and discontinuities, in Randall pp. 113–34.

Chalmers, D.A., 1977. The politicised state in Latin America, in Malloy pp. 38–60.

Chaloemtiarana, T., 1979. *Thailand: The Politics of Despotic Paternalism*, Thammasat University, Social Science Association of Thailand.

Clapham, C., 1988. Epilogue: political succession in the Third World, *Third World Quarterly*, Vol. 10, No. 1: 281–8.

Clapham, C. and Philip, G. 1985. *The Political Dilemmas of Military Regimes*, Croom Helm, London.

Coad, M., 1988. Chile's regime bids farewell to alms, *The Guardian*, 30 September, p. 14.

Cohen, Y., 1987. Democracy from above: the political origins of military dictatorship in Brazil, *World Politics*, Vol. 40, No. 1 (October): 30–54.

Collier, D. (ed.) 1979. *The New Authoritarianism in Latin America*, Princeton University Press, Princeton, New Jersey.

Crouch, H. 1978. *The Army and Politics in Indonesia*, Cornell University Press, London.

Crouch, H., 1988. Indonesia: the rise and fall of Suharto's generals, *Third World Quarterly*, Vol. 10, No. 1 (January): 160–75.

Dallas, R., 1987. Will Latin American democracy last?, *World Today*, April: 70–2.

Danopoulos, C.P., 1980. From military rule to civilian government in contemporary Greece, *Armed Forces and Society*, Vol. 3 (Summer): 614–24.

Danopoulos, C.P., 1983. Military professionalism and regime legitimacy in Greece, *Political Science Quarterly*, Vol. 98, No. 3 (Fall): 485–506.

Danopolous, C.P. (ed.) 1988. *Military Disengagement from Politics*, Routledge, London.

Dekmejian, R.K., 1982. Egypt and Turkey: the military background, in Kolkowicz and Korbonski pp. 29–51.

Delury, G., 1987. *World Encyclopaedia of Political Systems and Parties*, Facts on File Publications, Oxford.

Diamond, L., Linz, J. and Lipset, S.M. (eds) 1988/1989. *Democracy in Developing Countries*, Vol. II, *Africa;* Vol. III, *Asia*, Adamantine Press, London.

Dikerdem, M.A., 1987. Introduction, in Birand, pp. 1–20.

Drake, P.W. and Silva, E. (eds) 1986. *Elections and Democratisation in Latin America*, Centre for Iberian and Latin American Studies, University of California, San Diego.

Dunkerley, J., 1985. Central America: the collapse of the military system, in Clapham and Philip, pp. 171–200.

Dyer, G. and Keegan, J., 1983. Pakistan, in Keegan, pp. 441–56.

Eatwell, R. and O'Sullivan, N., 1990. *The Nature of the Right*, Pinter, London.

Eckstein, H. 1966. *Division and Cohesion in a Democracy: A Study of Norway*, Princeton University Press, Princeton, New Jersey.

Evin, A., 1988. Changing patterns of cleavages before and after 1980, in Heper and Evin, pp. 201–13.

Featherstone, K. and Katsoudas, D.K. (1987). *Political Change in Greece: Before and After the Colonels*, Croom Helm, Beckenham.

Finch, M.J.H., 1985. The military regime and dominant class interests in Uruguay, in O'Brien and Cammack, pp. 89–114.

Finer, S.E. 1962. *The Man on Horseback*, Pall Mall Press, London.

Finer, S.E., 1982. The morphology of military regimes, in Kolkowicz and Korbonski, pp. 281–309.

Finer, S.E., 1985. retreat to barracks: notes on the practice and theory of military withdrawal from seats of power, *Third World Quarterly*, Vol. 7, No. 1 (January): 16–30.

Fleischer, D., 1986. Brazil at the cross-roads: the elections of 1982 and 1985, in Drake and Silva, pp. 299–327.

Gamarra, E.A., 1988. Bolivia: disengagement and democratisation, in Danopoulos, pp. 47–78.

Gardezi, H. and Rashid, J. (eds) 1983. *Pakistan: The Roots of Dictatorship*, Zed Press, London.

Garreton, M.A., 1986. The political evolution of the Chilean regime and the problems of transition to democracy, in O'Donnell *et al.*, pp. 95–122.

Gauhar, A. 1985. Pakistan: Ayub Khan's abdication, *Third World Quarterly*, Vol. 7, No. 5 (January): 102–31.

Gillespie, C., 1986. Uruguay's transition from collegial military–technocratic rule, in O'Donnell *et al.*, pp. 173–95.

Gott, R., 1989. Twilight of the generals, *Guardian*, 12 May. p. 12.

Hale, W., 1988. Transition to civilian governments in Turkey: the military perspective, in Heper and Evin, pp. 159–75.

Han, S-J., 1989. South Korea: politics in transition, in Diamond *et al.*, Vol. III, pp. 267–303.

Handelman, H., 1981. Uruguay: military authoritarianism and political change, in Handelman and Sanders, pp. 215–36.

Handelman, H., 1986. Prelude to elections: the military government's legitimacy crisis and the 1980 constitutional plebiscite in Uruguay, in Drake and Silva, pp. 201–14.

Handelman, H. and Sanders, T. (eds) 1981. *Military Government and the Movement Toward Democracy in South America*, Indiana University Press, Bloomington.

Handy, J. 1984. *Gift of the Devil*, Between the Lines, Toronto.

Harris, G.S., 1988. The role of the military in Turkey in the 1980s: guardians or decision-makers?, in Heper and Evin, pp. 177–200.

Heper, M. and Evin, A. (eds) 1988. *State, Democracy and the Military in Turkey in the 1980s*, de Gruyter, New York.

Heywood, R., 1987. Spain: 10 June 1987, *Government and Opposition*, Vol. 22, No. 4 (Winter): 397–8.

Hoadley, J.S. 1975. *Soldiers and Politics in South East Asia: Civil–Military Relations in Comparative Perspective*, Schnenkman, Cambridge.

Hojman, D.E. (ed.) 1985. *Chile after 1973: Elements for the Analysis of Military Rule*, Centre for Latin American Studies, University of Liverpool, Liverpool.

Huntington, S.P. 1968. *Political Order in Changing Societies*, Yale University Press, New Haven, Connecticut.

Huntington, S.P., 1984. Will more countries become more democratic?, *Political Science Quarterly*, Vol. 99, No. 2 (Summer): 193–218.

Huntington, S.P. and Nelson, J.M. 1976. *No Easy Choice: Political Participation in Developing Countries*, Harvard University Press, Cambridge, Massachusetts.

Im, H.B., 1987. The rise of bureaucratic authoritarianism in South Korea, *World Politics*, Vol. 39, No. 2 (January): 231–57.

Kahane, R., 1976. The problem of institutionalisation of military government: the case of Indonesia 1965–74, in Schriffrin, pp. 229–57.

Karakartal, B., 1985. Turkey: the army as guardian in the political order, in Clapham and Philip, pp. 46–63.

Karl, T.C., 1985. After La Palma: the prospects for democracy in El Salvador, *World Policy*, Vol. 2, No. 2: 305–30.

Karl, T.C., 1986. Imposing consent: electoralism versus democratisation in El Salvador, in Drake and Silva, pp. 9–36.

Karpat, K.H., 1988. Military interventions: army and civil–military relations in Turkey before and after 1980, in Heper and Evin, pp. 137–58.

Keegan, J. (ed.) 1983. *World Armies,* Macmillan, London.

Kim, C.E., 1976. Transition from military rule: the case of South Korea, in Bienen and Morrell, pp. 24–38.

Kim, S-J. 1971. *The Politics of Military Rule in Korea,* University of North Carolina Press, Chapel Hill, North Carolina.

Kolkowicz, R. and Korbonski, A. (eds) 1982. *Soldiers, Peasants and Bureaucrats,* Allen and Unwin, London.

Levine, D.H., 1988. Paradigm lost: dependence to democracy, *World Politics*, Vol. 40, No. 3 (April): 377–94.

Lewis, P.H. 1980. *Paraguay under Stroessner,* University of North Carolina Press, Chapel Hill, North Carolina.

Lewis, P.G. and Potter, D.C. (eds) 1973. *The Practice of Comparative Politics,* Longman, Harlow.

Linz, J.J. and Stepan, A. (eds) 1978. *The Breakdown of Democratic Regimes,* Johns Hopkins University Press, Baltimore, Maryland.

Lipset, S.M., 1959. Some social requisites for democracy: economic development and political legitimacy, *American Political Science Review*, Vol. 53, No. 1 (March): 69–105.

Lissak, M. 1976. The politics of military intervention in Burma and Thailand: two prototypes, in Schriffrin, pp. 151–75.

Loveman, B., 1988. Government and regime succession in Chile, *Third World Quarterly*, Vol. 10, No. 1 (January): 260–81.

Luckman, A.R., 1971. A comparative typology of civil–military relations, *Government and Opposition*, Winter: 8–34.

Mainwaring, S., 1988. Political parties and democratisation in Brazil and the Southern Cone, *Comparative Politics*, October: 91–120.

Makin, G., 1984. The Argentine process of demilitarisation: 1980–83, *Government and Opposition*, Vol. 19, No. 2: 225–38.

Malloy, J. (ed.) 1977. *Authoritarianism and Corporatism in Latin America,* University of Pittsburgh Press, Pittsburgh, Pennsylvania.

Malloy, J.M., 1987. The politics of transition in Latin America, in Malloy and Seligson, pp. 235–58.

Malloy, J.A. and Gamarra, E.A., 1987. The transition to democracy in Bolivia, in Malloy and Seligson, pp. 93–120.

Malloy, J.M. and Seligson, M.A. (eds) 1987. *Authoritarians and Democrats: Regime Transition in Latin America,* University of Pittsburgh Press, Pittsburgh, Pennsylvania.

Maniruzzaman, T. 1971. Crisis in 'political development' and the collapse of the Ayub regime in Pakistan, *Journal of Developing Areas,* Vol. 5, No. 2 (January): 221–38.

Marks, T.A., 1980. October 1976 and the role of the military in Thai politics, *Modern Asian Studies,* Vol. 14, No. 4: 603–44.

Mazzella, F., 1988. Guatemala: the politics of military withdrawal in a polarised society, in Danopoulos, pp. 139–76.

McDonald, R.H., 1975, the rise of military politics in Uruguay, *Inter-American Economic Affairs,* Vol. 28 (Spring): 25–43.

McDonald, R.H., 1985. Confrontation and transition in Uruguay, *Current History,* February: 57–88.

McDonald, H. 1980. *Suharto's Indonesia,* Fontana, London.

MacDougall, J., 1982. Patterns of military control in the Indonesian higher central bureaucracy, *Indonesia,* Vol. 33 (April): 89–121.

McKinlay, R.D. and Cohen, A.S., 1975. A comparative analysis of the political and economic performance of military and civilian regimes: a cross-national aggregate study, *Comparative Politics,* Vol. 8, No. 1: 1–30.

McVey, R.M., 1971. The post-revolutionary transformation of the Indonesian army, Part I, *Indonesia,* Vol. 1 (April): 131–75.

McVey, R.M., 1972. The post-revolutionary transformation of the Indonesian army, Part II, *Indonesia,* Vol. 2 (April): 147–81.

Meisler, S., 1977. Spain's new democracy, *Foreign Affairs,* Vol. 56, No. 1: 190–202.

Millett, R.L., 1981. The politics of violence: Guatemala and El Salvador, *Current History,* Vol. 80, No. 463 (February): 70–88.

Mitchell, C., 1981. The new authoritarianism in Bolivia, *Current History,* Vol. 80, No. 463 (February): 75–89.

Morris, J.A. 1984. *Honduras: Caudillo Politics and Military Rulers,* Westview Press, Boulder.

Mowzelis, N., 1987. Continuities and discontinuities in Greek politics, in Featherstone and Katsoudas, pp. 271–87.

Noman, O., 1989. Pakistan and General Zia: era and legacy, *Third World Quarterly,* Vol. 11, No. 1 (January): 29–54.

North, L., 1976. The military in Chilean politics, *Studies in Comparative International Development,* Vol. 11, No. 2: 73–106.

O'Brien, P., 1985. Authoritarianism and the new economic orthodoxy: the political economy of the Chilean regime 1975–83, in O'Brien and Cammack, pp. 144–83.

O'Brien, P. and Cammack, P. (eds) 1985. *Generals in Retreat: The Crisis of Military Rule in Latin America,* Manchester University Press, Manchester.

O'Donnell, G., 1979. Tensions in the bureaucratic authoritarian state and the question of democracy, in Collier, pp. 285–318.

O'Donnell, G., 1986. Introduction to the Latin American cases, in O'Donnell *et al.,* Part II, pp. 3–18.

O'Donnell, G., Schmitter, P. and Whitehead, L. (eds) (1986). *Transitions from Authoritarian Rule in Latin America*, Johns Hopkins University Press, Baltimore, Maryland.

O'Kane, R.H.T., 1989. Military regimes: power and force, *European Journal of Political Research*, Vol. 17 (Spring): 333–50.

Ozbundun, E., 1989. Turkey: Crisis, interruptions and re-equilibriations, in Diamond *et al.*, Vol. III, pp. 187–229.

Painter, J., 1986. Guatemala in civilian garb, *Third World Quarterly*, Vol. 8, No. 3 (July): 818–44.

Painter, J., 1987. *Guatemala: False Hope. False Freedom*, Latin American Bureau, London.

Perlmutter, A., 1980. A comparative analysis of military regimes, *World Politics*, October: 96–120.

Perlmutter, A., 1986. 'The military and politics in modern times: a decade later', *Journal of Strategic Studies*, Vol. 9, No. 1: 5–15.

Philip, G., 1984. Democratisation in Brazil and Argentina: some reflections, *Government and Opposition*, Vol. 19, No. 2: 268–76.

Philip, G. 1985. *The Military in South American Politics*, Croom Helm, Beckenham.

Pinkney, R., 1973. The theory and practice of military government, *Political Studies*, Vol. 25, No. 2 (June): 152–66.

Pion-Berlin, D., 1985. The fall of military rule in Argentina 1976–83, *Journal of Inter-American Studies and World Affairs*, Vol. 28, No. 2 (Summer): 55–73.

Randall, V. (eds.) 1988. *Political Parties in the Third World*, Sage, London.

Rathamarit, N. 1984. Military governments in Thailand: their policies toward political parties, 1977–83. Ph.D. thesis, University of Pittsburgh, Pittsburgh, Pennsylvania.

Reed, C., 1988. Cerezo's uphill reform task, *The Guardian*, 12 March, p.7.

Reid, M. 1989. Bolivia's ruling centre-right party heads for victory, *The Guardian*, 9 May, p.6.

Remmer, K. 1989. Neopatrimonialism: the politics of military rule in Chile 1973–87, *Comparative Politics*, Vol. 21, No. 2 (January): 149–70.

Rizvi, G., 1985. Riding the tiger: institutionalising the military regimes in Pakistan and Bangladesh, in Clapham and Philip, pp. 201–36.

Rocha, J., 1989. Brazil leader pledges sweat and sacrifice in war on inflation, *The Guardian*, 17 July, p.8.

Rose, L.E., 1989. Pakistan: experiments with democracy, in Diamond *et al.*, Vol. III, pp. 105–41.

Rosenberg, M.B., 1987. Political obstacles to democracy in Latin America, in Malloy and Seligson, pp. 193–215.

Rustow, D.A., 1973. How does a democracy come into existence?, in Lewis and Potter, pp. 117–32.

Rustow, D.A., 1988. Transitions to democracy: Turkey's experiment in historical and comparative perspective, in Heper and Evin, pp. 239–48.

Samundavanija, C-A., 1989. Thailand: a stable semi-democracy, in Diamond *et al.*, Vol. III, pp. 305–46.

Sanders, T.G., 1981. Chile: military government and national organisation, in Handelman and Sanders, pp. 287–306.

Schmitter, P.C., 1986. An introduction to the southern European transition from authoritarian rule, in O'Donnell *et al.*, pp. 3–16.

Schriffrin, H.Z. (ed.) 1976. *The Military and the State in Modern Asia*, Academic Press, Jerusalem.

Seligson, M.A., 1987. Democracy in Latin America: the current cycle, in Malloy and Seligson, pp. 3–12.

Simons, M., 1981. Guatemala: the coming danger, *Foreign Policy*, Vol. 43: 93–103.

Sivard, R.L. 1983. *World Military and Social Expenditures*, World Priorities, Washington.

Skidmore, T.E. 1988. *The Politics of Military Rule in Brazil 1964–85*, Oxford University Press, Oxford.

Stepan, A. 1971. *The Military in Politics: Changing Patterns in Brazil*, Princeton University Press, Princeton, New Jersey.

Stepan, A. (ed.) 1973. *Authoritarian Brazil*, Yale University Press, New Haven, Connecticut.

Stepan, A., 1978. *State and Society in Peru in Comparative Perspective*, Princeton University Press, Princeton, New Jersey.

Stockholm International Peace Research Institute 1987. *SIPRI Yearbook 1987: World Armaments and Disarmament*, Oxford University Press, Oxford.

Sunar, I. and Sayari, S., 1986. Democracy in Turkey: problems and prospects, in O'Donnell *et al.*, pp. 165–86.

Sundhaussen, U., 1984. Military withdrawal from government responsibility, *Armed Forces and Society*, Vol. 10, No. 4: 543–62.

Sundhaussen, U., 1989. Indonesia: past and present encounters with democracy, in Diamond *et al.*, Vol. III, pp. 423–74.

Sundhaussen, U. and Green, B.R., 1985. Indonesia: the slow march into an uncertain future, in Clapham and Philip, pp. 99–127.

Tachau, F. 1984. *Turkey: The Politics of Authority, Democracy and Development*, Praeger, New York.

Tahir-Kheli, S., 1980. The military in contemporary Pakistan, *Armed Forces and Society*, Vol. 6, No. 4 (Summer): 639–53.

Thomas, M.L., 1988. Limited disengagement of the military from Thai politics, in Danopoulos, pp. 111–37.

Turan, I., 1988. Political parties and the party system in post-1983 Turkey, in Heper and Evin, pp. 63–80.

Vacs, A., 1987. Authoritarian breakdown and redemocratisation in Argentina, in Malloy and Seligson, pp. 15–42.

Valenzuela, A., 1978. Chile: the Chilean military, the 1973 election and institutional breakdown, in Linz and Stepan, pp. 81–110.

Veremis, T., 1985. Greece: veto and impasse 1967–74, in Clapham and Philip, pp. 27–45.

Veremis, T., 1987. The military, in Featherstone and Katsoudas, pp. 214–29.

Weiner, M., 1971. Political participation: crisis of the political process, in Binder *et al.*, pp. 159–204.

Welch, C.E. 1987. *No Farewell to Arms?*, Westview Press, London.

Whitehead, L., 1985. Whatever became of the Southern Cone model, in
 Hojman, pp. 9–28.
Whitehead, L., 1986. Bolivia's failed democratisation 1977–80, in O'Donnell
 et al., pp. 49–72.

Index